Rupert Guinness is a Walkley Award-commended senior sports writer at the *Australian* newspaper who has covered fifteen Tours de France. He is a former editor of *Winning Bicycle Racing Illustrated* magazine, European correspondent for *VeloNews* (USA) and a contributor to *Cycling Weekly* (UK) and *Velo* (France). He is also the author of six other books on cycling including *The Foreign Legion*, *Tales from the Toolbox: Inside a Pro Cycling Team* and *The Dean Woods Manual of Cycling*. Rupert, who lives in Sydney, also writes on rugby union and rowing and has covered two Olympic Games.

Aussie Aussie Aussie
OUI, OUI, OUI!

Australian cyclists in 100 years
of the Tour de France

Rupert Guinness

RANDOM HOUSE AUSTRALIA

Random House Australia Pty Ltd
20 Alfred Street, Milsons Point, NSW 2061
http://www.randomhouse.com.au

Sydney   New York   Toronto
London   Auckland   Johannesburg

First published by Random House Australia 2003

National Library of Australia
Cataloguing-in-Publication Entry

Guinness, Rupert.
Aussie Aussie Aussie, oui! oui! oui!: Australian cyclists
in 100 years of the Tour de France.

Bibliography.
ISBN 1 74051 245 6.

1. Tour de France (Bicycle race) – History. 2 Bicycle
racing – France – History. 3. Cyclists – Australia. I.
Title.

796.6208924044

Front cover image: The Australasian team for the 1928 Tour de France,
Courtesy Robbie McEwen.
Cover design by Darian Causby/Highway 51
Typeset in 12.5/14.5 Adobe Garamond by Midland Typesetters, Maryborough, Victoria
Printed and bound by Griffin Press, Netley, South Australia

10 9 8 7 6 5 4 3 2 1

To my wife Libby

Table of Contents

Foreword   Phil Liggett   ix

Chapter 1 Le départ   1
Chapter 2 Two men with a dream: Don Kirkham and
               Snowy Munro   9
Chapter 3 'Allez, Oppy, Allez': Sir Hubert Opperman   20
Chapter 4 'Mocka' (The Geelong Flyer):
               Russell Mockridge   42
Chapter 5 A Tale of two Tours: Don Allan   58
Chapter 6 Thirteen out of thirteen: Phil Anderson   81
Chapter 7 The slave trade: Allan Peiper and
               Neil Stephens   105
Chapter 8 Yellow fever: Stuart O'Grady   127
Chapter 9 Winning Lotto: Robbie McEwen   148
Chapter 10 Rising to the top: Brad McGee   166
Chapter 11 Reading the stars: Baden Cooke and
               Cadel Evans   183

Honour roll and statistics   194
Acknowledgements   205
Bibliography   209

Foreword

Let there be no mistake. The Tour de France is the greatest annual sporting spectacle anywhere in the world. In 1903, the very idea of racing around France's hectagon was seen as the shortest way of killing off, literally, an ambitious group of sportsmen. In fact, the riders were so afraid that the race was almost cancelled without a wheel being turned due to lack of entries. When it did go ahead, bribery, corruption and sabotage of the riders by placing tacks on the roads in the 1904 edition caused its French founder Henri Desgrange to declare his race 'dead' before it had hardly begun.

Le Tour, or *la Grande Boucle* (the big lap) has survived to become an annual French spectacle that brings twenty million people to the roadside every July, each straining to catch a glimpse of the men who have long since passed the human endurance test as they battle the mountains, heat and cold of an event that would break the spirit of most.

Lance Armstrong, the American who has won the race more times than any of his countrymen, has a saying: 'If you don't like pain, then don't ride.' Armstrong knows all about pain. After all, he battled through a life-threatening cancer to return and triumph in the toughest event of all. Pulling on the *maillot jaune* – yellow jersey – of race winner at the finish on the Champs Elysées, Armstrong knows that to succeed, you must always be humbled first.

I first saw the Tour in 1973 when a young Spaniard, winner Luis Ocaña, combined with the daily dose of warm sunshine, made me think: 'If only I could have ridden this race.' As a journalist I have followed the Tour ever since, making 31 Tours in 2003.

Everyone wants to ride the Tour, but only a few can; and of those who start the race, another twenty percent will never see the sacred cobblestones of the Champs Elysées three weeks later. If they are lucky they will go home partway through, either sick or tired, but at least they are not the few who view the finish from a hospital bed after a crash has ruined their life-long ambition.

Most among the English-speaking media – brought up on a diet of soccer, Australian Rules football, rugby league and union, cricket or the like – have never known the intense pleasure of reporting an event in which the competitor pitches himself more against the race than the man he is racing against. Survival rather than winning is uppermost in the mind of the Tour rider – so much so that even those on competing teams will share their drinks and food if it means their rival will finish the stage to fight on another day. Armstrong, chasing his third victory in 2001, showed the respect in which each competitor is held when he waited for his main rival, the German Jan Ullrich, after Ullrich crashed on a mountain descent, saying: 'No one should win this way.'

Rupert Guinness is one of the few antipodean journalists who knows and understands what the Tour means to a rider and his family and how he is regarded by those around him. The Tour rider is more than just a 'professional sportsman'. He is one who has become a super-human in the eyes of us mortals. People are proud to associate with him. To a European, it is the ultimate achievement just to participate in the Tour, so can you imagine what it meant to the pioneers from Australia who went to France not knowing what horrors lay along the unmade roads of the Alps and the Pyrénées. In 1914, with World War I imminent, Iddo 'Snowy' Munro and Duncan 'Don' Kirkham took the Aussies into their own battle – one against the elements – which they both conquered by reaching the finish in Paris in a year when of the 146 who started, only 54 made it to the end.

Britain doesn't beat Australia at much in sport these days, but against the twenty-seven Australians who have crossed the world to ride the Tour, Britain can boast 51, although we weren't brave enough to try until Bill Burl and Charlie Holland gave the race their best shot in 1937. I have to report that they did not get far before bad luck and falls ended their race: Burl quit on day two, Holland made it through the Alps, but not the Pyrénées.

Australian cycling is now on a high it has never known before and soon there will be an Australian winner of the Tour. Until then though, spare a special thought for Phil Anderson who rode the race thirteen times and finished every time, on the way wearing the yellow jersey for a total of ten days from two spells in 1981 and 1982 and winning two stages in a career that still rates him as Australia's greatest ever road racer. In many ways, Anderson was Australia's modern day pioneer in the annals of Tour history. When an Australian does win the Tour one day – and I am sure it will happen – I hope the Australian media sitting behind their desks will realise just what that rider has achieved. Rest assured, Europe certainly will.

Phil Liggett
Hertfordshire,
UK

Chapter 1

Le départ

The world was a vastly different place in 1987. Eastern Europe was still under communist rule and the Soviet Union was alive and well. Still standing in its ugly defiance to liberty and freedom was the Berlin Wall, erected in 1961 by the East German government to separate its people from capitalist West Berlin.

This is where the 1987 Tour de France began, signifying for me an adventure that would continue for years.

On the eve of the Tour, I recall the suspicious looks from rifle-clad East German guards standing atop the Wall. You only had to look through Checkpoint Charlie in the American zone to see the distant East Berliners walking back and forth among drab state-owned buildings. There they were, virtually imprisoned on one side of the Wall, seemingly oblivious to the hype and excitement building on the other side in West Berlin where the next day the world's greatest and toughest bike race was to start.

It seemed surreal not so much because the Tour was starting outside the nation it is named after; rather, that it was to start at such a volatile political crossroad. Due to the West Berlin government paying an estimated $3 million for the right to host the start of the Tour and its first two stages, the issue of difference and sufferance caused by the Wall became a talking point in those first days amongst the 1000-strong press-corps who had gathered from all around the world.

The Tour has always been more than a sporting event. It was first held as a promotion for the French daily sports newspaper *l'Auto*. On July 1, 1903, outside the au Reveil Matin café in Montgeron, 17 km south-east of central Paris, 60 riders set off for the first edition before 600 or so onlookers.

First proposed to the paper's owner, Henri Desgrange, by his cycling editor, Geo Léfèvre in late November 1902 at a lunch in Restaurant Zimmer near the paper's Rue Faubourg Montmarte offices, the Tour suffered many early problems. Cheating and skullduggery were rampant, as was apparent in the 1904 race when the first four riders overall were among a number to be disqualified for taking trains and cars to shorten stages, while many spectators sabotaged the course. Desgrange even thought of discontinuing the race.

But in the 89 editions raced in the last 100 years, the Tour has developed into the biggest annual sporting event in the world and is watched by an estimated one million people a day. The famed *maillot jaune*, or yellow jersey, of race leader – introduced in 1919 and its colour chosen to match that of the paper used to print *l'Auto* – is one of the most identifiable garments in world sport.

Since its early days, the Tour has undergone many revisions. The rules have changed, distances have been refined and the make-up and numbers of the teams who race it have altered. Now run by the Société du Tour de France, which in turn is owned by Amaury Sport Organisation, it has also transformed into a marketing locomotive. The only events in world history to stop it have been World War I and II.

But from its inception in 1903 to its Centenary year in 2003, the Tour has always remained a platform of social and political expression. In 1992, the Tour passed through seven of the then twelve European Economic Community member nations to celebrate the 35th anniversary of the 1957 opening of the EEC. The same year when the Tour started in the Basque city of San

Sebastian, organisers even allowed an allocated number of Basque flags to fly at the official start to stem fears of an outbreak of unrest among nationalist groups. In 1994, the Tour visited England via the Channel Tunnel to celebrate its opening. In 1998, it began in Dublin, Ireland, because it clashed with the World Cup of soccer being held in France; in doing so organisers seized the chance to champion the feats of Ireland's two greatest cyclists, Stephen Roche and Sean Kelly. Organisers have also allowed the Tour to be used as a platform by striking workers or protest groups. 'There are political, social and technical events which happen and the Tour has to participate,' said Tour race director Jean-Marie Leblanc, a former cyclist and journalist. 'When there is a town with high unemployment, or things are going badly on the economic front and the mayor wants the Tour [to pass] to boost morale, I say yes. Or if there is a very poor department with a small population or not much money or industry, when the Tour comes it gives a bit of pride back to these people. Rather than being a place of confrontation, the Tour is a means of bringing the people together.'

Yes, as I was to learn, the Tour is much, much more than a bike race. When covering it in 1987, I never imagined it would become a race I would follow year after year. But I was hooked. And on each return I brought with me the same strong hope for Australian success.

As the Tour celebrates its Centenary, it isn't difficult to find that hope again. Australian riders have proven to be legitimate forces in the fight for victory, having won stages and enjoyed spells in the yellow jersey of overall leader. Collectively, no year has ever been as successful for Australian cyclists as 2002. The nation ended the year ranked sixth in the world for men's elite road racing. In the Tour, Queensland's Robbie McEwen, NSW's Brad McGee, South Australia's Stuart O'Grady and Victoria's Baden Cooke won three stages, the sprinter's green jersey (*maillot verte*) and claimed nineteen top-ten places in stages.

Enter another Victorian, Cadel Evans. A gifted climber who in 2002 was the first Australian to wear the pink jersey (*maglia rosa*) as overall leader of the Giro d'Italia – the second-biggest race in the world after the French Tour – he planned to race the Tour for his first time in 2003. In him, there is every reason to consider the prospect of the cycling world finally celebrating the first Australian overall winner in the not-too-distant future. But let us not put the cart before the horse.

In this book, I hope to describe the emergence of the Australian rider in the Tour – and not only in numbers. Today, the collective power of Australian riders makes them a major force to be reckoned with alongside more traditional cycling nations. However, with recent Australian success, it is easy to forget the journey of Australian riders before them. From the first Australians to ride the Tour in 1914 – Duncan 'Don' Kirkham and Iddo 'Snowy' Munro – every Australian rider since has contributed in some form to today's success. Their results and first-hand experiences have inspired many of those Australians who followed.

It is heartening to hear today's stars like the 2002 green jersey champion, Robbie McEwen, acknowledge their role in this story. Talking of the early riders, McEwen says, 'You can liken them to explorers, like the guys who first went to Antarctica. It was a pure adventure, not having a clue about what they would come up against. For us it has been different. We have been a lot more groomed. We've come through a national team. We raced in Europe a bit. It has built up, our road to the Tour. Those guys just jumped on a boat, landed in France after seven weeks and raced with basically no preparation.'

Looking back, I regret not having covered the Tour earlier than 1987. I regret not having seen first-hand the sheer rage with which Anderson raced in the prime of his career as a Tour rider. By his retirement in 1994, he could boast thirteen finishes from thirteen starts, ten days in the leader's yellow jersey, five top-ten places overall (including two fifths), victory in the white-jersied best young rider category (1981) and two stage wins (1984 and 1991).

I was prompted to turn my attention to Anderson by a wire agency report about his first of two claims to the yellow jersey. It happened in the sixth stage of the 1981 Tour after a torrid battle against the French hero and eventually five-times winner of the Tour, Bernard Hinault, to the summit of Pla d'Adet (1680 m) in the Pyrénées. I was in the infancy of my journalistic career, working as a cadet journalist on Sydney's *Daily Telegraph*. Little did I know what the impact of seeing the report transform from a three-line brief to a one-page feature would have on me. Until then, my passion for the Tour had been untapped. I first heard of the race in 1976 as a fourteen-year-old when my French teacher produced a slide of the cyclists passing by a roadside picnic where baguette-eating, red wine-toasting cycling fans cheered on. The most recent Australian to ride the Tour then was Victorian Don Allan who raced it in the 1974 and 1975 editions. But Anderson propelled me to move to Europe to follow it.

First impressions always count. And mine were formed at the start of the 1987 Tour in West Berlin. The afternoon of July 1 also happened to be the day when a blond, short and lightly built Australian rider became the centre of attention of the entire Tour entourage, let alone this journalist covering the race for the very first time. For a minute or two, Shane Sutton led the Tour. As the first starter in the 6.1 km prologue time-trial, he was the only rider who mattered for the thousands who lined the Kurfurstendamm route, a wide and seemingly endless boulevard in the fashionable end of West Berlin.

But Sutton, then making his Tour debut with the soon-to-be-doomed British ANC-Halfords trade team, quickly dropped down the order as 207 riders recorded better times in the time-trial that kicks off most Tours as a way to formalise a starting order for the next day's opening stage. In fact, by the day's end, Sutton was placed fifth from last – in 202nd position and 1 minute and 5 seconds behind Dutch winner, Jelle Nijdam. Nevertheless, such was our excitement that, even if it was thanks to the lucky chance of being drawn first in his team to ride off, an Australian leading the Tour was something worth celebrating! In a race that until then had been dominated by Europeans, only one Australian had experienced that honour. This was Anderson in 1981 and 1982 when, more legitimately, it was due to his trademark aggressive riding rather than sheer luck of the draw.

Not that Sutton had it easy. The image of him nervously steadying himself on the starting ramp in those few seconds is as clear to me today as it was then. As a wave of humidity smothered West Berlin in 32-degree (celsius) heat, he braced himself for three weeks of torture, and the pressure of being the first rider off. He knew that as soon as he shot out from the shadows of the starting ramp, his name, face, and every effort on the pedals would be the first to be seen and spoken of in the 1987 Tour. The attention of millions would be focused on him alone.

Similarly, as the starter counted down the last 5 seconds before Sutton rode off, I too was preparing to begin an event that to this day is my *raison d'être* for the whole month of July. As soon as Sutton gripped the handlebars, hauled himself forward and made his first wobbly pedal-strokes down the ramp, my first sweat-dripped, hesitant notes about him represented my entry into a new world.

Sutton was not the only Australian in the 1987 Tour. Also in the race was Anderson and Victorian Allan Peiper on the Dutch Panasonic team, and Omar Palov, a teammate of Sutton's born in Czechoslovakia but an Australian citizen after defecting. However, Sutton was the first of them to abandon. As the prologue and stages one and two got underway, it became clear that his brief foray as Tour leader would be my sole moment of celebration. Sutton, then one of the best riders in Australia, never made it to the first mountain, let alone over it. On the day the race was to enter the Pyrénées – stage thirteen from Bayonne to Pau – he came to a halt by the side of the road 70 km into the 219 km stage and retired. Not that it was a surprise. Twenty minutes before the stage began, Sutton, then placed last overall, was standing alone on the start-line, staring blankly down at the road ahead to where the giant forested peaks of the Pyrénées bordering France and Spain awaited. He was like a condemned man facing execution. Like many of his teammates, he had drained his reserves in races before the Tour to impress upon organisers that the team was worthy of a start.

Palov, on the other hand, did make it over the mountains and to the finish in Paris. He came 103rd, 2 hours 59 minutes

4 seconds behind Irish race winner, Stephen Roche. But my lasting image of Palov is from much earlier than Paris. It is at the finish of stage nineteen to Villard de Lans (1150 m) in the Alps where, exhausted, he crossed the finish in 100th place and stopped metres after the line and right in front of me. His shaking head and glazed, ghostly look said it all. He was at the brink.

Peiper spent his Tour busily (and painfully) doing what 'domestiques' like him do: racing to help their team win. It is a task requiring many duties, from fetching drink bottles, offering up their own wheel or bike if needed and, providing cover in head- and cross-winds to chasing down any dangerous break-aways who could pose a threat if they gained time. It was a Tour that came at personal costs for Peiper: exhausted and suffering from a week-long fever and upset stomach, he quit in the Alps on stage twenty-one to La Plagne (1970 m).

As for Anderson, the man I had banked on to report more yellow jersey feats and stage wins, the Tour marked a phase in his comeback from a debilitating back injury at the end of 1985. All I heard from experienced Tour journalists was how good Anderson *was*, rather than *is*. By the time we took the now defunct corridor through East Germany and back into the west of Europe for stage three from Karlsruhe to Strasbourg, it was clear many felt Anderson was past his prime. After the stage ten individual time-trial from Saumur to Futuroscope near Poitiers, his Panasonic team director, Peter Post, was even overheard accusing a startled and later very angry Anderson of having ridden like a retarded human being. I was astounded that a rider Post had so eagerly sought to recruit and who rose to become the world number one-ranked rider in 1985 before his back injury, could be so swiftly dismissed. Such is the professional bike game, I was to learn.

It is fitting that as the Tour embarks on its Centenary, one Australian – if not more – is being touted as the overall winner. For Cadel Evans, a former mountain biker, the anticipation of what awaits in his career is unparalleled.

Four-times Tour winner and defending champion, Lance Armstrong, sees Evans as one of the few major threats in the new generation of riders. It is a big ask to expect Evans to win on first attempt. But it has happened before in the modern Tour (since World War II): Eddy Merckx in 1969, Frenchmen Laurent Fignon in 1983, Bernard Hinault in 1978, Jacques Anquetil in 1957, and Italy's Fausto Coppi in 1949. Unless he retires first, Armstrong has to lose sometime and to someone. It might as well be an Australian.

Chapter 2

Two men with a dream

DON KIRKHAM AND SNOWY MUNRO

In the darkness of early morning on June 28, 1914, two young men stood nervously on the ancient cobblestones in the Saint Cloud area of Paris. Straddled over their bicycles, Duncan 'Don' Kirkham and Iddo 'Snowy' Munro waited to begin the adventure of their lives: racing the twelfth edition of the Tour de France. They may have been poles apart in appearance and background but as Victorians, teammates and – most importantly – the first Australians and English-speaking riders to ever race the Tour, they were definitely as one.

Born in Lyndhurst, Kirkham was a tall, lean, broad-shouldered and dark-haired man of about 72 kg. The owner of a dairy farm at Carrum southeast of Melbourne, Kirkham was brought up under the hard-working ethics that characterise farming life. He won his first bike race in 1904 at the age of seventeen. He then toiled away at the sport with the same diligence and defiance he used on the land and quickly become a benchmark of excellence for many Australian riders. Up until the 1914 Tour, the unassuming and modest 27-year-old was known in Australia for his two wins in the Goulburn to Sydney classic in 1910 and 1911, and the 1910 Scone to Newcastle race, as well as for his many world road unpaced records.

Iddo 'Snowy' Munro, one of nine children, was a short, golden-haired 'runt' who weighed 60 kg dripping-wet. He was born in the country town of Warrnambool, but unlike Kirkham, he was brought up as a city lad in the Melbourne suburb of Coburg. But he still knew how to do a hard day's work. As a teenager, Munro worked as a tinsmith making tin trunks at McEwan's crockery and pan store on Elizabeth Street, Melbourne. In his lunch-breaks he used to entertain the staff by running up and down the stairs as training.

The effort paid off. Munro went on to win many races between 1906 and 1909, one of the greatest being his 1909 victory at age twenty-one in one of Australia's most prestigious one-day races: the 264 km Melbourne to Warrnambool handicap classic in Victoria. His win was a world record for the distance and was faster than the scheduled train from Melbourne to Warrnambool. Then came his win on corrected time in the 1909 Australasian road championship that boasted an incredibly large start-list of 548 entries. First to finish was W. Knaggs, but Munro – riding a fixed gear bike (52 × 16) – crossed the Flemington Road finish in Melbourne in 7 hours 12 minutes 51 seconds. The celebratory words of Sir Albert Spicer regarding both were poignant: 'You have beaten a world record. You have learned to keep your body in subjection. You have shown pluck, nerve and endurance. I hope that those good qualities which you have cultivated so early will benefit you in life, and that yours will be a prosperous life.'

Five years on, Munro and Kirkham had eaten their final pre-race meal for the Tour and arranged their clothes and bikes in readiness for the great race. They and the 143 other riders at the 3 am start weren't to know that 2000 km away, in the Serbian city of Sarajevo, seven would-be killers were soon to commit the murderous act that would change the world. Gavrit Princip, a member of Serbian activist group, the Black Hand, was hours away from assassinating Archduke Franz Ferdinand, third in line to the Austro-Hungarian throne, and his wife, Sophia, the Duchess of Hofenberg. Of the seven assailants, Princip was the only one to get close to the royals, shooting them in an ambush as their car backed up after taking a wrong turn to the Sarajevo Town Hall.

By the time Princip struck, Kirkham, Munro and all the riders from thirteen teams in the Tour were well into the first of fifteen stages from Paris to the port of Le Havre in northeast Normandy. They had ridden through the night, past dawn and well into another summer day. As they raced, on their already exhausted minds was not the act that would lead to the declaration of World War I on August 3 – five days after the Tour finished in Paris – but their own awaiting torture in the kilometres ahead. During a month that would be known as the 'July Crisis' as one by one the major powers allied themselves either with Austria–Hungary or Serbia in readiness for war, the Tour carried on with its agonising 5405 km journey toward Paris.

Far from everyone's mind was the possibility that for some riders, this race would be their last. Following the Tour, a number of them fought and died in the war. Come 1919 when this ugly chapter of world unrest was closed and the Tour was held again, three past Tour winners were among the hundreds of thousands killed in action: Frenchmen Lucien Petit-Breton who won in 1907 and 1908; Francois Faber, the 1909 champion; and Octave Lapize, winner in 1910. The other times the Tour would not be raced was from 1940 to 1946 due to World War II.

Kirkham and Munro owed their Tour start to a string of impressive early season results. They were the stand-out riders from a six-man Australian team who ventured to Europe in late 1913 with a view to earning a start for the 1914 race. It was a bold idea, hatched by Munro after he returned from a motorcyle trip through Europe in 1913 with trainer Percy Power. So bold was it, many of the Australian riders he approached to come on board dismissed it. To finally press-gang enough participants, Munro wasn't completely straight with his pitch: he started telling riders that others he'd invited had agreed when they hadn't. Soon enough, he was hearing: 'Count me in.' Finally on the roster were the names: Munro, Kirkham, Charlie Piercey, George Bell, Charles Snell and Fred Keefe, whose Tour hopes would be cut short when he fractured his skull in a race.

The day before they began the seven-week sea voyage to France on December 10, 1913, the Australian team met in Melbourne at the Collins Street offices of solicitor W.R.R. Blair to formalise their union. Each rider signed a contract they had all helped to draw up. Each agreed to pay their own way and share any prize-money won in races.

The next day, full of dreams and ambition, they embarked on their journey to Toulon in the south of France. Munro even took his favourite 'Thistle' bike which was specially built to measure for him by the Coburg Cycling Club president, Andrew Johnston. Not that Munro was superstitious. On the contrary, he was a down-to-earth bloke who, according to his daughter, Olga Rothleithner, went to France because, 'He had a job to do, as well as to fly the flag.'

It wasn't long after arriving in France that the Australians were approached with their first sponsorship offer. Monsieur Vinot, a representative of the Société Française des Cycles Clement and Gladiator from Paris, made contact with Munro. The deal was for the Australians to first race on the firm's bikes in six races: Paris–Roubaix, Paris–Tours, Paris–Menin, Paris–Brussels, Bordeaux–Paris and in the Tour. Then, rather than focus on winning, they were expected to carry out the job of a domestique by pacing French riders such as London-born Georges Passerieu who Munro and Kirkham would eventually be signed to ride the Tour for. In return, the offer stated that the Australians would be offered payment of 1000 French francs in five instalments to commence upon their arrival in January to July 31, 1914. A bonus incentive scheme was also put on the table: in the Tour it was 1000 francs for a stage win and 100 francs for finishing within the time limit. Also on offer was the option for the contract to be renewed between both parties for 1915.

For the Australians – who became termed the 'Britishers' by the English cycling magazine *Cycling* – their campaign began in Italy with the 281 km Milan–San Remo classic. It was a promising start. Kirkham placed ninth (the best result by an Australian until 1992 when Scott Sunderland was fifth) and Munro twentieth and 10 minutes down on winner Ugo Agostoni of Italy.

Apart from their own joy for the good result, the marathon event taught them a major lesson: the need for goggles to deflect dust and debris sprayed from the gravel and potholed roads.

A week after Milan–San Remo the Australians lined up again – with their new goggles – for the famed Paris–Roubaix classic which was then raced mostly on dirt roads but with about 50 km of bone-jarring Napoleonic-era cobblestones that became as slippery as ice when it rained and like a dust bowl when it was dry. This time Munro placed best among the Australians in the 274 km race, in 37th at 7 minutes to the French champion and winner, Charles Crupelandt, who led a group of seven riders into the famed velodrome of Roubaix and outwitted them in the sprint.

Munro's effort in one of the two hardest races in the world was timely. Midway into the race, he was still in the lead group that then numbered about 50 riders from 153 starters at Arras. Also in the group alongside Munro was Passerieu who, like many of the more noted Europeans, was now growing in admiration for this Australian as the race charged on towards Roubaix. Meanwhile, Snell was 57th, Bell was 64th and Kirkham and Piercey both failed to finish due to broken bikes.

From Paris–Roubaix, the Australians – buoyed by their strong showing so far – backed up for the two-week Tour of Belgium, followed by the Paris–Brussels and Paris–Nancy one-day classics. Meanwhile, as the European spring edged towards summer, the Tour beckoned and conversation about the race heightened. The Tour may have only been held eleven times previously since its inception in 1903, but by 1914 it had well and truly become a household event in Europe. As riders began hitting their straps at events in Belgium, Holland, France and Italy, the media increasingly interpreted their performances as a premonition of who would do well in the Tour and who would not.

An offer of a Tour start was finally made to the Australians. However, it was not for the whole team. Only Kirkham and Munro were invited to ride, and this time under the sponsorship of the French Phebus bicycle and Dunlop tyres. Their role was to be helpers or domestiques for Georges Passerieu – *l'anglais de*

Paris – who was then still highly regarded as a challenger for overall victory even though it had been five years since he last proved to be a threat. In 1906, Passerieu was second overall behind Frenchman, René Pottier, and also won two stages. He returned in 1907 to place fourth, again taking two stages; and then in 1908 to finish third, with three stage wins.

In the 1914 race, however, Passerieu was unable to improve on his previous best, or even emulate past results. He was not even among the 54 finishers having abandoned the race on the 405 km third stage from Cherbourg to Brest. Instead, Kirkham and Munro led home the team in a Tour that celebrated Belgian Philippe Thys' second of three wins in 200 hours 28 minutes 48 seconds, netting him 5000 French francs from the total 45,000-franc prize purse. Joining Thys on the podium was the French duo of Henri Pélissier (at 1 minute 50 seconds) and Jean Alavoine (at 36 minutes 53 seconds). Australia's debut in the Tour ended with Kirkham placing seventeenth at 11 hours 53 minutes 39 seconds, and Munro taking twentieth place at 12 hours 34 minutes 57 seconds.

As with the first editions of the Tour, the 1914 route was characterised by marathon mind- and leg-sapping stages over rough cattle trails that ranged in distance from 323 km to 470 km. (Today stages are rarely over 240 km in length and held on much smoother bitumen roads.) There were also as many as fourteen rest days, allowing for the stages to be held on every second day. And unlike the late morning starts of today, each start was held between midnight and 3 am – increasing the risk of crashing as the country roads were often dirt tracks and unmarked for hazards.

The Tour started on a promising note for Thys. His win over Frenchman, Jean Rossius, on the first stage to Le Havre saw him become the first overall race leader.

Rossius took joint leadership of the Tour with Thys the next day by winning the 364 km second stage from Le Havre to Cherbourg, but then Thys moved back into sole first place in the Pyrénées on the 326 km sixth stage from Bayonne to Luchon, which was won by Fermin Lambot. It was a punishing stage, highlighted by climbs over the Col d'Aubisque (1709 m), Col du Tourmalet (2115 m), Col d'Aspin (1489 m) and Col du Peyre-sourde (1569 m). On the Col d'Aspin riders took the 12 km-long descent so fast that official race cars could not keep up with them – except for riders like Munro who unluckily broke a wheel and finished 2 hours down on Lambot.

However, from the Pyrénées, along the heat of the Côte d'Azur of southern France and then across the savage ascents of the Alps to the finish at the Parc des Prince velodrome in Paris, Thys had to fight off a mighty challenge from Henri Pélissier, who had lost time in the Pyrénées. Both men raced for Peugeot, but Pélissier really put Thys under pressure on stage twelve from Geneva to Belfort: his stage win saw him take back 2 minutes 37 seconds on the Belgian.

It was a time gain that became even more important three days later when Thys crashed and broke his wheel on the stage to Dunkirk. He ran to the next town where he was given a new wheel. While warned of the possible punishment – it was illegal to get mechanical assistance – he took the risk and was soon pursuing the stage leader. However, later, as warned, he was penalised 30 minutes for breaking the rules. The penalty could have been fatal for Thys' winning chances. When he led Pélissier to the finish in Paris, their margin was only 1 minute 50 seconds. Ironically, throughout their closely fought battle, it was Pélissier's own supporters who proved to be the biggest hindrance to his brave efforts to win the race. They were so excited by Pélissier's late charge out from the Alps in the last days that they swarmed onto the road to pat him on the back and encourage him. But on the second last stage their well-intended actions near the finish at Dunkirk led to Pélissier blaming them for blocking his path.

For Kirkham and Munro, it was soon after starting that first stage, when they rode out through golden-beam gaslights into the darkness of night, that the Tour began testing their minds and bodies – Munro, in particular, judging by one early stage record. Stricken with thirst at one of the mandatory control checks and short of fluent French to communicate, he pleaded to someone for a drink of water by cupping his hands together and raising them to his mouth. His request for help was apparently well-understood – until he drank out of the bowl he was given in return. Munro soon discovered that he was not swigging water but fresh cologne with which he was meant to wash himself. He soon fell ill.

Munro recovered from his error and survived the two days in the Pyrénées. But he and Kirkham were still unable to smile during the passage along the sun-baked holiday region of the Côte d'Azur. Their respective eleventh and sixteenth places on the 370 km eighth stage from Perpignan to Marseille provided a timely boost for their confidence and belief that they could win a stage. But then the 338 km ninth stage from Marseille to Nice saw the podium taken by Rossius, Pélissier and Thys respectively. It was a result not without some controversy; furthermore, it was sparked by the two Australians. Finishing almost 2 hours behind on the stage, they accused the local stars of foul riding, claiming their tactics robbed them of a historic stage win. What occurred exactly is not known, but their protest failed to convince officials and led to Kirkham and Munro threatening to quit the race until officials convinced them against taking the drastic step. By now the Tour was really starting to take its toll on them, mentally as well as physically. They were so exhausted after one stage that they couldn't dismount from their bikes and were carried off by officials to their bedrooms.

However, their decision to ride on paid off. Kirkham managed to finish ninth on stage thirteen to Longwy. And on the last stage to Paris, Munro, who had lost 6 kilograms, placed tenth, thereby allowing them to end the first chapter of Australia's history in the Tour on a high note. Kirkham and Munro proved that contrary to public opinion, Australian riders were more than capable of racing. Being so far from Australia and living in an unknown country where English was not spoken, they proved their mental as well as physical toughness.

After the Tour, Kirkham and Munro joined the exodus from France as war became imminent. Both riders returned to Australia, but unfortunately, awaiting them there were mixed fortunes despite their indisputable legacy. Foremost was their impact on the career of a future star – Hubert Opperman who would emulate their achievement with impressive twelfth- and eighteenth-place finishes in the 1928 and 1931 Tours. Opperman – ever the adventurer – was a rider who loved nothing more than discovering new frontiers and learning from those who had broken them. Kirkham and Munro also helped open doors for other Australians to earn starts in the race. Among them were Munro's fellow Coburg Cycling Club colleagues, Ernest Bainbridge and Richard 'Fatty' Lamb who would help Opperman.

Kirkham and Munro were introduced to Opperman by Bruce Small who owned Malvern Star bicycles, and was also Oppy's manager. The celebrated pair made instant impressions on Opperman. He was particularly taken with Kirkam's staunch belief that: 'You're never as tired as you think you are.' In 1922, Opperman and Kirkham became training partners and as they pedalled kilometre after kilometre, they often chatted about the 1914 Tour. Opperman became a sponge for Kirkham's knowledge on training, gears, speeds, position, tactics and diet. Opperman described Kirkham as 'the pinnacle of pedalling achievement' in his 1977 autobiography, *Pedals, Politics and People*. '[He was] tall, angular and straight-eye, off the machine he was just one of the crowd, but on it he epitomised rhythm. His legs and feet dropped and turned without a quiver, as smoothly at the end of a long ride as when he first left the mark. His experience fell on me like a tailor-made coat.'

Sadly, Kirkham's career and life met a tragic end. After the Tour, he stopped racing, but made a brilliant comeback in 1920, winning the 100-mile Cycle Traders' race from scratch. However, fate then betrayed him in the same event four years later. While riding back from the 1924 race in wet conditions along Point Nepean Road, a drunk driver struck him down. Kirkham broke his leg in the crash. Apparently there was an inexplicable delay by the driver in helping get an injured and soaked Kirkham to hospital where he remained for eight weeks. It is believed that the delay played a part in Kirkham coming down with pneumonia. The condition impaired his ability to do farmwork and developed into tuberculosis from which he died in 1929.

Munro tried to serve in the Australian forces in World War I. A long-time member of the Coburg Cycling Club, he twice attempted to join the Australian Flying Corps. But despite his impeccable sporting pedigree, he was rejected both times on medical grounds, the reason being that his feet – while good for pedalling over some of the world's toughest roads and mountains – were simply too flat for flying!

Such a rejection would not be the only blow for Munro. After arriving back in Australia, he soon lost his will to continue racing. He attempted to further the cause of Australian cycling by providing personal insights into the world of European racing, but Munro felt Australia's cycling establishment was dismissive of what he could offer. It was a setback after all he had done to ensure Australian riders raced in the Tour.

However, Munro's disillusionment didn't stop him from helping others. As well as creating his own business by founding the Embassy Taxi service in Australia, he continued to push the sport domestically and always remained in contact with the clubs in Victoria. His intuitive mind also fuelled his development of derailleur gears that allow riders to have a choice of gears, rather than the fixed block he used. He was also a force behind the birth of the *Herald Sun* Tour of Victoria that celebrated its 50th anniversary in 2001, and invested time and energy into his son's cycling career.

Alan Munro followed in his father's slipstream – almost. He was a champion cyclist and raced in Europe in 1947. Starting in the world's biggest race became the dream it once was for his father, but for Alan, it did not become reality. Unlike 1914, the Tour organisers would only allow national teams, not individuals, to enter the Tour. And despite some promising form, Munro junior's bid to impress a team to take him on as a guest or replacement rider was marred by the misfortune of mechanical problems in a number of important lead-up races. In three events, he punctured twice, and in the Paris–Tours one-day classic, his chain broke. There is, however, one heartening result of Munro junior's attempt to race in the Tour, besides his personal satisfaction of having competed against the best in other events. This was the positive response he received from Tour organisers to his application for a place on a team. They told him they wanted nothing more than to see an Australian team compete in their event.

This response prompted the then retired Opperman to go public with claims that Australia should invest more time, money and energy into training up a six-rider team to race in the 1950 Tour. Opperman's proposal was for the League of Victorian Wheelmen to call for a levy on local races for two years to raise the required funds. He proposed the LVW conduct a series of races of the calibre of a Tour stage in order to select a team. Then, with the team chosen by the end of 1948, it would have all of 1949 to prepare for the Tour. Sadly, Opperman's enthusiasm fell on deaf ears, and to this day, while attempts have been made to set up Australian trade teams, no one has managed to get one on the start-line at the Tour.

Sadly, 'Snowy' Munro never heard of the greatest exploit of them all by an Australian on the Tour: Phil Anderson's historic claim to the yellow jersey in 1981. In September 1980, Munro suffered heart problems and was hospitalised in the Alfred Hospital in Melbourne. After spending one month there, he was transferred to Freemasons Centennial home where he passed away on October 27, 1980.

Chapter 3
'Allez, Oppy, Allez'
SIR HUBERT OPPERMAN

In the centre of the north-central Victorian town of Rochester, two memorials – a statue and a museum – celebrate one of Australia's greatest sportsmen. The hero is Sir Hubert Ferdinand Opperman.

Born on May 29, 1904, the native of Rochester was an atypical adventurer. The son of a butcher – himself a former amateur cycling champion – Opperman spent much of his free time chasing dogs and rabbits and riding horses. At school he was a natural sportsman, vice-captaining both the cricket and Australian Rules football sides. But it was during his youth in the town of Melton where his family moved that he fell in love with cycling.

'From bare-kneed boyhood days I was drawn magnetically to cycling. I can recollect gazing at the village lads of Melton as they rode down the wide main street, with similar feelings to those which stirred me years later when I saw Nicolas Frantz and André Leducq in the Tour de France,' Opperman recalled in a five-page feature titled 'Opperman's Spectacular Story' published in the *Bulletin* magazine on August 24, 1960.

As well as developing into Australia's greatest bicycle racer of the time, Opperman continued to be a leader in his post-racing career. A former telegraph messenger boy who plied his trade delivering telegrams on his bicycle before becoming a copy boy on the *Melbourne Herald* (now *Herald Sun*), he joined the RAAF in 1940 and was commissioned as a flight lieutenant in 1942 during World War II. After the war, Opperman was then approached by Lord Casey to begin a career in politics with the Liberal Party. In 1949, he sat for the seat of Corio and won – he then held it for seventeen-and-a-half years, fighting off many a strong Labor foe, including the future prime minister of Australia, Bob Hawke. Serving under Prime Minister Robert Menzies, Opperman was also appointed as chief government whip in 1956 before taking up post as minister for shipping and transport in 1961 and then minister for immigration in 1964 before accepting his appointment in 1967 as Australia's first high commissioner to Malta and a year later his knighthood.

It was at the age of fifteen while living in Melton that Opperman first raced the bike, a 42 km handicap. He finished way back in the field, with the dusk setting. But his effort to continue when he could easily have quit earned him praise from his new club-mates. It was the same dogged effort that would see Opperman endear himself to so many fans around the world. A year later, in 1921, he won his first race – the 10-mile Senior Cadet Championship of Victoria. And soon after that, he claimed the win that would become a major turning point in his life – first place in the Cycle Trader's 80-mile race. Opperman was awarded a Malvern Star bicycle donated by the bike firm's young and promising manufacturer, Bruce Small. As soon as he was given the bike, Opperman sold it back to Small, but he also placed an order for a new custom-made one, and Small soon became Opperman's manager and close friend.

Their partnership would take both of them on a sporting adventure around the world. Small and his two brothers, Ralph and Frank, began by looking after Opperman's cycling career from their shop in the Melbourne suburb of Malvern. In return, Opperman rode their bikes around the world and with his many successes, helped to establish the Malvern Star brand as a mark of Australian excellence in a very competitive cycle trade industry. Opperman quickly became a household face. Many said his small stature, dark hair, hangdog eyebrows, thin lips, beedy eyes and long pointed nose bore a stark resemblance to another Australian sporting icon who had yet to rise to prominence – cricketer Don Bradman. Either way, Australians could not get enough of their 'Oppy'.

Opperman's last days were spent living with his wife, Lady Mavys, in Wantirna, Melbourne. He had fulfilled his pledge to Mavys that at age 90 he would stop riding his bicycle on the road, and ride his indoor bike instead. He could not have come to a more fitting end than to die at age 91 from heart failure while riding it on April 18, 1996 on the eve of the Australian road championship. His life was celebrated and his death mourned nationally.

Before Opperman died, former Tour de France director Jacques Goddet who met Opperman in the 1928 Tour said of him in his book, *L'Equipée belle* (The Great Escapade): 'The champion Australian of light build and stylish pedal-stroke was a veritable phenomenon of endurance.' They are words of tribute to a cycling career that ended in 1940 at age 36 when – before joining the RAAF – Opperman rode for 24 hours non-stop at the Sydney Sports Arena to set 101 state, national and world records. But in many ways, those same words also stand as testimony to Opperman's life as a whole.

It was Goddet who in 1965 presented Opperman with the Tour organisation's 'Medaille de la Reconnaissance' for his services to cycling. The award was made during a rare visit from Opperman to the Tour, just before stage one from Cologne in Germany to Liege in the Belgian Ardennes. For Opperman, the moment presented a stark reminder of how the Tour had changed, as he recalled in his autobiography:

'It was plain that Continental cycling, from my days, had stepped into seven league boots. Increased speed with improved roads, multiple gears, feather-weight silk tyres, lighter frames and equipment had raised their average like inflation . . .

'To my veteran astonishment, it was not obligatory for riders to carry spare tyres. Mechanics were ready, only seconds behind, with wheels or bicycles when called up on shortwave radios by the race directors. True to old-timer tradition, I grumbled critical comparisons ... I felt like Rip Van Winkle waking up to the realities of modern years.'

1928 – Four against the rest

Opperman's first of two Tour campaigns in 1928 was financed by a fund-raising campaign run by *The Sporting Globe* newspaper. Readers contributed the then generous sum of £1250 to send Oppy and three teammates away, a sponsorship due largely to Opperman's popularity from his previous feats on the track and the road. Most notable were wins from 1922 to 1928 in the Launceston–Hobart road race, the first of three Melbourne to Warrnambool classics titles, the Dunlop Grand Prix stage race, Goulburn to Sydney classic, Cycle Traders 100, Australian motor-paced championship, Wonthaggi to Melbourne road race, the first three of four career Australian road championships (1924, 1926, 1927 and 1929) and the first of two 24-hour unpaced world records.

The four-man contingent to Europe included Opperman; Melbourne rider, Ernie Bainbridge; a Victorian potato farmer, Percy Osborne, from Koo-wee-rup; and New Zealander, Harry Watson. The Australasian quartet who travelled as the Malvern Star team was to have teamed with a contingent of French riders, but upon arrival in France they discovered the French riders were not there. This forced them to race the Tour – of which fifteen of the twenty-two stages were raced as team time-trials – heavily undermanned against the permitted ten-man teams.

As was always the case for any Australian sporting side going to Europe, travel was long and arduous. While in 1914 it took Don Kirkham and Iddo 'Snowy' Munro seven weeks by ship, for Opperman and his team it took five weeks on board the 20,000-tonner, the *Otranto*. They did not travel in first class, as did the then amateur Australian Davis Cup tennis team of Harry Hopman, Adrian Quist, Don Turnbull and Len Swartz who were coincidentally onboard, but in steerage where their six-bunk cabin was way below the sealine.

The trip was made harder by two lengthy train trips from Melbourne to Perth and from Toulon in the south of France to Paris where they would be based while racing in the lead-up to the Tour.

One major problem for any travelling cyclist at sea was remaining in shape. All they could do was ride their bikes on stationary rollers and go for countless walks on the deck. Another difficulty on that first trip was coping with the humidity and noise of sleeping deep in the *Otranto*'s under-belly. To overcome this, Opperman and his teammates slept on deck, the frustration of any discomfort appeased by the novelty of watching the ocean at night and the moon rising in cloudless skies.

The long trip also allowed Opperman to temporarily forget the attention and expectation on him – until the *Otranto* docked at Ceylon. There he was reminded of his celebrity status in Australia by a telegram informing him that his secret marriage earlier that year on January 14 to Mavys – his eighteen-year-old childhood sweetheart – had been leaked to the press. The pair had wanted to keep their marriage under wraps, preventing it from becoming the public spectacle that characterised Opperman's every move. He was not that surprised to learn of the breaking news and grateful that their attempt to keep the marriage quiet had lasted until he had left.

Upon arrival in Toulon, a representative of the Dunlop tyre company, their sponsors, accompanied the Australasians on the train trip to Paris from where they were taken to their base at the Velo Club Levallois in Les Loges-en-Josas, located in a forest 5 km south of Versailles. The Velo Club Levallois was like a sports institute. Residing there were some of the French Tour de France stars and French amateur riders preparing for the upcoming Olympic Games in Amsterdam. The French riders were living in relative luxury while training to strict schedules that had them awake at 6.30 am and in bed with lights out at 9.30 pm.

The Australasians, however, weren't met with any creature comforts. Their quarters were a cramped loft with little headroom and no running water. Instead, they had to collect their own water and washed by standing in an iron hot tub which they purchased themselves.

As they tried to learn the intricacies of European racing under the tuition of Paul Ruinart, the Velo Club Levallois trainer, Opperman, Osborne, Bainbridge and Watson also came face to face with their first cultural – or rather, gastronomic – obstacle: the lack of the big breakfast of eggs, bacon and toast on which they had been brought up in Australia and New Zealand. In an article he wrote on the Tour de France for the Australian magazine *Boys Manual* in 1948, Opperman described the French *petit déjeuner* of bread rolls and coffee as, 'a bleak and austere few moments for us, and we used to leave [for training] feeling that our hunger had been roused instead of appeased.'

To match the inadequacies of an empty stomach, the Australasians then discovered that their fitness upon leaving Australia had disappeared at sea. Worse still, they became something of a laughing stock among the local French riders who not only mocked their inferior and outdated equipment, but their riding techniques.

After five weeks, the Australasians began planning their pre-Tour race program. With such a long boat trip and their lost condition, they knew they couldn't start the Tour without some racing miles in their legs.

First up was the 390 km Paris to Rennes road race. They sensed it would be a baptism of fire as they convened for the 2 am race start at a hotel on the Champs Elysées. But they performed beyond expectation – surpassing even their own. Opperman was the best-placed, finishing eighth. He also learned much from the many world-class cyclists he raced against, such as the Luxembourg rider Nicolas Frantz who would later win the 1928 Tour; but so too did the French learn about Opperman and his small team. The French newspaper *l'Auto* glowingly wrote: 'The Australian riders made an excellent debut.' Another report more reluctantly credited Opperman who became known as 'La Camionette' [the van] because of his staccato rhythm while racing. 'He isn't as good as they think in Australia but he's a long way better than we thought he'd be.'

In his next race, the Paris–Brussels one-day classic – of similar length but rated harder and more prestigious because of its history and a stronger field – Opperman proved he was as good as Australians rated him. He placed third, one length behind the winner and soon-to-be world road champion, Belgian Georges Ronsse, and ahead of another Belgian, Armand Van Brauene – the remnants of an original six-man break down to four with 80 km to go.

It was an important race for Opperman. He earned the respect of his new peers who tried to work him over and drop him until Ronsse put in one last effort to do so before looking at Opperman with a wry smile and saying in broken English: 'Our war is finished Oppy, we must work together now or the big bunch will catch us.' For Opperman the moment was a turning point: 'With those words I knew that the accolade of Continental cycling had been conferred upon me. It was an admission that the top-liners had accepted me into their class.'

When the 5476 km Tour began on June 17, the French still gave little credit to the prospects of Opperman and *les Australiens* who rode as the Ravat Wonder-Dunlop team. 'They took one look at our out-dated bikes and laughed at us,' said Opperman. And if he needed any more convincing of their scepticism, he had only to read the French newspaper headline that said: 'They'll be back in Paris after three days', before the first stage over 207 km left Paris for Caen.

In fact, their long odds were justified considering they were just four riders racing teams of ten. Against them was the race formula: fifteen of the twenty-two stages were contested in team time-trial fashion where each squad started at 10-minute intervals and riders could save energy or recover from efforts by slipstreaming each other. It was a system many cycling observers had already discredited as unfair and were lobbying with Tour founder Henri Desgrange to change well before the Australasians arrived to race. Too bad for them, it was only in 1929 when there was no Australian team in the Tour, that Desgrange took heed of the criticism and ruled out the controversial team time-trial formula.

The lack of manpower was an overwhelming obstacle. Making it worse was that it could have been prevented had there been correct measures of communication between the Australian management and Dunlop in France. It was also one of only several problems faced by an angry Bruce Small, the Australian manager, when he arrived in France one week before the Tour started. Others included the Australasians having to pay for equipment and essentials that other teams got for free, poor regard for their general welfare and alleged misuse of the Australian-raised funds by Dunlop's appointed French team manager. But the attempt at resolution ended as it had begun: as an argument, made worse by the language differences and an empty promise to find six French riders to fill the void.

Despite these setbacks, Opperman couldn't help but be swept up in the pre-Tour hype. 'For three days prior to the start there was an armistice with training, but consistent activity in other directions kept life at a fast tempo,' he wrote. One of those activities was for every rider to collect a cap and a hat from a race sponsor and have a photograph taken in readiness for publicity in return for a bonus payment should he produce a good result. Another was for a rider to go to the Tour race headquarters in the office of *l'Auto* and receive official race clothing and autograph memorabilia. Riders also had to take their bicycles to the same race headquarters and have them 'plumbed' – a mandatory official process where a lead seal was fixed onto the tube and a race number inserted onto the frame to avert illegal bike changes. It was an atmosphere that helped the under-manned Australasians to temporarily forget their problems and their slim chances of winning.

It didn't take them long to remember, however. To many, they looked like paupers on stolen bicycles as they pedalled courageously for the first eight days to the foot of the Pyrénées, their faces covered in ever-present dirt, backsides blistered and raw from saddle sores, their poor quality shirts, shorts and shoes wearing thinner with every pedal-stroke. Other teams rode within themselves, knowing that the Pyrénées and Alps were ahead. But the Australasians, desperate to prove their critics wrong, rode every stage as if the Tour was a one-day race. And as they painfully pushed on, all they had to draw on were encouraging words from Small who followed them in a car patriotically adorned with the Southern Cross flag and an image of a kangaroo. Each stage they survived was regarded as a win, proving wrong those who had anticipated they would quit after three days.

One day blended into another. They began each stage in the chilly darkness of early pre-dawn hours. Each day, eagerly awaiting fans would greet the mass of stone-faced, dead-tired riders mounted on their single-gear bikes that had been cleaned and repaired by mechanics while they slept. They would have already signed on at the start-line before collecting a daily *musette* or feedbag containing cheese, chocolate, rice cakes and cutlets on a cool day and oranges, bananas, chicken, raw eggs and raisins on a warm day; two *bidons* of drink and at least two spare 'single' tyres of which one had to be worn over the shoulders and the other behind the saddle. Then as the flag dropped to start another stage, they would begin up to ten more hours of torture in the saddle. The pain was relentless; for Opperman, the first few minutes of each stage was especially tough. As he recalled, 'Before the warmth of exertion seeped between the wooden arteries, there were minutes of agony when flesh and sinew seeming to be tearing from the bones.' Each day ended with the riders prising themselves off their bikes, which were checked for their officials' seals, before they hobbled to their hotel rooms, washed and dressed into their pyjamas in which they remained – no matter if they were in their bedrooms, the dining room or even strolling down local village streets.

The Australasians were battered and near-broken after making their way around the west coast of France from Caen, Cherbourg, Dinan, Brest, Vannes, Les Sables-d'Olonne to Bordeaux in desperate daily bids to finish within the time limit which was then fifteen percent of the stage winner's time. The one day that brought a smile to their faces was the eighth stage from Bordeaux to Hendaye (near Bayonne) on the French–Spanish border which they nearly won. Opperman credited the near-upset to their team interpreter, René de Latour, who had finally been allowed to officially follow the race. His presence alone helped to dismantle the language barrier they faced with their French manager. It also meant they had an extra set of ears to hear the whisper of planned moves – one being that the Alycon team was going to race the 182 km stage easy to fully rest up for the first Pyrénéan stage two days away. This rumour prompted de Latour to encourage the Australasians to throw all they had into the stage to try and win it. They heeded his words and led until 80 km to go when Alycon was suddenly ordered to go for the win when the sponsor's manager arrived to watch the stage. The result: Alycon first, Australia second at 4 minutes 23 seconds.

Despite that one result, the risk of elimination against ten-man teams had been constant since the Tour began. There was little room for error as Osborne embarrassingly discovered after puncturing in one stage. Telling his teammates not to wait, he was confident of being able to make it to the finish alone and within the limit. But he did so within a whisker of elimination. Opperman asked Osborne to explain, puzzled at the poor result. He learned that after stopping at 70 km at an earlier town, signing another of the several mandatory control sheets along the route and eating a meal, Osborne thought he had reached the finish. He realised his error by asking for the whereabouts of his teammates, only to be told they were kilometres away at the finishing town. Osborne was distraught, as Opperman recalled his teammate's words at the time. 'He said to me: "I've seen these other blokes cry, and I reckon it was little Percy's turn and I had a real good weep and felt better. I know now why they turn it on now and again." '

With the mountains of the Pyrénées to come, the field was now allowed to start *en masse* – in one group – rather than race in team time-trial formation. The rest day at Hendaye on the Atlantic coast was more than welcome for Opperman who was then two hours down overall. In an interview after the Tour he said: 'We rested for 24 hours to prepare for the Pyrénées, but we were dead beat. If it hadn't been for the fact the newspaper raised the money to get us there, I'd have pedalled up a French country road and stayed a naturalised Frenchman.'

Mountain roads of the Tour were still more like cattle tracks in Opperman's era. If wet weather prevailed, they became cascading fountains of slush, especially on peaks where glacial ice and snow was still melting. In the heat, the same tracks were slippery with loose gravel and characterised by long plumes of dust as riders descended precariously to the bottom. Falls are regarded as an ever-present danger today. But in Opperman's era they were common. 'You'd dare not stop or ease up or another rider would hurtle down the mountain straight over the top of you,' said Opperman who, as with all riders in that era, raced during the night – unlike today when stages are only held in the day.

Despite much of his career spent racing overnight – and his ability to overcome it being a key to many of his wins – Opperman didn't hide his dislike for night-riding. It was always terrifying: riding out from a small town after midnight, knowing the tunnel of light from street lamps would lead to the pitch-black of the rural outdoors where danger lurked around every corner. Aside from the blinding flash from the lights of an occasional official race car, all Opperman could see were the black silhouettes of other riders, not knowing who they were, as one incident in the 1928 Tour proved.

With the field spread out to all distances and wanting to liven up the loneliness of the 387 km eighth stage from Hendaye to Luchon, Opperman tried to get some conversation going with a nearby rider he couldn't recognise. He yelled out to the rider in French: 'C'est dure,' (it's hard). The only reply Opperman got was a grunt. Then after a few minutes of silence he yelled in French again: 'This Tour . . . it is very difficult – all are weary.' But once more, all Opperman got in return for his effort was a gruff snarl. Not to be beaten and determined to get some response, Opperman tried once more, telling his silent companion, 'It is very dark and you are too tired to talk.' Then to Opperman's surprise came the one reply he never expected: 'Shut up, you Froggie gasbag. I can't understand a flaming word you're jabbering.' The response was in English. To his surprise, it was Opperman's teammate, Bainbridge.

The shock for both riders turned to welcomed humour during a night in which they crashed repeatedly on the tricky descents until dawn arrived, and with it the much-appreciated sunlight that made staying upright a more realistic prospect. With daylight, all but one in the pack regrouped, even Leducq who had lost 17 minutes during the night due to crashes and punctures. The sole rider away was the Belgian, Camille Van de Casteele, who was 15 minutes ahead of the pack; but after leading across the painfully long ascents of the Col d'Aubisque (1709 m) and Col du Tour-malet (2115 m) he was finally brought undone and caught in a stage that saw the Belgian finish third, 6 minutes behind Frantz and 12 minutes down on stage winner, Victor Fontan.

In Opperman's era, one time-costing factor was changing gears. Next to having to change their own tyres, it is one feature of road racing that has truly benefited from modern technology. Today, changing gears is a simple, ever-so-quick and largely under-esti-mated action, requiring the discrete flick of a finger on the gear lever attached to the brake lever, which leads by cable to a derailleur that shifts the chain from one sprocket to another. But derailleurs weren't in general use at the Tour until 1937 so shifting gears was a very deliberate and slow affair because cyclists rode with single gears. The only way to change gears was to stop, undo the rear wing nuts, turn the wheel around and then slip the chain onto a bigger sprocket to get a lower gear. The next crucial move was deciding *when* to change gears. Little wonder that most riders followed the example of noted climbers when they decided to stop and change, thereby destroying the element of surprise for many of them.

In his autobiography, Opperman describes his first passage across the Pyrénées as 'traumatic':

'As the abrupt bends with sheer drops came closer, one would panic and with brakes jammed on hard, skid to a halt. Yet as we timidly steered around corners, hugging into the safe compan-ionable cliff face, there were shouts from behind: "Attention, guardez-vous", and the flying figures hurtled past grim-faced, tense eyes glaring through goggles, bikes swinging from right to left, to the very edge of the abyss and back towards the rocky wall, searching for wheel holds in the jolting surface.'

Opperman was more relieved to have survived the danger of descending rather than to have endured the physical demands of climbing the Aubisque and Tourmalet. He let it show too by sitting up to stretch and warm his frozen limbs and muscles as he hit the valley run to Luchon. But Opperman had barely relieved his agony when the Belgian Julian Vervecke rode up to tell him: 'Never, never *retard* [delay], Oppy. We must fight for every minute.' For Opperman it was a lesson he would not forget and was thankful to the Belgian when he reached Luchon in seventeenth place, again best of the Australasian team which saw Watson place 38th, Osborne 39th and Bainbridge in 50th after crashing head-on into a car. At 37 years of age, Bainbridge was worse for wear, as he told his teammates: 'Believe it or not, when I was sprawled on the bonnet I saw the broken wheel and thought, "I hope to God I have broken my leg too and I won't have to ride any further." '

Bainbridge's 'wishes' would come true. Saddle sores and infected wounds from such crashes forced his withdrawal as the Tour left the Alps on the fifteenth stage from the mineral water centre of Evian to Pontarlier. 'Bainy', as he was known, could ride no further. It didn't help that by the time the Tour reached the foot of the Alps, the surviving field had been further tested by the boosted race speed caused by the controversial inclusion of fresh 'reserve' riders allowed to make up numbers in the ten-man teams that had lost personnel.

Amazingly, the Australasian quartet did not qualify for this luxury of new pedal power, and they did not welcome the return of time-trial stages. It also meant that Opperman could not put into practice the intricacies of what he had learned about riding in the pack. In the two Pyrénéan stages and following them, the stages across France, Opperman had not only earned the respect and friendship of many European riders, he had picked up tips every day. He was warned when to get ready for a change in fixed gears, when to be ready for attacks or accelerations, when to relax, and which upcoming race controls were compulsory or not. While fatigued and pained, he was fully fuelled on the camaraderie of the European peloton when under fire. But with the team time-trial stages, he and his teammates were once more alone.

However, as the end approached, the thought of finishing became more real for Opperman, Osborne and Watson. As Paris drew near and mass starts returned, they noticed moods lighten up between all the riders, barr the ever-cautious and wary race leader, Frantz. Suddenly, after a month of feeling nothing but rough mountain roads, bone-jarring cobblestones and slippery rural lanes, they were rolling over the smooth Parc des Prince velodrome in Paris.

The three Antipodeans were not Tour winners, but they were welcomed as heroes by the now-adoring French public and media who, only four weeks earlier, had regarded their participation in the Tour with incredulity. The tenacity of Opperman and his teammates was akin to the united resolve of the French a decade earlier following the outbreak of World War I. Opperman – the best-placed finisher of the trio – made no secret of what it took for him to finish: 'I never suffered in my life like I did in that race. I lost my goggles on the last day and my eyes were burned red raw. At the finish I rolled in agony on the roadway.'

Opperman placed eighteenth overall at 8 hours 34 minutes 25 seconds to Frantz who won his second successive Tour in 192 hours 48 minutes 58 seconds. Meanwhile, Watson finished 28th at 16 hours 53 minutes 32 seconds; and then in 38th at 22 hours 1 minute 49 seconds came the ever-tenacious Osborne who Don Kirkham once described as riding 'like a Belgian peasant' – a comment Opperman realised was a compliment, not an insult.

Soon after the Tour, Opperman was further rewarded for his efforts with numerous invitations to track meetings around Europe. The most prestigious was racing in the Bol d'Or race in Paris.

A non-stop 24-hour event, the Bol d'Or was one of cycling's most prestigious events. To make the race faster, each starter had a team of riders who would set the pace for their leader. The pacers would take turns resting while the leader continued on. The Bol d'Or attracted all the Tour stars, much as the shorter post-Tour criteriums – or exhibition races – do today. But unlike the Tour, the last thing anyone was doing at the start was laughing about the Australian's prospects. In fact, so feared was Opperman as a potential winner, that somebody who had bet on another rider sawed half-way through the chains on his two bicycles. When they inevitably broke, Opperman was forced to ride a heavy roadster while his manager Small repaired the broken chains. Job done, Opperman was seventeen laps down and facing the prospect of defeat when he rode furiously for 11 hours straight to catch the field and then another hour to take the race lead before miraculously winning in a record of 565 miles (909 km) claiming seven other intermediate records along the way. He finished 106 laps (53 km) ahead of the runner-up. So impressive was Opperman in the Bol d'Or that he even continued to take the 1000 km world record. Upon the urging of Small and a Parisian crowd chanting 'Allez Oppy, Allez', he defied his senses, remounted and rode another 79 minutes to break the 1000 km mark.

By the time Opperman boarded the ship back to Australia, France had taken him into its heart. Such recognition was formalised when Opperman was voted the most popular sportsman in Europe in a readers' poll conducted by *l'Auto*. To get the award, Opperman was voted ahead of French tennis stars, Henri Cochet and Jean Borotra. According to *l'Auto*, it was, 'Because the public admires and appreciates his courage, his perfect loyalty and his eternal smile.'

Opperman believed that any fame and fortune should be used to help others, rather than improve his lifestyle. When asked about his future in an interview published on September 4, 1928, Opperman said: 'I don't know what yet I shall do. I have a job, almost a duty, to fulfil in Australia – the lecturing of younger riders, giving of advice and the forming of fresh clubs. One has no right in life, when chance gives one some authority over younger riders, to neglect the good one can do in wielding this influence.'

Coming during the Great Depression, Opperman's charitable words were inspirational, especially among the poor who identified with the working-class image of cycling, personified by the suffering experienced by riders.

1931 – The best, but what if . . .

It was three years before Opperman returned to Europe for the
Tour de France. After arriving back in Australia from his 1928
campaign, he focused on setting numerous record rides on point-
to-point courses, including a new mark for Sydney to Melbourne,
567 miles (912 km) in 39 hours 42 minutes 12 seconds. But
when he did return to Europe to compete in the 1931 Tour,
Opperman soon showed that his tenacity for lengthy rides was
arguably stronger. He placed twelfth overall at 1 hour 36 minutes
43 seconds to French winner, Antonin Magne, who clocked
177 hours 10 minutes 3 seconds. However, due to an illness, it
was not the result Opperman had expected. But it at least served
to prepare him well for the Paris–Brest–Paris race in September
in which he achieved a career-best performance in the gruelling
745 mile (1200 km) event.

One aspect that struck Opperman during his second tour of
Europe was the wide use of drugs – whether to stem the rigours
of the Tour or through desperation to win it at all costs. Years
later, reflecting on the trend in an interview, Opperman said he
was totally against drugs, even though the sport was then years
way from drug-testing riders:

'I'm dead against drugs. There was doping among riders even
back in the thirties. I saw fellows with their eyes popping out. I
hate to think of anyone taking some substance that might make
him perform better than his natural ability. It's like putting in an
engine that is too powerful for the car. It is just as likely to
explode. No. They've had all their warnings. If anyone is caught
taking drugs, he or she must be rubbed out for life.'

Opperman raced the 1931 Tour in a combined Australia–
Switzerland team – one of five national squads (the rest were
regional). The Australians with him were Richard 'Fatty' Lamb,
the last of 35 finishers at 5 hours 29 minutes 5 seconds; Oserick
'Ossie' Bernard Nicholson; and Frankie Thomas – the latter two
failing to finish.

As in 1928, the Australians – sponsored by Malvern Star rather
than by funds raised by *The Sporting Globe* newspaper – travelled

to France by ship; this time it was a four-week trip to Marseille in the company of Opperman's wife Mavys and Lamb. The sea voyage was one week shorter but Opperman still faced the same frustrations: the lack of space and the difficulty of maintaining his fitness. The sight of the Australians riding on their rollers every day on the windswept deck attracted plenty of curiosity. When one female passenger asked a ship-hand what Opperman was doing, he replied, 'He's producing the electricity for the ship, madam.'

When Opperman arrived for the June 30 start at Le Vesinet in Paris, he did so all the wiser for his experience in 1928. He also noted a number of changes to the Tour since 1928, besides its shorter route and greater number of stages (twenty-four against twenty-two). First off, the Australian contingent had a full compliment of eight teammates to increase their chances. Their Swiss teammates were Jules Gillard, Roger Pipoz, Georges Antenen and Albert Buchi. The Australians and Swiss knew little of each other when the race began and ended up placing last of the five national teams. Opperman later said it was a team in name only. But finishing three of the eight riders was still a credit considering their language differences. Also different was the race formula: gone was the team time-trial rule that devastated Opperman's undermanned four-man team in 1928. Furthermore, about 900 km of road on the course had been improved, including the disappearance of some hellish sectors of cobblestones. Sadly, another difference in 1931 was the wet and cold weather.

However, back home in Australia it wasn't just the expectation of good results that attracted publicity. As soon as the Tour got underway, the Australians created interest. The first major story came with the abandonment of Thomas due to illness. Tallest of the four, he started the Tour well below the form he showed in Australia. On the circuit of Bourbonnais on stage one he did well to bravely chase and rejoin the pack after puncturing. But by the end of stage three from Dinan to Brest he was out of the race.

Then Nicholson helped to perpetuate the image of the Tour in Australia as the grand adventure it is with the story of his agonising bid to avoid elimination on the 206 km stage three from Dinan to Brest. The crank on his pedal broke in a fall during the leg, forcing him to walk 18 km with his bike to get a new one. Once fitted, Nicholson remounted and rode doggedly to the finish to come in last of the 70 surviving riders. However, despite his courage, Nicholson was way outside the time limit and thus not allowed to continue the Tour from stage five.

Nicholson came into the team after he and Opperman fought out a strong rivalry in Australia. Born in Tasmania and the shortest of the Australians, the twenty-three-year-old of inno-cently boyish looks was nicknamed the 'pocket Hercules' for his stocky 165 cm build. He seemed to come from nowhere in 1929 when he won three races in three weeks – one of them controversially overturned in Opperman's favour. After moving to the mainland, Nicholson had ridden with the Prahran Amateur Cycling Club before turning professional in 1928 after winning the club 25-mile championship. This marked the beginning of his tumultuous relationship with Opperman that would bring them together as teammates on the Tour.

A week after winning the Warrnambool 75-mile race in September, Nicholson – who then rode Pasco bicycles – was awarded victory in the Warrnambool to Melbourne classic after protesting that Opperman blocked him in the sprint. He won his protest, resulting in the disqualification of Opperman and West Australian, Horrie Marshall. But then Opperman successfully appealed to get the win back and force Nicholson's relegation to third. The controversy set the scene for a classic duel between Opperman and Nicholson in the Wangaratta to Melbourne race sponsored by Malvern Star.

Opperman was fancied to win until he crashed and withdrew when he found his forks were bent. Coincidentally, Nicholson met a similar fate when a flock of sheep drifted onto the road and he crashed. He escaped serious injury by landing on a sheep and continued riding. Then, despite puncturing further down the road, he won the race in a sprint. With Nicholson riding a Pasco bicycle, Malvern Star representatives were left red-faced at the presentation ceremony. But some quick negotiation soon had

Nicholson switching allegiances and agreeing to join Opperman in the Malvern Star stable.

Nicholson's loyalty to Malvern Star continued, even well after the 1931 Tour. Racing for Malvern Star in Australia, he set many records, his most incredible being a 365-day world best of 70,000 km in 1933 during which he rode around the country while at the same time appearing at Malvern Star promotions. During World War II he worked for the firm, supervising its production of radio location devices as part of the essential war service industry. After the war, he continued to push Malvern Star, appearing on ads and at shopping centre promotions with bike and rollers in tow.

However, if there is one unfortunate aspect to Nicholson's career, it is his inability to finish his one and only Tour due to mechanical problems, which were often the cause of his misfortunes.

Opperman and Lamb fought on bravely in a Tour that was won by the reserved Magne, a farmer who by tradition always got up at 6 am to throw a stone to the end of his garden for good luck. Magne's superstition paid off. He took the yellow race leader's jersey by winning the 231 km ninth stage from Pau to Luchon in the Pyrénées. His margin on the stage over Italian Antonio Pisenti of 4 minutes 42 seconds also brought the added reward of a 3-minute time gain. It was a bonus awarded that year to any rider who won a stage by more than 3 minutes and left Magne holding a 9-minute 32-second lead on Pisenti and 10 minutes 44 seconds on Belgian Jef Demuysere. It helped Magne keep the yellow jersey all the way to Paris where he won the Tour by 12 minutes 56 seconds on Demuysere, and 22 minutes 51 seconds on Pisenti.

The fortunes varied between Opperman and Lamb. Neither were noted climbers. Lamb was definitely the least credentialed, especially with his extra weight. He finished near the back of the field on every climb.

Opperman rode more consistently. On the overall classification, he even reached sixth place after stage fourteen, the

132 km stage from Cannes to Nice in the hilly Alpes Maritimes overlooking the Côte d'Azur. Opperman also sensed that this time he was regarded as a threat: 'When I punctured or shed a chain and raced to the group, the field had quickened, with the team belonging to those just above or just below me pacing furiously in the front. In the cycling vernacular they had begun to "work out" on me.'

However, it was not Opperman's rivals who would ruin his Tour, but illness. During the rest day on the eve of the first Alpine stage – the 230 km seventeenth stage from Grenoble to Aix-les-Bains – he was struck down with dysentery. He struggled through the next stage – including passage of the Col du Galibier (2556 m) – to finish 41st and drop to eighteenth overall. It was a result that would have left Opperman devastated were it not for the mid-race shock of being told that his manager, Bruce Small, had narrowly escaped death. Small jumped from a photographer's car as it ran off the road and down into a ravine. For a period, Opperman thought Small had been killed when defending Tour champion, André Leducq, told him so while passing the Australian. Opperman was preparing to abandon the Tour in distress when suddenly he saw Small waving from the back of another van. As he later recalled, 'Emotionally relieved, I was physically back then into the misery of drawn-out time-losing miles.'

Opperman's health improved over the next days. He even claimed his best placing in the Tour of fourth on the twentieth stage from Belfort to Colmar near the German border where Leducq won in a sprint. By then Opperman's mind was focused on finishing the Tour healthy and strong – in time for his next challenge, the Paris–Brest–Paris marathon in September. By managing to reach Paris in twelfth place overall, Opperman at least reassured himself and his fans that he would be ready for that.

In Paris–Brest–Paris, Opperman was not only tested against twenty-eight of the finest bike racers in the world, but against the physical and mental rigours of riding without sleep, throughout the night and in horrendously wet and cold conditions. The event was first raced in 1891 and in 1901 it was taken over by *l'Auto* newspaper. It has not been held since 1951 due to a lack of entrants, but at the time it was held only every ten years because of sheer difficulty and the toll it took on those who raced it. However, Opperman showed he could handle everything that Paris–Brest–Paris could throw at him, and managed to win the race by the narrowest of margins.

The race started under torrents of rain, but the first half to the turn-around at Brest went relatively smoothly for Opperman. However, on the return leg and into his second night on the saddle, things started going awry for him and for most in the field. Sleep deprivation, fatigue and the inevitable soreness of every limb from sitting in the saddle for so long began to take their toll. Riders started zig-zagging across the road, many straight off it as they lost their sense of direction and became delirious. Opperman was leading the pack and – under the instruction of Small – took long hard turns at the front to try and tire out rivals. Opperman gained in spirit, knowing he was causing fatigue in a bunch full of Tour de France stars, as he recalled, 'These giants of the road, those of the Tour of 1928 and 1931, who had carried their bursts of speed and strength of the team, were weakening under the pressure of miles, and the duration of time, into a combined fear of me.' Later when Opperman was alone and in front, he repeatedly smacked his head and drank large amounts of black coffee to stay awake. With Small by his side, he also sang songs through the night while holding a 3-minute lead with 80 km to go.

The race was far from over though, as Opperman discovered. Behind him came four riders, the image of their enlarging silhouette indicating that they were closing in. If he needed further proof that they were going to catch him, it came via the clock as it showed his lead dropping to 2 minutes as Paris came in sight, and then to 30 seconds as he laboured his way past the Palais de Versailles. With 5 km to go, the four chasers – the Belgian pair Emile Decroix and Leon Louyet, Frenchman Marcel Bidot and Italian Giuseppe Pancera – suddenly swooped passed Opperman in formation.

Miraculously, Opperman found the energy and will to lunge out of the saddle, grip his handlebars with life-saving desperation and stamp on the pedals in a bid to generate enough speed to

catch their slipstream and keep up with them. Despite succeed-
ing to do so, this feat and Opperman's earlier work led the others
to discount him as a threat for the sprint finish. Therein was
their biggest mistake. For on the final bend, Opperman rode up
the bank from last wheel and, milking every click of speed the
G-forces could provide, suddenly swooped down and passed
them all to cross the finish-line first. Opperman's win in 49 hours
and 21 minutes was regarded as his greatest ever victory.

Chapter 4

'Mocka' (The Geelong Flyer)

RUSSELL MOCKRIDGE

Russell Mockridge should never have participated in the 1955 Tour de France. A crash on a mountain descent while training near his home in Nice five days before the start in Le Havre seriously injured his left knee. Doctors thought it unlikely he would race, but two hours before the start on July 8 he defied them and took his place among the 130-strong field. Mockridge was further disadvantaged by his poor eyesight. It made him a hazard on the narrow, winding, cobbled and mountainous roads of France – if not to himself then to everyone else in the 4495 km race. After all, we are talking about a person who took up competitive cycling after being discouraged from playing Australian Rules football at Geelong College when his defective eyesight exposed a serious weakness for carrying out rudimentary ball skills. But as the sporting world was to discover, Australian football's loss was definitely cycling's gain. On the bike, Russell Mockridge was anything but defective. He was superb.

Away from the bikes, Mockridge was a quiet man who didn't drink, smoke, swear or carry the playful Ocker swagger that has long been the image of many Australian sports stars. He loved reading English literature, Chaucer's *Canterbury Tales* and Oliver Goldsmith's classic essays among his favourites. On the bike he astounded many with his versatility. From the wooden boards of the velodrome where he excelled in sprints and time-trials to the roads of the Tour de France, Mockridge seemed to have a bottomless supply of strength and natural class. It was often said that the one person who never knew how good he was, was himself. 'His essential failing at the time was confidence – a confidence to match his phenomenal ability,' said long-time friend and manager Gino Bambagiotti in a tribute published in Mockridge's autobiography, *My World on Wheels*.

Mockridge's life was tragically cut short on September 13, 1958 when a bus struck and killed him during the Tour of Gippsland in Victoria, Australia. On the day of his death it seemed many more victories were destined for him. The Tour of Gippsland was to have been one of his last races in Australia before returning to Europe for the winter Six Day track season which lead to the 1959 road season there. Who knows, maybe another Tour de France? But 3.2 km into the race, on the inter-section of Dandenong and Clayton Roads in the suburb of Clayton North, those expectations suddenly counted for nought.

Mockridge had titles in so many disciplines of cycling – both the track and road. Most observers still agree that his sudden passing left Australian cycling history with many blank pages of unwritten history. From the moment Mockridge competed and won his very first race – a 40 km Geelong Amateur Cycling Club handicap event in 1946 – he found himself stepping up to the winner's podium in Australia and around the world. Throughout his career, he was remarkably humble, even when on the attack. It is Geelong folklore that Mockridge, soon after the halfway mark of his first race, politely asked a rapidly tiring Don McGregor who started with him and on a handicap of 16 min-utes behind the front marker, if he would mind if he rode off alone in pursuit of the leader.

Throughout his youth, Mockridge was torn between various choices. After school, he contemplated a career in journalism and worked as a cadet reporter on the *Geelong Advertiser*. He also once aspired to become a Church of England minister. But it was cycling that beckoned Mockridge strongest and finally won him over. And it wasn't long before he was winning races wherever he went. He won the 1947 Australian road title to earn selection for the 1948 Olympic Games road race in Rome. In Rome, two punctures foiled his winning chances and he finished twenty-fifth from 101 starters. But he continued to impress and at the 1950 Empire Games in Auckland he excelled on the track, winning gold medals in the sprint and 1000 m time-trial and silver in the 4000 m individual pursuit. Once known as 'Little Lord Fauntleroy' for the baggy clothes, spectacles and pink school cap he wore for his first race in Geelong, and then as 'The China Doll' and 'Mother's Little Boy' for his sensitive, fresh boyish looks, Mockridge – known by his close mates as 'Mocka' – now saw his name being billed in Australian newspapers as 'the Geelong Flyer'.

It wasn't long before Mockridge fell into conflict with the then Australian Olympic Federation over their wish that he remain amateur for at least two years after the 1952 Olympics by signing a fidelity contract. One of Mockridge's key supporters in what became a public and parliamentary debate was former Tour star, Sir Hubert Opperman who was then in federal politics.

A compromise was reached between the AOF and Mockridge who agreed to remain amateur for one year. In return, he went to the 1952 Olympics at Helsinki and won two gold medals: one in the tandem sprint with Lionel Cox, and one in the 1000 m time-trial. It was a period in which a strong and respected rivalry developed between him and Italian sprinter, Enzo Sacchi. The pair raced each other in 1951, Sacchi beating Mockridge in both the world championship and in a promoted grudge match race challenge by the Australian. Before the 1952 Games, Mockridge avenged those two losses by defeating Sacchi in the Grand Prix de Paris.

In France, memories of how Mockridge became the first rider to win both the professional and amateur divisions of the Paris Grand Prix were still fresh. And with the prospect of earning some good money, he turned professional in 1953. With his fiancée Irene, who he would marry that September, Mockridge moved to Europe and on New Year's Eve that year, arrived in the Flemish cycling capital of Ghent. He raced on the track and in as many road events as possible, but due to a bout of glandular fever, found tapping into his winning vein impossible. But by 1954 when he moved to Nice in the south of France with his pockets nearly empty, Mockridge's fortunes began to pick up. He came close to winning the 240 km Grand Prix de Monaco, but a wrong turn with 400 m to go cost him the victory and saw him finish seventh. The next day he took fifth place in the 220 km Tour de Monaco. The wins were not yet his, but with improving results in finishes and in the various intermediate sprints offering prize money, his pockets were a little heavier.

Come early 1955, so were his hands – with the weight of a trophy for winning the Paris Six Day in an Australian team including all-time track greats, Reg Arnold and Sid Patterson. That win and a successful road race schedule to follow became the foundation behind Mockridge's brave showing that July in the Tour de France.

1955 – All that for a handshake

Whether Mockridge would have ever shone in the Tour – as was predicted by the French – the world was never to see. However, in 1955 he did become the first Australian in the post-World War II era to finish the Tour and his courage against tremendous odds earned him widespread praise. Despite overcoming his poor eyesight and knee injury, Mockridge also suffered a bout of chronic bronchitis that nearly saw him eliminated in the second week after the Tour passed the Alps and reached the Pyrénées.

The French media predicted future glory for Mockridge even after he finished 64th overall amongst the 69 survivors. He was 4 hours 14 minutes 46 seconds behind the enigmatic French winner and world road champion, Louison Bobet, who claimed his third successive win in 130 hours 29 minutes 26 seconds. One French newspaper tipped Mockridge to return for 1956 to finish in the top ten overall. The big Paris daily newspaper, *Parisien*

Libéré wrote: 'Mockridge has filled us with admiration. When you think that this man, who wears spectacles, dared to descend the 7000 ft mountain sides as quickly as all the others, it send shivers up our back. The Australian had all the disadvantages in the race, yet he stuck out to the finish while other riders – and several famous ones – gave up. We have adopted you, Russell, for good. You have proved yourself worthy of your glorious predecessor, Hubert Opperman. Next year you will finish among the top ten.'

At the same time, Australian riders in general were beginning to be recognised collectively as tough and tireless against the adversity of the Tour, as the French sports daily *l'Équipe* intimated with its commendation of Mockridge: 'Mockridge is entitled to all of our esteem. He showed all the qualities of the Australian people: strength of will, endurance and fortitude. So the gates of the 1956 Tour de France are wide open for him.'

The race for the yellow jersey in the 1955 Tour was fancied to go Bobet's way once the race began in Le Havre. Besides being in great form (having won Paris–Roubaix), the French national team – including his brother Jean – was extremely strong and dedicated to him. One of his teammates, Antonin Rolland, became the caretaker wearer of the yellow jersey for two weeks. He surrendered it to Bobet in the Pyrénées during the 206 km eighteenth stage from St Gaudens to Pau. It was the decisive stage won by the Belgian, Jean Brankart, who finished second overall while third overall was a twenty-one-year-old Tour revelation, Luxembourg's Charly Gaul.

Bobet hung on to win by 4 minutes 53 seconds over Brankart and 11 minutes 30 seconds from Gaul, drawing added admiration for having fought off the painful effects of a saddle sore in the last week. His fortitude was never stronger than in the twenty-first and penultimate stage from Chatellerault to Tours, a 67 km individual time-trial. Bobet still finished third in the stage, won by Brankart, and reached the finish at the Parc des Princes velodrome in Paris to become the first person to ever win the Tour three times in succession.

It was a timely moment to make history. That year, all of France shared in Bobet's glory thanks to television coverage of the Tour for the first time.

That Mockridge gained so much praise amongst such national-istic French fervour says a lot about his performance, despite his low place overall. During an era when national and French regional teams were still competing in the Tour, Mockridge and his close friend and training partner, Victorian John Beasley – the 1951 Australian road champion who started but did not finish the 1952 Tour – were selected for the Luxembourg–International team. With them were two Germans, two Austrians and four Luxembourgers – one being Gaul, who would win the Tour in 1958.

Mockridge and Beasley found it hard to settle into the composite team managed by the 1927 and 1928 Tour winner, Nicolas Frantz. He was a stern German-speaking disciplinarian from Luxembourg. According to Mockridge, Frantz was a hard man who 'you could imagine finishing 100 Tours and asking for more'. He also believed Frantz deliberately left him and Beasley out of team discussions during dinner each night. As Mockridge says in his autobiography, Frantz 'obviously felt that John and I were excluded from the plans made by the four Luxembourgers, who were the force of the squad. Not being told any of their plans made it quite obvious that whatever money [they] did win would not be shared.' It was only later in the Tour when the team was lacking riders and Mockridge was still in the race that Frantz approached him one-to-one with directions to protect Gaul who was about to make a long-awaited challenge to Bobet.

It was later suggested that Mockridge and Beasley would have been better off riding for the British team, the first to compete in the event. They would have shared a common language, mixed in more intimately with teammates and possibly enjoyed greater success. Mockridge believed the British didn't want them in the team because of contractual difficulties. Nevertheless, it was a choice they may well have rued because after fourteen stages, the British had only two riders left: Brian Robinson and Tony Hoar.

Mockridge and Beasley prepared for the Tour by racing in Europe beforehand. Mockridge rode the Paris–Roubaix classic won by Bobet – also known as 'l'Enfer du Nord' (Hell of the North) because of its harsh cobblestone course – and finished 42nd. A few days later, he claimed his first major win in the Tour du Vaucluse that included the gruelling passage up Mont Ventoux (1909 m). Mockridge outsprinted fellow breakaway companion, Frenchman Raoul Remy, to win and thus earn his benediction as a respected road racer.

After returning to Nice, Mockridge was then invited to join a select field to compete in the Rome–Naples–Rome five-day stage race. He raced well enough to convince his team manager, Gino 'Bamba' Bambagiotti, that he could be up for the Tour. It was a prospect Mockridge had not really given much thought to at the time. But after fulfilling a number of track engagements around France, it was with that in mind that he and Beasley rode the Midi Libre race – then a 290 km one-day race near Montpellier rather than the five-day stage race it is today – followed by the prestigious and mountainous Dauphiné–Libéré stage race in France for the Vampire Cycles team.

Mockridge did not finish the Dauphiné–Libéré because of previously signed contracts to compete in a number of clashing track meetings. He rode well though, and on the day he retired – stage six – he was second in the points competition to Bobet, the eventual overall winner. The standout man, though, was Beasley, especially in the mountain stages. He was fifteenth overall when Mockridge quit and was poised to improve come the last stage of the race when he broke a brake cable on a dangerous descent and crashed. He miraculously avoided serious injury, but the 15-minute delay while waiting for a new bike cost Beasley any chance of causing an upset.

However, such frustrations were quickly forgotten once Mock-ridge and Beasley knew they had the Tour to race. Overcoming injury and illness in the final days leading up to the Tour took priority over their disappointment over the Dauphiné–Libéré.

For Mockridge the main worry was his knee injury. It required constant treatment – including an anti-tetanus injection that 'Bamba' tried to argue him out of. It left his place in the Tour under a cloud until he was given the green light by Tour medico,

Doctor Pierre Dumas, two hours before the start. On first inspection the day before, Dr Dumas told Mockridge he could not race, as he recalls in his book: 'After taking the bandages from my leg, he frowned, made a close inspection and said that he could not let me start the Tour. It seemed useless to plead with him, as he did not appear to be the type to be persuaded by a layman on the wisdom of a clinical decision. However, as I somewhat disconsolately left his office, he told me to return the next morning just before the race started. Maybe there was till hope?'

To make matters worse, Mockridge and Beasley both came down with a bout of food poisoning after devouring a feast of seafood two nights earlier upon their arrival at Le Havre. Beasley was the worst affected and the problem would play a large part in his eventual abandonment of the Tour.

Despite the learning curve Mockridge had ridden so far, he was still stunned by the frenetic pace of the Tour as soon as it began. Beasley at least had the experience of 1952 to help prepare him. Mockridge had been swept away by the fanfare of a Tour start, especially in the days leading up to it at Le Havre. More like a spectator than a participant in one of the world's biggest sporting events, he said, 'I wished that I could have been an outside observer to more fully appreciate the spectacle. These professional road cyclists must surely be the greatest collection of superbly fit athletes in existence.'

As the 130 riders convened among the mass of spectators still seeking autographs, Mockridge recalled the advice of the great Italian cyclist Fausto Coppi to conserve as much energy as possible: 'Never stand to sign an autograph. Sit down and sign.' Mockridge did, but was up on his feet and chasing quicker than he had ever imagined once the signal – in French, which he could not understand – was given for the Tour to start stage one (a).

But chase was all he did of the pack that splintered several times under numerous attacks. By the finish at Dieppe where Miguel Poblet won to become the first Spaniard to claim the yellow jersey, Mockridge was last and 10 minutes 30 seconds down. It was the worst possible start to his Tour. And to think there was still a team time-trial – stage one (b) – to contest later that day. Recalling that first night, Mockridge later wrote: 'Never had I dreamed of winning the Tour, but I had not expected to be last either. I could not get over the fact that we had lost 10 minutes in our chase. Surely they could not keep this up for 3000 miles?'

Mockridge improved on stage two, a 204 km race to Roubaix where he placed sixteenth. The experience of having raced Paris–Roubaix on many of the same torturous roads helped and, placed 91st from 128th place, he began to settle down – unlike Beasley who was still feeling the effects of food poisoning and finished 123rd. Beasley had taken charcoal tablets as treatment, but the effort of racing was taking its toll on his weakened body. His chances of staying in the race were slim with heat, dust and a punishing 210 km in stage three from Roubaix to Namur to look forward to.

The stage was as action-packed as expected, with Bobet using it to launch his first major bid for Tour victory. After attacking soon after the start, he won the stage, moving up to fourth overall at 4 minutes 11 seconds to Dutch leader, Wout Wagtmans. Mockridge placed 29th at 11 minutes 30 seconds. But of more concern to him was the tempered ride of his team leader Gaul who had been tipped to challenge Bobet on the stage. Gaul, known as the 'Angel of the Mountains', had yet to spread his wings as he came in 33rd (17 seconds after Mockridge) on the steep finish to hold 34th position overall at 17 minutes to Wagtmans.

It was during this stage that Beasley was forced to quit the Tour. Exhausted and suffering from food poisoning, his problems began when he and a number of other riders crashed. He escaped serious injury and with the others, formed a chase group of the main pack. But as they began their pursuit, Beasley punctured and found himself distanced again – this time alone and desperately trying to rejoin the chasers against a hot and strong headwind. His efforts were futile, or deemed to be. As Beasley continued his lone struggle to catch the group, race officials following him believed he would not make the required time limit so they forced him to stop and quit the Tour. Mockridge criticised the officials for acting 'too harshly'. As he later wrote: 'Not far ahead of John was another group of chasing riders and they arrived at Namur outside the time limit but were reprieved and allowed to start the next day.'

The next day, stage four from Namur to Metz, brought mixed emotions for the Luxembourg–International team. It was a forlorn-looking Frantz who greeted his riders at breakfast – not for Beasley's abandon, but because Gaul was not turning out to be the rider of providence he had hoped for. Mockridge remembers how Frantz's gloom swept through the Luxembourgers as they prepared for the stage.

However, the day was saved by Willy Kemp who won the stage from seven other breakaway riders and finished 11 minutes ahead of the pack. Among them was Bobet's teammate, Antonin Rolland, the new race leader. But for Mockridge and Beasley, any celebration of Kemp's win was tempered by their parting of ways. Race rules required the abandoned Beasley to leave the Tour caravan after dining with Mockridge who regarded him as his only close friend in the event.

If Beasley's departure was a mental blow for Mockridge, the physical one came the next morning when he woke for the 229 km fifth stage from Metz to Colmar, the first climbing stage that passed through the Vosges mountains. He was a wreck and later said that had he known he would get worse, he would have followed Beasley and returned home to Nice. He believed his condition was due to the combined effects of the anti-tetanus injection he took for his cut knee before the Tour and the rigours of racing so far. As he wrote: 'Night had brought no recovery to tired limbs and every part of me ached. I did not know that each day my condition would deteriorate. Maybe if I had known this I would have abandoned. But I hoped the next night would bring me complete rest and freshness in the morning.'

Early into the stage Mockridge was actually invited by a French rider, Roger Hassenforder, to join a planned breakaway. Hassenforder, who had a penchant for playing up in the peloton, was certainly no joke as a rider. He wore the yellow jersey for four days in the 1953 Tour and would win eight stages in his career. In 1955, he was also the national pursuit champion. When asked to go with him, Mockridge knew he wasn't kidding but kindly rejected the offer claiming his poor state would be of no use to any breakaway. Hassenforder went ahead with his plan nonetheless and attacked, taking three others with him. They were later caught by Bobet's brother Jean but managed to stay away to the finish. The winner? Hassenforder. Ironically, on a day when Mockridge felt so bad upon waking, he finished with his best result for the Tour – twelfth.

When the Tour arrived at the Alps two days later, Mockridge sensed anxiety throughout the pack. Stage eight was brutal, 253 km-long from Thonon-les-Bains to Briançon and highlighted by three giant mountains, the Col des Aravis (1498 m), Col du Télégraphe (1566 m) and the Col du Galibier (2645 m). Mockridge didn't understand the conversation between Frantz and Gaul at dinner the night before. But he understood enough about how the Tour was unfolding to know that the stage was to be his team leader's big chance of challenging Bobet. Mockridge's challenge, he saw, was to simply survive the long and arduous stage to race another day.

Gaul finally gave Frantz reassurance of his form. He produced a magnificent attack on the first of the three climbs and won the stage by almost 14 minutes. The 'Angel of the Mountains' – pedalling at an incredibly high pedal cadence (much as what American Tour champion Lance Armstrong does today) of 120 rpm – moved up from 37th place overall to third and 56 seconds ahead of Bobet who was sixth overall.

The day even paid dividends for Mockridge. Despite his fatigue, he wisely rode at his own tempo and rose to 47th place at 44 minutes to the race leader, Rolland. Mockridge's ride earned the praise of the 1930 and 1932 Tour winner, André Leducq, who was now writing daily columns about the Tour. Of the Australian who he regarded as a sprinter, Leducq wrote: 'I did not have much time for sprinters in the Tour, but if Mockridge finishes I will shake his hand as warmly as I shake that of the winner.'

Mockridge later admitted that he was suffering badly at this point and wondered if the demands of the Tour would leave serious after-effects on his health. Stage nine from Briançon to Monaco wasn't going to provide any physical relief either, with 6830 m of climbing. But the stage did provide some psychological solace. Mockridge knew the roads near Monaco from training in the region. He was also looking forward to reuniting with his wife Irene and daughter Lindy on the rest day at Nice that followed.

By the time he arrived in Monaco, Mockridge's longing for the rest day and family reunion was even stronger. The stage was as challenging as the race book indicated. At 275 km in distance, it was the longest of the Tour. It was mountainous, and making it tougher was the heavy rain causing 63 of the 98 riders still in the race to crash.

For one of them, Mockridge's teammate Gaul, the price of such an accident was doubled: the stage win and a potentially Tour-winning moment. After throwing down the gauntlet at 50 km and on the first major climb, the Col de Vars (2110 m), Gaul extended his 30-second lead at the top to more than 3 minutes over the Col de la Cayolle (2326 m) and to 4 minutes 15 seconds by the time he passed the summit of the Col du Vasson (1700 m) at 154 km in the Alpes Maritimes. It was on the descent of the Vasson that the crashes came. Among the many victims were Mockridge and Gaul, the latter skidding off the road and passed by eventual winner, French veteran Raphaël Geminiani, and Bobet. They beat third-placed Gaul on the stage by 3 and 2 minutes respectively. The outcome was a success for Bobet even though he didn't win the stage. His teammate Rolland still had the yellow jersey and he was still third overall behind the Italian, Pasquale Fornara, and Gaul who – for all his attacking – was fourth.

Still driving Mockridge as the Tour neared its halfway mark was his ambition to become the first Australian to finish the Tour since Opperman in 1931. The goals of today's Australian riders may appear loftier: stage wins, green and yellow jerseys and possible overall victory. But for Mockridge – or any Australian at the time – finishing the Tour was a feat of Everest proportions. And with the Pyrénées still to come, Mockridge, who was now doubting his preparation for the Tour, knew finishing was not certain, as he said, 'If I did not finish? It was a distinct possibility. I was not riding myself in like the other riders who seemed to be going better as the days wore on. But surely there could be no worse hell than the last nine days. And if there was not – I would reach Paris.'

If Mockridge thought the next three days to the Pyrénées would provide a little respite, he was in for a shock. The stages between the Alps and Pyrénées are often termed as 'transition' stages, but for the riders they very rarely mean an easy day on the saddle. There are few giant mountains to tackle, but the passage is littered with repetitive ups and downs, many long, twisting and steep. Adding to the mix is the oppressive summer heat and the hectic race pace caused by opportunistic riders not in overall contention trying to snare a stage win.

Mockridge discovered the difficulty of the 'transition' as the Tour journeyed from the Alpes Maritimes into Provence and then the Pyrénées – from Monaco to Marseille, Avignon, Millau, Albi, Narbonne, Ax-les-Thermes and Toulouse where the race stopped before entering the Pyrénées on stage seventeen. By fate, it was on his twenty-seventh birthday – July 18 – that Mockridge confronted one of the most feared mountains in Provence – Mont Ventoux. Known as the 'Giant of Provence', this opaque-white limestone massif awaited the pack on the 198 km eleventh stage from Marseille to Avignon. Mockridge, who rode it that spring in the Tour du Vaucluse when snow rather than the haze of a sweltering heatwave draped its summit, recalled sighting the 21.1 km-long climb as the field approached it from the north: 'It looked just as I had imagined it would look in a Tour de France – a giant, smouldering 6000-foot-high (1909 m) slagheap.'

The heat that day had already caused much concern for the riders and their teams. Elsewhere in Europe, people were dying from the hot weather. But race director Jacques Goddet was unsympathetic to pleas to start the stage later. When racing got underway at 10 am, the temperature had already passed 33 degrees celsius and bitumen had started to melt, looking more like a volcanic lava-flow than a road. It was a sign of worse to come.

Most riders were feeling the effects of the heat, among them Mockridge. He started feeling weak and drained of energy as the image of Mont Ventoux rose ominously from the horizon. Way before the day's serious climbing began, a stretch of rural road that crossed a series of small rises felt more like mountains with every pedal-stroke.

Mockridge struggled on. But outside Malaucène, a quaint fourteenth-century town just north of the foot of Mont Ventoux, he suddenly felt his legs wobble, his breathing strain and noticed riders passing him one by one. Soon he stopped and dismounted his bicycle where a local farmer was hosing down exhausted riders. Taking a spray, Mockridge started eating handfuls of sugar to try and stoke his energy source. Replenished, he took the farmer's offer of a push, but within seconds felt sapped of his strength and again came to a halt. He was alone, the race was gone and Mont Ventoux still towered above him. Instinct directed him to a house and into the cooling shade of its kitchen. His entrance was no intrusion to the family that lived there. He was a Tour rider, after all. They handed Mockridge drink and food, and within a minute or two he was back on his bike, chasing the race again.

Mont Ventoux, meanwhile, was mercilessly punishing many of the riders who had dropped Mockridge earlier, as temperatures reached 45 degrees celsius on the barren moon-like slope. Replenished by his earlier stop, Mockridge passed up to 30 riders on the climb. He saw many of them collapsed on the ground in various states of exhaustion and attended to by Dr Dumas. He recalls how one rider, Frenchman Jean Malléjac who was second in the 1953 Tour, 'lay by the roadside, grey-faced, mouth foaming, eyes bulging.' Malléjac was put on a drip, given oxygen and whisked away to hospital in delirium. Others to suffer badly included Gaul and the Swiss star, Ferdi Kübler, who had attacked earlier on the climb. Kübler made it over the summit overlooking the Rhône Valley behind him and down its long, twisting descent where the Luberon awaited – but not before long he collapsed in a heap less than 1600 m shy of the finish line in Avignon.

Mont Ventoux had lived up to its promise. Even the stage winner Bobet – whose win lifted him to second overall behind his teammate Rolland – could not help but comment on how tough the stage was. 'A day like that takes years off our lives,' he said, not knowing how poignant his words would be. Twelve years later, Mont Ventoux took an entire life. In 1967, English rider Tom Simpson – leader of the Great Britain team which also included Australian Bill Lawrie – collapsed and died on the very same climb. A monument still stands in his memory today.

Having conquered Mont Ventoux, Mockridge began to feel valued by his team. With Gaul still placed well and the Pyrénées to come, the chances were that every team member would be needed to get him to Paris in as high a place as possible. Mockridge knew he would be of little use in the Pyrénées; he was feeling terrible. But so were most of the 78 riders still in the race as the Tour continued towards the mountains. Nevertheless, he was confident he could still help Gaul in the flatter portions by offering drinks, food or his wheel should Gaul puncture and need a quick change.

But Mockridge discovered that no amount of confidence can overcome rapidly depleting health in the Tour. And it was more than the cocktail of fatigue, tired limbs and saddle sores that was troubling him. Breathing problems later diagnosed as chronic bronchitis contributed to him being dropped by the diminishing pack and then finishing last on the fourteenth stage from Albi to Narbonne, 21 minutes behind the stage winner, Louis Caput. It was the first time Mockridge had finished last since stage one, but this time he was outside the time limit, signalling his elimination from the Tour.

As is so common for ill or injured riders who struggle to finish a stage – only to find out that they have missed the time limit – Mockridge was swept by mixed emotions. He was relieved the agony would be over, but upset over losing his chance of finishing the Tour. Later that night, however, he was snapped out of his conflicting emotions by the news that Tour organisers had overturned his elimination and were letting him stay in the race because he finished the stage 'under extreme difficulties'. The reprieve gave Mockridge one stage and a rest day to recover as much as possible before the Pyrénées. For the first time, he also found himself becoming part of Frantz's tactical plans to support Gaul. As expected, his job was to be Gaul's support on the flat.

Once in the Pyrénées, Gaul did attack. On the 254 km seventeenth stage from Toulouse to Saint Gaudens, he broke free midway and led by 3 minutes on the Col d'Aspin (1489 m). However, by the summit of the Col de Peyresourde (1569 m), that advantage was down to 2 minutes on Bobet who was chasing alone after dropping everyone else. Gaul was caught on the descent, but fate favoured him. Bobet punctured at Luchon, allowing Gaul to stay away and take the stage by 1 minute. However, with Rolland coming in at 7 minutes 30 seconds, Bobet was able to take the yellow jersey from his teammate and secure a commanding overall lead. The next day, stage nineteen from Saint Gaudens to Pau, saw no threat to Bobet's lead. Gaul attacked again on the Col du Soulor (1474 m), but Bobet was able to remain with him all the way to the finish on a stage won by the Belgian, Jean Brankart.

With the Tour virtually decided and mountains behind him, all that was left for Mockridge in the final days was to remain on his bike, avoid injury and lap up the satisfaction of a likely finish at the Parc des Princes velodrome in Paris. It was a task Mockridge had no trouble fulfilling after all the agony he had endured. He reached Paris in the main group, 14 seconds behind the lone breakaway, Spaniard Miguel Poblet, who was first on stage one. After pedalling his heart out for 4495 km, Mockridge's Tour was finally over.

Later, as he sat on the grass taking in the atmosphere before 35,000 fans while waiting for his team's turn to ride a lap of honour around the 454 m velodrome, Mockridge saw a victorious Bobet in discussion with his team director. He noticed that with them was Leducq, the former Tour winner-cum-journalist who had praised Mockridge earlier in his newspaper column. Leducq noticed Mockridge and wandered over in his direction. Then, just as he had promised, Leducq warmly shook his hand.

Chapter 5

A tale of two Tours

DON ALLAN

Don Allan stopped dead in his tracks on the sun-baked, sticky bitumen mountain road, high in the Alps bordering France and Italy. He could go no further on the fifteenth stage of the 1975 Tour de France. Standing, legs astride the top bar of his bike and torso slumped over his handlebars, he slowly looked up to the mountain summit and winced as he saw the hellish glow of blinding sunlight shrouding the crowd-covered peak. It was as if he were pleading for mercy, for the pain to end there and then. Allan was only a few kilometres from the top and another long cooling descent to the foot of another climb. But he may as well have been at the bottom of this twisting mountain where his torture had begun. He had made so little advance on the nearest stragglers, let alone leaders, that Allan thought he might as well not be on the Tour. He shook his head and dismounted.

After spending most of the previous stages in the mountains riding off the back of the race, Allan's mind was too dizzy from the effort to know where he was placed on the stage. Even today, he still can't say where he was. When asked, he replies that it was somewhere on one of four mountains that lie between the city of Nice on the

French Riviera and the ski station summit of Pra Loup (1630 m) where the 217 km stage finished. What he did know was that he was once more alone, in his now daily struggle to make the finish within the allocated time limit and avoid elimination by the race organisers.

Allan soft-pedalled to the side of the road, prised himself off the saddle, and then threatened the Dutch driver of the car behind him that he would have no further part of the Tour – unless he could get a chicken sandwich, a glass of beer and a 25-sprocket gear for his rear wheel to make climbing the mountains ahead more possible, if not easier. All these items are supposedly unattainable in the mountain wilderness; it was as if Allan was taking hostage of his fate and, hoping the ransom would not be delivered, be forced to carry out his threat. 'I just spat the dummy and was naming something they couldn't come up with. They all started laughing,' recalls Allan, adding that he didn't see the humour. 'The team director said, "Where am I going to get that?" and toddled off. Then the mechanic said, "I haven't got a 25 [sprocket] but a 24", so I said, "That'll do." They didn't make a 25. Then the director came back with a chicken sandwich and an old French lady in a black coat had a glass of wine for me. So I got on [my bike] again. I wasn't really going to give up. I was just being cantankerous.'

That night as Allan and his Frisol teammates ate dinner in their hotel, conversation focused on the performance of their protected team leaders and how effective everyone else was in helping them. It was from the stage victories of the team leaders and their successes in various categories that team helpers (or domestiques) like Allan reaped their share of prizemoney. It is customary in any team to pool all prizemoney and share it out at the finish in Paris.

Included among Frisol's arsenal of leaders was their number one rider for the overall general classification and the Tour winner's yellow jersey, a Dutchman named Hennie Kuiper, the 1972 Olympic road champion. He was a gifted climber who was recruited to the team to possibly challenge the reigning five-times winner, Eddy Merckx of Belgium.

Across the hotel dining room, other teams continued to eat their dinner, one of them being the Dutch team whose car followed Allan that day. Between mouthfuls of pasta, salad, meat and bread, word jokingly spread of Allan's episode on the mountain. The Dutch team director who miraculously supplied Allan with his stage-saving chicken sandwich approached the Frisol table to give his account of the incident. While it was at Allan's expense, his story boosted the morale of the Frisol team. The ever-affable Kuiper was in fits of laughter and then told their team director, Piet Liebregts: 'I am going to ride with Don one day, sounds like he has a lot of fun.' Allan shook his head. Fun? Maybe, if you call earning the right to go through all the pain again for another day. At least this time, Allan thought, the reward would be making it one day closer to the finish in Paris on his first attempt at the world's biggest bike race.

At home as a member of the Blackburn Amateur Cycling Club in Melbourne where he was known as 'Blacky', Allan was regarded as a reserved person who took his time opening up to people. Yet he revealed his sarcastic wit to those close to him and, once within the inner-sanctum of a closely knit team or group, loved nothing more than playing up.

He was also a great bike rider. He could match his rivals in races across the country, in the tours and one-day road races – even on the climbs. Despite sustaining a broken spine in 1970 that half paralysed him, he recovered and was still able to compete. In 1972 Allan finished second in the Australian road championships, won the seven-day *Tasmanian Examiner* Tour on a course full of tough climbs and made the Olympic Games road race team.

In Australia, Allan didn't fear hills or climbing. But as he would discover, it was a very different story in France against the world's greatest bike racers. The pain, the loneliness and the fear of finding yourself off the back and chasing time limits was a relentless struggle. Allan says that even before he felt the first incline of a mountain under his lightweight wheels, he knew the only way up would be agonisingly slow: 'I was quite a good climber in Australia. But the Tour is so hard. A bloke may be half a centimetre per hour quicker than you, but you just can't get on [his wheel]. It gets to another limit. You are right on the edge and you can't do much about it. I just suffered and knew I was going to go out the back and ride my own tempo.'

In the years to come, Allan would become better known for his partnership on the track with Australian cyclist Danny Clark in the European Six Day circuit – the pair won seventeen races together. He never rode the Tour again, believing that Six Day racing was a better deal financially.

However, despite his suffering and modest results in the Tour – 103rd from 105 finishers in 1974 and 85th from 86 finishers in 1975 – road racing was Allan's passion. And by riding and finishing those two Tours, he can say one thing that no other Australian can: he was a player in one of cycling's most poignant eras – when the career of one of the sport's greatest champions, Belgian Eddy Merckx, began to unfold.

In the two Tours he rode, Allan was the sole Australian and one of only two English-speaking riders in the race. Both tours were historic. The first in 1974 ended with the final and record-equalling fifth career victory by Merckx – a.k.a 'the Cannibal' because of his ferocious appetite for winning every race. Allan's second Tour in 1975 marked the start of Merckx's downfall when Frenchman Bernard Thévenet – who would later become friends with Allan as well as the darling of France – won for the first of two times.

Because he was always dropped in the mountains, Allan saw little of Merckx or Thévenet during the 1975 Tour, as in 1974 when Merckx's main challenger was Frenchman, Raymond Poulidor. But competing in the same race as these champions was a scenario he never thought possible in 1973 when he went to Europe as an amateur.

Allan's move to Europe after his selection in an Australian road racing team was organised by Ron Webb, an Australian who now lives in the south of France and is best-known for designing many of the world's premier velodromes. Allan arrived in Amsterdam from racing in Britain with $4 in his pocket (from selling his return train ticket back to London), a bike, a dream and promise of a place to stay – a claim that the suspicious

Dutch customs officer seriously doubted as Allan got off the train. 'He asked if I had money and I said no, so he said I was going back to England. I told him I wanted to be a bike rider. He said: "Not with my money you are not", recalls Allan who was finally allowed entry when the family of Dutch *soigneur* (masseur) Hans Halderman backed him up.

In his first season in Europe, Allan, then twenty-three, bagged seven stage wins in major amateur races, one being in the Peace Race where he became the first Australian to win one in a field dominated by the Eastern Bloc nations. He also excelled in the Tours of Austria, Sweden, Denmark, Switzerland and Scotland.

Halderman saw Allan win and rated him a stand-out choice for a new professional Dutch team to be sponsored by the car-oil brand, Frisol, the following year. He passed on Allan's name to the team's *directeur-sportif*, Piet Liebregts. Winning a criterium at The Hague where the 1973 Tour prologue was to start the next day tied the knot.

Allan signed with Frisol in November 1973. The prospect of racing against the likes of Merckx was still a distant thought; the bright pull-out colour posters of riders such as the champion Belgian and others like Thévenet, Poulidor, Kuiper and Patrick Sercu was still as close as he could get to them. Frisol offered Allan a minimum contract of one year with an option and a salary of 450 guilders (Aus $125) a month. Despite the meagre pay, Allan was thankful for the offer when many riders then signed up for the simple gain of a team jersey, shorts and bike and the right to say they were professionals.

It didn't take long for Merckx – in the flesh rather than in print – to impress Allan. He saw 'the Cannibal' live up to every praise-worthy word said about him, and noticed the devotion he drew from his Molteni teammates. Such dedication, Allan believes, helped to create the very first of the cycling super teams. 'I grew up reading about Merckx. I idolised him. To later ride with him and against him was awesome. You couldn't help but be awe-struck by Merckx, the strength of him. He just seemed to roll away. I saw him do some incredible things like attack at the finish and hold the whole bunch off in the last few kilometres. I had so much respect for him. He wanted to win everything in every way. Twice, he won eight stages in the Tour (1970, 1974). He also had a super team, one of the first super teams.'

Allan is adamant that if Merckx was still racing, he would be as dominant as he was in the 1970s when he began amassing a professional career total of 426 wins from 1582 professional race starts. He also believes Merckx would not have been deterred from winning the Tour by modern riders focusing solely on it and downplaying the one-day classics and small stages races. 'People have said he wouldn't do as well in it today because [other riders] specialise in the Tour. But there were riders [in Merckx's era] who specialised in it. The Spaniards and Italians didn't ride the classics in Belgium. They were Tour riders. One year he won 54 races. If Merckx had chosen to specialise in Tour he may have even done a lot better in it.'

1974 – Matching up with Merckx

When the 1974 Tour started its 4098 km clockwise excursion around France in Brest, a fishing port on the west coast of Brittany, Merckx, then twenty-eight, and Allan, then twenty-four, were poles apart in their expectations. Merckx was aiming to join Frenchman Jacques Anquetil as one of only two riders who had won five Tours. Allan's objective, besides finishing the Tour in Paris after its twenty-two stages, was to help his Dutch team and its leader, neo-pro Fedor Den Hertog, place highly in the overall classification.

Merckx quickly began to impress Allan with his early fight to win the intermediate sprints. All offered time bonuses and, ultimately, his early claim for the race leader's yellow jersey. But for a rider of the stature of Merckx to race so hard so early when he could have saved energy for the time-trials or mountains was a monumental display of panache.

Allan quickly learned, however, that rather than focus on Merckx's brave feats, he had better focus on getting through the Tour himself. Just as opportunity lay around every corner, so too did many hazards, hiccups and headaches. As is tradition, the first week of any Tour is tense. The environs of northern France where the Tour often starts are littered with sinewy, narrow and potholed or cobblestone rural roads. Add some strong head-, tail- and cross-winds, a heat wave or a cold front with some bone-chilling wet weather, and the early stages can become a platform for danger.

It is not surprising that the overall favourites for the yellow jersey are often racked with nerves, fearing they may crash or lose vital time as less credentialed riders – or the sprinters who will take a back step in the mountains – vie for any winning chance that arises. Risks are plentiful in the speeding pack, with riders darting and weaving within centimetres of one another for gaps that don't seem to exist. With only the slightest touch of wheels, a pack of riders can fall like dominoes, putting an end to any rider's Tour in a second.

For Allan and the Frisol team, the first week of the 1974 Tour was a case in point. After celebrating a win on stage two by Dutch teammate Henk Poppe at Plymouth, England, Frisol backed up after the Channel voyage to France and stage three from Morlaix to St Malo by losing Dutch champion Cees Priem in a spectacular crash on the finish line. In a mad, high-speed dash down the left-hand side of the barriers, Priem took down several other riders with him – including another Frisol teammate, Dutchman Piet Van Katwijk, who needed stitches to his head. Although he gained ninth place, Priem suffered a hairline fracture to the pelvis, and was unable to start the next day's stage to Caen.

Boldly, Merckx continued his war against the sprinters for the yellow jersey he claimed in the prologue but then lost, reclaimed and lost again before the start of stage six (b), a 9 km team time-trial out and back from the Flemish town of Harelbeke. Meanwhile, Allan kept his head low: 87th in the prologue, followed by 41st on stage one, 26th stage two, 106th on stage three, 114th on stage four, 90th on stage five, and 19th on stage six (a).

The team time-trial exposed another major difference between the statures of Merckx and Allan: the condition of their teams. The win by Merckx and the Molteni squad enforced the domination of the champion Belgian's henchmen. The opposite was true for Frisol who finished eighth from thirteen starters. The team time-trial is a specialised discipline requiring all team riders to stay together for as long as possible while racing collectively and in each other's slipstream at the fastest possible speed. For Allan and Frisol, it was a day of frustration. Ironically, as Allan recalls, most of it was caused by their team leader, Den Hertog, whose sheer strength was their undoing: 'There was probably not a rider who rides as strong as him, but he wasn't very intelligent. In the team time-trial, he would often go out [too hard] and create gaps. We would always have trouble just sitting on. He had enormous strength but would use it at the wrong time.'

Making it worse for Frisol, the team time-trial came just hours after Den Hertog caused angst on stage six (a) from Dieppe to Harelbeke. A rain-soaked and windswept stage saw up to 200 punctures among the pack. Incredibly, 29 of them were for Frisol riders, of which Den Hertog had eight. This meant work for his domestiques, too much of it wasted for Allan's liking. Repeatedly, Allan found himself dropping back to wait for Den Hertog when the Dutchman punctured and got his wheel changed by a mechanic, in readiness to tow him back to the bunch in his slipstream. But there were times that day, Allan says, when the unwittingly strong Den Hertog may as well have carried out the entire task himself and let his domestiques save their energy: 'He would puncture. We would drop back to get him back on. And then he would go straight past us.'

Merckx took outright ownership of the yellow jersey on stage seven, the 221.5 km leg from Mons through the forested Belgian Ardennes to Châlons-sur-Marne. From there to the finish he did not relinquish cycling's most prized garment, despite being bravely pursued by Poulidor. His seventh stage win was later labelled opportunistic, for Merckx reportedly jumped from the pack at a corner on the finishing circuit and into the slipstream of a television motorbike. The slipstream gave him the gap he needed to win.

That day, Allan claimed his best place for the week (fourteenth) after helping set up his sixth-placed Dutch teammate Van Katwijk for the sprint finish. But with the Alps approaching and another two weeks to go, he knew the Tour had only begun, even if his exhausting role as a domestique told him it should almost be over. 'It is hard when you are a domestique. You do your job properly, like getting the *bidons*, the raincoats . . . When you get to the mountains [it feels like] you've ridden one-and-half races already,' he said.

Allan was not alone in expressing the rigours endured by domestiques – of which Australian riders are reputably some of the best. Their feats may often go unnoticed as all the praise is aimed at the winner who stands on the podium, spraying the crowd with champagne. But inside any team, the domestique is recognised as a vital element to winning a race. Even the mercurial Eddy Merckx needed them.

As the Tour edged towards the Alps, Allan was pleasantly reminded of the esteem in which domestiques are held by his team *directeur-sportif*, Piet Liebregts. Liebregts felt that workers like Allan deserved more public recognition for their efforts. He was especially angry about the lack of kudos they received compared to soccer players who, Liebregts felt, had it all too easy. According to Allan, 'Piet said he would love to get them to follow the Tour for a couple of days; not the leading riders, but the last few and then they would learn what suffering was about.'

Once the Alps arrived, Allan also learned a thing or two about suffering. The three days spent ascending and descending their peaks were action-packed. It was in the Alps that the real battle for the yellow jersey began, and so too for Allan the battle to survive and make it to Paris.

From the moment the start-flag dropped, attacks began in the first stage in the mountains – a 241 km run from Besançon to Aspro Gaillard. The Spaniards launched their first assault on Merckx, and Poulidor also dealt his first cards. But Merckx and his Molteni henchmen were onto every move on a stage that included five climbs of varying lengths and grades, the first coming after only 5 km. With each of Molteni's measures to control the race, the pace crept up a notch. Hour by hour, riders began dropping off the back. They were shell-shocked by the sudden increase of tempo after a week on flat roads, and by the sheer demands of the ascent.

By the foot of the final climb up the 14 km-long Mont Salève, the first in the Alps, Merckx had accounted for every move. Unsurprisingly, when the climb arrived, all eyes were focused on him. This opened the door for Spanish champion, Vicente Lopez-Carril, to try his luck. He attacked with 9 km of the climb to go, hoping he could escape as the attention remained on Merckx. But his efforts to break Merckx's hold were in vain. However, when Lopez-Carril was caught, his compatriot and Kas teammate, Gonzalo Aja, attacked just short of the summit. But with 15 km to go – and most of it on the descent – Aja's lead was not enough. He soon found Merckx, Poulidor, Italian Wladimiro Panizza and Portuguese Joaquim Agostinho with him for the finishing sprint home which Merckx finally won.

Merckx's victory at Aspro Gaillard ensured he kept the yellow jersey. But of more significance to a long-discarded and rapidly tiring Allan, Merckx's sprint set the clock running for him to finish within the time limit. As the field finished in groups of ones, twos and threes, Allan and Frisol teammates, Van Katwijk and Poppe, reached the finish 43 minutes down on Merckx. Their reward was to endure it all again the next day.

Allan rued such an early fast pace in the mountains. The option of quitting was always open to him. Four riders left the race that day. Allan admits the idea always became tempting when he saw riders abandon.

But quitting the Tour is certainly not a ceremony of pomp and pageantry. The rider first slows to a halt, dismounts and often slowly straightens his aching back. Then, after pausing for a final moment of solitary reflection (or second doubt), he nods to an attending race *commissaire* (judge) to signal that, yes, he may now unpin his race number. Once made, this decision cannot be reversed. It is simple and swift, with few words spoken. More often than not, it is an act of surrender that leaves the rider in tears in front of a swarm of photographers trying to capture the moment. The day after, some riders feel guilt and shame, an experience Allan says he wanted no part of: 'I spent a lot of time on my own in the mountains. You see them giving up but you think that is the easy way out. I am a fighter. I don't like giving up.'

Also pushing Allan was his desire to join the shortlist of Australians who have finished the Tour. Up until 1974, only six Australians from the eleven starters had finished in Paris: Don Kirkham (1914), Iddo 'Snowy' Munro (1914), Sir Hubert Opperman (1928, 1931), Percy Osborne (1928), Richard 'Fatty' Lamb (1931) and Russell Mockridge (1955). Allan wanted his name among them. But for that to happen he knew he had to hang on through the Alps, a task that was made harder by the aggressive assault on Merckx's race lead by Poulidor and the Spanish riders.

The rest day couldn't come sooner for Allan – or anyone for that matter – after Merckx won the relatively short 131 km tenth stage from Aspro Gaillard to Aix-les-Bains. He did so by out-sprinting three fellow breakaways, a group he joined on the descent of the Col du Chat. Eighteen minutes later Allan arrived, second last and again with two Frisol teammates, Poppe and Van Katwijk.

After the rest day, Allan struggled through the eleventh stage, a 199 km run from Aix-les-Bains to Serre-Chevalier which Merckx began with a 2 minute 1 second overall lead on Poulidor. It was a brutal leg that saw seven riders quit the Tour, leaving it with 115 riders. Among those who abandoned was the 1973 runner-up, and the next year's winner, Thévenet, who had fallen ill overnight. To the dismay of the French, he was forced to stop on the slopes of the Col du Télégraphe just as the aggression began to take shape. Allan came home third-last.

But the Col du Télégraphe was only a precursor to what lay ahead – the more demanding rise up the summit of the Col du Galibier (2556 m) which began 5 km after the Télégraphe summit where the first serious group escaped. But it was an attack by Frenchman, Roger Pingeon, and Lopez-Carril with 10 km to go on the Galibier that really set the stage alight. The move forced Merckx to lead the chase – an effort that left Poulidor floundering under the pace.

The last 5 km of the Galibier unleashed carnage on the front-runners who were now a threesome of Merckx, Lopez-Carril and Aja. Lopez-Carril again attacked and was first over the summit.

Behind him came Merckx with Aja and another Spaniard from the Kas team, Francisco Galdos, in tow. In their wake was a string of riders leading all the way back to Allan.

With a Spaniard in front and two more in tow, Merckx again had no choice but to lead the chase of Lopez-Carril down the winding Galibier descent and then along the valley for the 20 km stretch to the ski resort town of Serre-Chevalier. Lopez-Carril still won, but Merckx – trying to minimise the time loss – rode as hard as he could to the finish and managed to win the three-up sprint for second place. Then came an exhausted line of riders. One was Poulidor who finished tenth at 6 minutes 17 seconds to Lopez-Carril and 5 minutes 23 seconds behind Merckx. After starting the stage second overall at 2 minutes 1 second to Merckx, the shattered Frenchman was now sixth and 7 minutes 24 seconds down overall. Closest on Merckx's tail were the Spaniards, Aja at 2 minutes 20 seconds, and Lopez-Carril at 2 minutes 34 seconds. Allan customarily finished at the tail-end, third-last at more than 30 minutes.

Leaving the Alps brought no respite. The Tour's entry into the steamy and sweltering region of Provence only heralded more pain. Highlighting the 231 km twelfth stage from Savines-le-Lac to Orange was the feared ascent up the scree-sloped rise of Mont Ventoux, one of the Tour's most fabled climbs and known as the 'Giant of Provence'. Mont Ventoux can be ascended from two directions: from the north and the south. Either way is a brutal challenge, and unsurprisingly, it was not until the race reached the 21.1 km climb that the stage saw any serious action. On this occasion, the field tackled the climb to its 1912 m summit from the south. The long, winding route began with the bunch being protected from the burning sun by the shade of pine trees that blanket the first 15 km of the climb. But cruelly, just as the route turns left and upwards at le Chalet-Reynard, the line of cooling shadows abates as the road leads into a vast furnace of heat, blue skies and testing Mistral headwinds, opening the riders to the hellish view of the barren, moon-like scree slopes.

For Allan and the Frisol team, it was a day of resounding success as the team very nearly celebrated their second win. For in second place – outsprinted by Spruyt – was their team leader, Den Hertog, finally using his power and strength wisely. With Spruyt already away, it was Den Hertog who ignited the main chase of Spruyt and four others, his effort even catching Merckx off-guard. In the finish at Orange, Spruyt – who had done little work in the bunch – won, but only with half a wheel to spare. Allan struggled to the finish, but at least he did so with more company than usual. He finished in a group of eighteen riders at 10 minutes 44 seconds to Belgian stage winner Jozef Spruyt, one of Merckx's teammates.

The Pyrénées would prove a harsher test for Allan. The two stages leading up to them were transition legs. For their respective winners, Barry Hoban (stage thirteen) and Jean-Pierre Genet (stage fourteen), they provided celebrations, but in the back of everyone's mind were the Pyrénées that border France and Spain and which Allan says were harder to climb than the Alps. Whether they *are* harder depends on the rider. Ask a Spaniard – climbers or not – and they will say they love the Pyrénées, spurred on by their proximity to home and the traditionally large, parochial and very loud local crowd that flocks to their slopes. Many others will say they prefer the Alps. Although they are longer climbs that reach higher altitude, the Alps are generally climbed on smoother roads with numerous switch-backs often helping riders – particularly those like Allan who are not natural climbers – seek a more even and manageable tempo. The climate can be cooler and less humid in the Alps, and this often helps. Other riders, however, prefer the Pyrénées as their climbing style is characterised by gusto and punch that can be so effective on short and sharper ascents.

That said, the Spaniards were hit by misfortune in the first of two Pyrénéan stages, the 225 km fifteenth stage from Colomiers to Séo-de-Urgel inside the Spanish border. Despite expectation of another Spanish assault on Merckx's yellow jersey, he still won the stage after a crash among the leading fifteen-man group 300 m before the end. But the passive riding by the Spanish contingent could have been due to Galdos' earlier crash at 132 km. Placed sixth overall and considered an outside threat to Merckx,

Galdos still rode the 100 km to finish in eleventh place. Many thought the Spaniards were easing up on their efforts in readiness for the next day, hoping that Galdos would recover to race again. But x-rays that night revealed he had fractured his femur. Galdos' Tour was over.

By now, Allan, who finished 99th at 18 minutes 9 seconds, was crossing off the stages in his mind. As he bedded down that night while torrential rain blanketed the Spanish Pyrénées, he had two counts running: the first, to when the last mountain would be behind him and the second to when his first Tour finish could become official. But Paris was still a long way away considering the hundreds of possible misfortunes.

At the end of the next day when the number of Tour survivors had dropped to 109, Allan and the entire Tour entourage came face to face with those unpredictable hazards in a terrifying fashion. It was not so much the race – a 209 km leg from Séo-de-Urgel that took the Tour 140 km to the Spanish–French border on the Col du Portillon on the way to Pla d'Adet – but the explosion of two car bombs. It happened at the end of the stage during the stay at St Lary-Soulan. Because of the massive worldwide publicity it generates, protesters wanting to champion their message have always used the Tour to air their grievances – from farmers, students and factory workers to political activists.

Two support team cars were blown up, as well as one belonging to the journalists of *Agence France Presse*. Fortunately, nobody was injured in the explosions which – according to David Saunders in *Tour de France 1974* – were claimed the next day by the International Revolutionary Group. According to Saunders, the IRG had also threatened two Spanish teams and planned to attack the race on the 119 km seventeenth stage from St Lary-Soulan to the finish at La Mongie – the famed Col du Tourmalet (2115 m).

The bombs created a major scare for the Tour, especially coming on the heels of a number of earlier incidents, such as Basque nationalists painting red slogans on cars and the explosion of a post office in Andorra where many of the Tour entourage were staying overnight after the stage from Colomiers to Séo-de-Urgel. With a threatened attack on the race itself, security was stepped up, foremost around the peloton as it rode out of the Pyrénées on stage eighteen from Bagnères-de-Bigorre to Pau. Worst affected were the Spanish riders, in particular Lopez-Carril, who was second overall to Merckx. Worried by threats from Basque nationalists, he refused to continue wearing his Spanish champion's jersey – as is customary of all national champions when they hold the title – and rode out the Tour in his Kas trade team strip.

Lopez-Carril survived the Pyrénées still in second place to Merckx, who had indicated all was not well by losing time to Poulidor on stage seventeen to the summit of the 20 km-long Tourmalet. It was a cold and drizzly day in which the final climb was preceded by the ascent of the Col d'Aspin. It was there, 1 km shy of the summit, that French stage winner Jean-Pierre Danguillaume made his winning solo move. Poulidor was second on the stage, 2 minutes 36 seconds behind; but he rode strongly to still take 42 more seconds on seventh-placed Merckx and move up to third at 5 minutes 18 seconds.

Allan finished with a group of 33 riders in 99th place at 17 minutes 16 seconds, safely inside the time limit. The prospect of reaching Paris was becoming more realistic.

But if he thought the Tourmalet was behind him, he was to think again. The final mountain stage began with another ascent up its slopes. Following it came the Col du Soulor where Danguillaume – still no major threat overall in sixteenth place – caught three early attackers to form the winning break and take out his second successive stage. Many in the peloton were happy for the outcome, even Merckx who had survived his weak spell and now knew that his fifth Tour was virtually safe with flat stages between Pau and Paris. After finishing the final mountain stage in 100th place at 11 minutes 3 seconds, Allan was now confident of reaching Paris. But he wasn't celebrating yet: 'Once they [the Pyrénées] were over I knew I could hang in there but it was still hard.'

The final days provided the sprinters with their last chance to savour a little of the glory they enjoyed in the first week. Also, riders who were still feeling strong after the mountains but had so far not shone were given a chance to salvage their Tour – if not their careers or trade team's image – with a stage-winning ride by going on the attack. Frenchman Francis Campaner was one of the latter, staying away alone for 115 km to win the 195.5 km stage nineteen (a) from Pau to Bordeaux. Allan was strong too, finishing sixteenth.

Merckx had not had his last say either. He won the second leg of stage nineteen, a 12.4 km time-trial around the lake at Bordeaux, to extend his overall lead on Lopez-Carril from 2 minutes 29 seconds to 3 minutes 26 seconds; and on Poulidor from 5 minutes 22 seconds to 5 minutes 42 seconds. He extended his advantage even further two stages later – stage twenty-one (a) from Vouvray to Orléans – with a solo win that saw him finish 1 minute 25 seconds clear of the peloton. In the main bunch led by Sercu – who would win the green-jersied points competition as best sprinter – Allan was seventh, giving him a best-ever finish of eighth.

Merckx, chasing a record nine stage wins in a Tour, struck again. But his bid for the record failed when he succumbed to a shock 10-second loss to Belgian Michel Pollentier in the 37.5 km stage twenty-one (b) time-trial at Orléans. But Merckx left his stamp on the Tour with an eighth win (equaling his own record of 1970) by taking out the final leg over 146 km from Orléans to Paris. It was a controversial finish though: Sercu was first across the line ahead of Merckx and Gustave Van Roosbroeck. But he was relegated to third for obstructing Van Roosbroeck, forcing officials to give Merckx the win and Van Roosbroeck second place.

For Allan, his 84th place in the same sprint was enough to get him home in 103rd place in 116 hours 16 minutes 58 seconds, third last and 3 hours 17 minutes 7 seconds behind Merckx whose winning time was 119 hours 33 minutes 51 seconds. His Frisol team was rewarded with two stages wins in the first week. Highest finisher overall was Den Hertog whose one great ride was on Mont Ventoux. But his 27th place overall at 50 minutes 28 seconds indicated his future as a Tour contender was limited.

It was a race that Allan admits 'opened his eyes' to the challenge of professional cycling. But despite his suffering and frequent solitude – physically, in the mountains and socially, as one of only two English-speaking riders in the race – he would return in twelve months to face it all again.

1975 – 'I don't want to finish last'

Merckx's pursuit of a record sixth victory was destined to be the talking point of the 1975 Tour – win or lose. Ever since he won his fifth Tour twelve months before, the pressure was on his broad shoulders.

Merckx didn't win the 1975 Tour; instead, the title went to Frenchman Bernard Thévenet. However, on a course rated as one of the most difficult in years, the race provided plenty of unexpected drama. Foremost was Merckx being physically assaulted by a crazed spectator during a stage in the Massif Central, and then his crash soon after which left him reaching Paris with a fractured jaw. However, those incidents aside, Allan concurs there was nothing hollow about Thévenet's win. The Frenchman took control of the race before Merckx's misfortunes, even though the yellow jersey had yet to be claimed. He reached the finish on the Champs Elysées in Paris 2 minutes 47 seconds clear of Merckx.

As for Allan, he was voted the Tour's most courageous rider by the European media who could have been excused for concentrating solely on the Tour's new champion and their reflections on the greatness of the Merckx era. However, the little-known Australian rider who finished 3 hours 24 minutes 38 seconds behind the winner attracted much praise for his gutsy performance.

Allan started his second Tour at Charleroi a far better rider than he was in 1974. He had one year's experience as a professional behind him, including one Tour finish. He was better prepared physically and mentally and had won a stage of the Vuelta a España (Tour of Spain) in Bilbao – the first Australian to do so. His Frisol team, also better for a year's experience, still had a strong arsenal of sprinters (Cees Priem and Theo Smit) and the valued strength of Den Hertog. But this time they also had a more legitimate overall contender, Dutchman Hennie Kuiper, the 1972 Olympic champion who would finish eleventh and in years to come twice finish second overall in the Tour. 'He was a very intelligent rider,' said Allan. 'It [having him] didn't mean more work for us. We had three or four protected riders, the sprinters and Kuiper for the mountains. Once we got him to the mountains there was not much I could do for him. He was on his own. But having him was good. It was thought he could be a real challenger.'

Allan's 1975 Tour was a similar story to 1974. Again, he kept his head low early, working for his sprinters. And the effort paid off. The champagne bottles were opened at the Frisol team dinner and the glasses were filled and raised after Priem and Smit respectively won the first stage from Charleroi to Molenbeek and the fifth from Sable-sur-Sarthe to Merlin-Plage. Smit repeated the feat four days later on stage nine (a) from Langon to Fleurance. And again Frisol opened, poured and toasted his victory with champagne.

Meanwhile, in the race for the yellow jersey, Merckx was in second place at the end of stage five, 2 seconds shy of an Italian Tour debutant and soon-to-be star, Francesco Moser, who would go on to become one of the world's greatest-ever riders. However, Merckx struck on stage six, winning the 16 km time-trial to take the yellow jersey from Moser and head into the second week with a 31-second lead which he held until the next time-trial on stage nine (b) from Fleurance to Auch. This extended his margin on Moser to 1 minute 39 seconds and on Thévenet to 2 minutes 20 seconds as the Pyrénées approached. But then Merckx took everyone by surprise with his relatively passive racing after the rest day on the tenth stage from Auch to Pau where he curiously allowed everyone else in the race to control the stage.

It was the first major mountain stage – stage eleven, 160 km Pau from St Lary-Soulan – that really saw a change in Merckx's fortunes. The stage finished at the summit of the Pla d'Adet (1680 m) after ascents of the Col du Tourmalet and Col d'Aspin.

It was on the final climb that the first chink in Merckx's armour was revealed: he made no response to an attack by Dutchman Joop Zoetemelk, followed by Thévenet. Zoetemelk won by 6 seconds from Thévenet. But the major upset was the sight of an exhausted Merckx labouring to the finish in fourth place, 55 seconds behind the winner. The result saw Thévenet ominously move up to second overall at 1 minute 31 seconds to Merckx.

Meanwhile, Allan was still finishing near the back of the pack: 115th from 119 riders on stage eleven. Like Merckx, he welcomed the more controllable paces of stages twelve and thirteen to Albi and Super Lioran. It was during stage fourteen, however, that unimaginable drama took place. The field was bunched together when they reached the foot of the steep and gruelling 13 km ascent to the finish at Puy de Dome where an all-out attack on Merckx was expected. But when people spoke of the attack, nobody foresaw that it would come from a spectator rather than a fellow rider.

As Merckx tried to chase the leading pair, he received a punch to the liver from a 68-year-old man in the last 300 m of the race. The blow left Merckx doubled-up over his handlebars as he crossed the finish-line. Miraculously, he didn't fall off and still finished third, 49 seconds behind a victorious Lucien Van Impe and 34 seconds after Thévenet.

After a rest day in Nice on the Côte d'Azur of southern France, the Tour prepared for its first major Alpine stage. It was a 217.5 km leg from the blue Riviera sea to the ski station summit of Pra Loup. The stage included four mountains that split the field one by one and then finished with a steep fifth climb – 7 km-long – up to the ski station. It was during the second-last climb, the Col d'Allos (2250 m), that Merckx arguably fired his final salvo in a bid to win the Tour.

After being tirelessly lead to the top by his teammate Jos Deschoenmaecker, Merckx attacked 1 km before the 2250 m summit. In his wake were Thévenet, Van Impe, Zoetemelk and Felice Gimondi. At the foot of the final climb to Pra Loup, Merckx was more than a minute clear after a huge downhill effort, but incredibly, he capitulated on the climb to the finish.

It was a turn of form that definitely surprised Gimondi when he caught Merckx, and then Thévenet – who seized the opportunity and attacked to leave Merckx struggling home in fifth place. As France rejoiced in Thévenet's stage victory and yellow jersey claim, the beaten defending champion crossed the line 1 minute 56 seconds later. With another brutal Alpine stage looming the next day, Merckx was now second overall at 58 seconds to Thévenet. His Tour was on tenterhooks.

Incredibly, Merckx gambled his last hopes of winning the Tour on the short 107 km sixteenth stage from Barcelonnette to Serre-Chevalier. Relying on the element of surprise, he bolted from the pack on the Col de Vars descent and rode with all his remaining fury along the valley towards the second and last mountain of the day, the giant Col d'Izoard (2361 m). The move sent Thévenet and his Peugeot henchmen into a panic and they unleashed a furious chase that succeeded just as the Col d'Izoard came into view.

Thévenet would not be caught out again. As soon as Merckx called for his Molteni team car on the early slopes of the giant climb to the finish, the Frenchman attacked to win back-to-back stages. By finishing 2 minutes 22 seconds ahead of Merckx he also extended his overall lead on the Belgian to 3 minutes 20 seconds. 'Thévenet smashed him again. Merckx just blew up and that was the start of [his fall],' says Allan who was then having problems of his own and looked like being eliminated from the Tour.

On the stage from Nice to Pra Loup, Allan finished 95th at 34 minutes 34 seconds to Thévenet. It was a torrid day, a blur of pain and emotion – hence his threat to quit the Tour unless he got a chicken sandwich, a cold beer and a 25-sprocket gear. He remembers the tug on his heartstrings as he reached the foot of the 7 km 'wall' to finish and heard the encouraging voice of an Australian – cycling journalist Dennis Lane. Unlike today when the Tour route is littered with Australian flags and cheering Australian tourists, that lone Australian voice carried the strength of a thousand for Allan.

Worse was to come, however, on the 107 km 'sprint' to Serre-Chevalier where the time limit was incredibly short in light of the fast pace. Allan was 96th and second-last, just ahead of Dutch teammate Gerard Kamper. They both finished at 21 minutes 55 seconds to Thévenet and outside the time limit. But their precarious future in the race was not solely due to the rapid pace up-front. Allan recalls how he and Kamper had taken a wrong turn during the stage: 'I remember packing my bag that night. I had wanted to finish but then I didn't really care, I was that buggered. The number-two team manager [Edgar de Maere] went to the organisers and pleaded. He put on a bit of an act, got the hanky out and cried. He told them we went the wrong way and punctured. Then they let us back in. He came back and said: "I've got good news." I thought, 'I don't know if it *is* good news.' We were at the end of our tether. We were that far back.'

With one more stage to go in the Alps, Merckx was also at rock-bottom. But if anyone doubted this, opinions would have firmed early in the 225 km seventeenth stage from Valloire to Morzine when he fractured his cheekbone. The injury was from a crash in the neutralised zone where attacks are banned to allow the Tour to safely roll out of a town and find open roads. When it happened, no one knew that Merckx had fractured the bone. But the spill left him looking groggy and ill enough for race doctors' orders to advise him to abandon. He refused and still finished third on the stage won by the Spaniard Lopez-Carril in a solo attack that bore no major changes overall.

Meanwhile, Allan was looking like a strong prospect to win the ignomious title of *lanterne rouge* – named after the red light at the back of a train and given to the rider who is last overall. For most, the title is worth vying for as the 'winner' is invited with the Tour stars to contest the post-Tour exhibition races, called criteriums, where appearance fees are regular. And because of the massive publicity the *lanterne rouge* attracts, winning it is highly regarded by a rider's team sponsor. That rider would often receive a bonus payment for the effort – or more accurately, lack thereof!

As Paris drew near, Allan publicly played along with the unexpected media attention that followed him. 'You have to have a first and last rider. I'll never be the first, so I might as well be the last,' he was quoted as saying in one French newspaper article titled: *Don Allan: Une 'lanterne rouge' and moral merveilleux (a 'lanterne rouge' with great morale)*. In the same article he continues to say: 'At least I will get a few contracts. If I stayed in the middle of the standings, my name would not be noticed. On the other hand, when it is on the last line of the classification, you see it . . .' During quiet moments of a stage, Allan also had his photo taken holding the lantern while dropping off the back of the pack and looking to check that nobody was behind him.

However, Allan says deep down the last thing he wanted was to be atop the podium in Paris waving the lantern in celebration. While he always believed that the last-placed rider is never last 'because riders abandon during the race', he says he never saw sense in celebrating the result: 'Everyone said, "It's great, you'll get a lot of publicity." The team said: "It's great, you'll get money." But I hated it. I didn't enter races to finish last.'

In many ways, while Merckx and Thévenet were poles apart from Allan on form and class, they shared the same stoic ethos. Allan has no qualms about labelling Thévenet's victory over Merckx as one earned rather than given. He reminds us that Merckx was already showing cracks before finding himself at the receiving end of his untimely misfortunes. Likewise, Allan sees it as a credit to Merckx that he defied doctors' orders after his crash and continued to ride on to Paris and chip away at Thévenet's lead. That Merckx could have easily pulled out without losing an ounce of pride and still finish second overall says something about the strength of character of the man Thévenet had to overcome.

As for Allan, his staunch opinion that finishing second-last in the Tour was better than finishing last was rewarded. He was fourteenth on stage nineteen, twenty-fourth on stage twenty, 38th on stage twenty-one and eighteenth on the final leg out and back from Paris in which he also attacked for two-and-half laps of the finishing circuit on the Champs Elysées in a brave bid to win the final leg.

His efforts were more praise-worthy than those of the rider who deposed Allan from last place, Frenchman Jacques Boulas.

According to his team masseur, Boulas hid behind a bush to lose 10 minutes. He punctured and waited. Allan's team told him it could have been him. But as Allan says, 'I would have hated it. I didn't want to finish last.'

Chapter 6

Thirteen out of thirteen

PHIL ANDERSON

Phil Anderson suffered more than his share of punishment en-route to paving the greatest professional road racing career of any Australian cyclist. In his fourteen years, he broke too many bones and was at the receiving end of too many injuries or illnesses to mention: in one season alone he sustained a fractured kneecap, dislocated shoulder, badly bruised ribs and index finger, torn chest muscles and bronchitis. After becoming Australia's first-ever Tour de France yellow jersey wearer in 1981, Anderson pushed his body and mind to its limits. One of a handful of Australians then racing in Europe in the 1980s, he also dismantled many of the cultural and social barriers that until then had hindered Australian cyclists. It is due to his efforts that today's Australian cyclists enjoy so many opportunities.

Anderson's career was so significant – including 85 professional wins and five top-ten overall placings from his thirteen starts in the Tour – that one could easily just focus on his victories, or at least the relentless pursuit of them. But it is a measure of the humble, fun-loving person Anderson is that when he looks back he remembers the lighter moments, the moments when he could laugh and which reminded him of his love for the sport and the camaraderie within.

One such moment occurred in a marathon 273 km stage in the baking heat of the Massif Central in 1985 when the peloton decided, of all things, to 'crash' *en masse*. The stunt was concocted for the sole reason of killing the boredom of another long and slow day on the saddle. As Anderson recalls, 'We were going along, getting slower and slower and then suddenly we all stopped, lay on the ground with the bikes up in the air – we were still strapped into the bloody bikes! Suddenly, all the mechanics were out of the cars and ambulances were rushing around and there were 180 guys all lying on their backs.'

Anderson's blue eyes light up as he speaks. You can see the larrikin who first took up cycling at age sixteen for a bit of fun – which is what cycling is to Anderson today where he and his wife Christi live at Ocean Grove on the southwest coast of Victoria. However, in between boyhood and today, Anderson forged the most glorious professional career of any Australian rider. At his prime in 1985, he was one of the most aggressive riders in the bunch. What he lacked in natural class he more than made up for in fighting spirit and an insatiable appetite to win. Along the way, there were disappointments – injuries, illness, disputes and form slumps – but he always survived to come through a winner until retiring in 1994.

It is fitting that when Anderson's career was nearing its end, the professional career of another rider on his Motorola team, Texan Lance Armstrong, was taking off the same way his did in 1980. Their union as teammates from 1992 to 1994 benefited both: Anderson saw a lot of himself in Armstrong, especially in the 1993 Tour when Armstrong upset French hopes by winning the first Tour stage of his own career. Armstrong struck on stage eight from Châlons-sur-Marne to Verdun, outsprinting a breakaway group that included Mexican Raul Alcala and the ever-popular Frenchman, Ronan Pensec. 'It reminded me of when I was his age, you know, the drive and [sense of] not being intimidated. He was like, "Fuck it, I'll attack whether you like it or not," ' Anderson recalls.

1981 – The breakthrough

It was in the week before the 1981 Tour de France that Anderson provided the first strong hint of his form. His French teammate, Jean-René Bernaudeau, had already secured leadership of his French Peugeot team with another win in the Midi Libre stage race. But Anderson's win in the four-day Tour de l'Aude in France indicated he would be a worthy helper for Bernaudeau. It was a further plus for the team that Anderson's victory in the Tour de l'Aude – his first in a professional stage race – coincided with the Peugeot team dominating the race. Two other Peugeot riders finished in the top-ten overall – Scot Robert Millar, fifth at 8 minutes 6 seconds; and Frenchman Jacques Bossis, ninth, another 48 seconds behind. It was a major boost for team morale, even though it also gave French race favourite, the much-feared Bernard Hinault, a good preview of their likely strength and potential threat.

It was on the 117 km sixth stage of the 1981 Tour de France from Saint Gaudens to the ski station of Pla d'Adet in the Pyrénées that Anderson, rather than the Peugeot team, rose up as a stand-alone danger for Hinault. Anderson was unsure of how to race his first mountain stage. He said he felt good before it began, but didn't know how good he felt. Furthermore, he was on-call to help Bernaudeau. He decided to follow someone with a steady rhythm like Hinault, rather than the more frenetic pace of the pure climbers like Belgian, Lucien Van Impe. The Belgian won the stage, but surprising everyone was Anderson who became the first Australian to claim the yellow jersey after a titanic tussle with Hinault.

Anderson and Hinault finished 27 seconds after Van Impe, and while the Australian stood proudly in yellow, Hinault had nothing but contempt for Anderson 'daring' to challenge him. It was even worse when Anderson just sat on his wheel – still hoping for news of Bernaudeau who had been long dropped – until Peugeot *directeur-sportif*, Maurice De Muer, told him he could work 'a bit' at the front. 'It was just as well, as Hinault was going off his block,' said Anderson, who had four other riders with him in the front group: Van Impe, Belgian Claude Criquelion, and the Spanish pair of Marino Lejarreta and Alberto Fernandez. Without knowing it, Anderson was to earn even greater wrath from Hinault by naively offering him a swill from his *bidon* (drink bottle). The Frenchman, taking the gesture as an insult, promptly swiped it from Anderson's hand. 'I didn't even know who Hinault was. I couldn't even pronounce his name. But I was there with him and when I gave him my *bidon* I was only trying to be sportsmanlike. I figured something was really up with him when he hit it away. I suppose I should have been intimidated by it all, but I wasn't. Heck, I was Australian and couldn't even spell Hinault, let alone know who he was,' says Anderson.

Anderson's gall of standing up to Hinault was an inspiration to a world accustomed to accepting 'the badger's' authority, as the fiery Breton was known. Peugeot, having seen Bernaudeau lose 4 minutes 30 seconds, seriously damaging any chance of winning the Tour, could not decide whether to defend the untested and relatively unknown Anderson, or to try and get their top star Bernaudeau back into contention. Opinions were mixed. Realising the sensitivity of his position, De Muer remained guarded. As Anderson tried to come to terms with his achievement, all of sporting France was in a fever over his feat that day. One significant vote in Anderson's favour came from former Tour race director, Jacques Goddet, who wrote: 'Peugeot should now play Anderson's card,' in his daily diary piece in *l'Équipe* newspaper.

Anderson was unprepared for the attention he received wearing his yellow jersey. One day he was just another face in the Tour, the next he was the name on everyone's lips. He faced a barrage of media interviews about him and Australian cycling; some television reporters even produced maps of Australia for him to point out where Melbourne was. It was a daunting change to his life: 'I didn't sleep too well because of the jersey. It was a dream, a dream come true. I never thought I would be riding in Europe let alone the Tour de France.'

The 'Australian phenomenon' had been analysed, questioned and judged in every possible way before the start of the next day's showdown – the stage seven 26.7 km time-trial from Nay to Pau. One obvious question was how Anderson, as an Australian in a French team, had adapted to the system – if he had at all.

The response of teammate Michel Laurent confirmed that even within his own team, Anderson was not the popular figure a yellow jersey wearer should be. When asked whether Anderson was popular, Laurent told *l'Équipe:* 'Yes and no. Yes, because he is a guy who always smiles, is nice and happy when all goes well. No, because he hardly speaks French so there is a barrier. At the table in the evening when we talk about the race, he can't take part in the conversation.' Anderson never heard such criticism from teammates like Laurent face-to-face. And one can only wonder how the French Peugeot riders would have fared on an English-speaking team if the tables had been turned. Certainly, Anderson sensed that official attitudes towards him changed after he took the yellow jersey. But he was readily aware of the 'barrier' Laurent was referring to. Citing Irishman Stephen Roche who spoke fluent French as an example, he said: 'Roche could understand all the jokes and everything that went on. I used to kind of go along and laugh, but then I would wonder, Shit, what are they laughing about,' he says.

From his experience on Pla d'Adet, Anderson would have sensed how badly Hinault wanted the yellow jersey back. However, while he ultimately surrendered it, the Australian didn't do so without a fight. Hinault won the time-trial stage and took the yellow jersey, but Anderson's third at 30 seconds after leading Hinault until 11 km and keeping the gap at only 3 seconds after 14 km was creating a lot of interest. And when he finally lost the jersey by only 13 seconds, even Hinault acknowledged that Anderson was a star for the future. 'I thought he had ridden very well. After all, the time-trial is one of my specialities. He proved today that he is going to be a very good rider indeed,' he said.

Anderson didn't lie down though. Hinault had a clear run to Paris and would clinch his third of five Tour victories. But in the days after that first time-trial, Anderson continued to be a thorn in Hinault's side by trying to chase down time bonuses in the intermediate sprints. Hinault was so annoyed he repeatedly tried to deal with him in a bid to stop his attacking style. 'He was infu-riated that I would challenge him and try and get it back, you know, and he kept coming back and trying to make deals. He was saying: "Listen if you sprint, I'm going to sprint, so why don't we just make a truce and save your energy for later in the mountains." But he would [still] send his riders up the road to try and win the bonifications, and I didn't have much help from my team.'

While never getting back the yellow jersey, Anderson confirmed his reputation by winning the white jersey as best young rider. He also proved he was a potential winner, as he was still second overall after sixteen stages before finishing tenth.

Anderson's feud with Hinault remained fairly dormant for the rest of the Tour, but picked up again at stage sixteen, the 38.5 km time-trial at Mulhouse where Hinault passed Anderson with 10 km to go to win. But Anderson, who was fourth, unwittingly stoked their rivalry by refusing to let Hinault get away, despite the intervention of race *commissaires* who felt he was slip-streaming and warned him of it during the stage.

Two days later in the Alps, stage nineteen from Morzine to l'Alpe d'Huez, Anderson was brought back to reality. His inab-ility to follow the best on the climbs was revealed as his biggest weakness and drastically changed the odds. He lost second place to Van Impe after finishing 44th, 17 minutes and 6 seconds behind stage winner, Peter Winnen of the Netherlands, and conceded the white jersey to the victorious Dutchman. However, Anderson never gave up hope of pegging back his overall place and claiming the white jersey. And by the end of stage twenty-one, after a series of strong stage placings, he was back to tenth overall and the white jersey was his again. He held his position right up to the finish on stage twenty-four at Paris, where Hinault was victorious once more.

Anderson's tenth place was the best ever by an Australian and his victory in the young riders' competition the first of any category in the Tour clinched by one of his countrymen. Peugeot may have been disappointed in Bernaudeau's sixth place overall, but their victory in the team's category, and Anderson's incredible results, kept the portly De Muer smiling as he looked to 1982.

Anderson was naturally a sought-after rider for the lucrative post-Tour criteriums. And his next objective was the world championships at Prague. But that goal and every other one pencilled in for the rest of the 1981 season were scrubbed when he broke his finger at the Chaam criterium in Holland in a crash that also killed a young spectator. Two operations and the inevitable period of recuperation gave De Muer no choice but to give Anderson an early mark for the season. Anderson didn't complain. He locked up his Belgian residence for the winter and returned to Australia where he married his American fiancée, Anne Robel.

Returning to Europe in 1982 with 4000 km training kilometres in his legs, Anderson found that Peugeot had added Sean Yates to its English-speaking force. There were now five English-speaking riders in the twenty-strong team – himself, Yates, Graham Jones, Robert Millar and Stephen Roche. Anderson's main aim was again the Tour, and he wanted to do better than his tenth overall in 1981. He felt the route was better-suited to his talents – or comparative climbing weakness. With two seasons behind him, he knew 1982 was his year for producing consistent results.

But the spring classics didn't see Anderson shine as expected. He was fifth in the Amstel Gold Race which was eventually won by Dutchman Jan Raas. Peugeot, however, notched up many wins and top placings: Laurent won the Mediterranean Tour and Dauphiné-Libéré, Gilbert Duclos-Lassalle was first in the Tour de l'Oise and second in Paris–Nice, Jones was second in Het Volk, Roche was third in the Four Days of Dunkirk and Bernaudeau won the Midi Libre after finishing second in the Route du Sud. Meanwhile, to secure his Tour berth, Anderson banked on his 1981 results and several early season appearances helping Peugeot riders to win races.

Come the 1982 Tour, Anderson soon found himself to be De Muer's favourite. De Muer believed that the only way to harass Hinault was to take the offensive, as Anderson did by winning the 246 km second stage from Bâle in Switzerland to Nancy – after attacking five other breakaways with 10 km to go. In the group with him were: teammate Laurent, Frenchmen Marc Madiot from Hinault's team, Bernard Vallet, and Dutchmen Henk Lubberding and Peter Winnen. Afterwards, Anderson was full of praise for Laurent: 'I was doing most of the work with Vallet and Laurent. But I owe him [Laurent] a lot because he was doing a lot of the work at the end, and it was he who did so much to get the breakaway.'

Anderson would not win a Tour stage again for another ten years. When he did, he took the yellow jersey from Belgian, Ludo Peeters. 'I intend to hang onto this jersey for a lot longer this time,' he said. And he did. The yellow jersey was his for the next nine days, despite challenges from Sean Kelly and imminent capture by Hinault who had won the Giro d'Italia a month before. As Anderson expected, his fate arrived on the stage eleven time-trial at Valence d'Agen. Hinault took back the jersey by placing second, but still 2 minutes 47 seconds clear of Anderson in the 68 km test.

De Muer didn't hesitate to declare Anderson team leader, despite Anderson saying he thought Bernaudeau would assume his role in the Pyrénées. However, circumstances left De Muer with little choice. Anderson was still third overall at 2 minutes 3 seconds when stage twelve from Fleurance to Pau began and it ended with Anderson finishing second to Kelly, and Bernaudeau being dropped on the Col de Soulor, finishing 3 minutes 53 seconds down after injury. The choice to protect Anderson to Paris was an obvious one – he was now second overall, still at 2 minutes 3 seconds, while Peugeot's next best rider overall was Bernaudeau in twenty-second place at 11 minutes 34 seconds.

Anderson needed help the next day in the Pyrénées too. In the stage from Pau to St Lary-Soulan, he took the race to Hinault by attacking the Frenchman twice. But then he paid for his efforts, blowing up as Hinault attacked. And were it not for the support of his teammate Laurent who had attacked earlier, Anderson may have lost more than the 1 minute 8 seconds he did on Hinault. But 24 hours later, after Hinault won stage fourteen, the 32.5 km time-trial at Martigues, Anderson was unable to call on team support again. In the 'race of truth' he was twentieth at 2 minutes

5 seconds to Hinault; and while still second overall, he was now 5 minutes 17 seconds down. With the Alps still to come, Anderson's threat to Hinault was quickly diminishing. He lost time on two of the three Alpine climbs, but on the third from l'Alpe d'Huez to Morzine – stage seventeen – he was seventh at 2 minutes 27 seconds to Winnen, beaten for sixth place in a sprint against Hinault. Still, Anderson had given 'the badger' a greater headache than anyone else in recent times.

That seventeenth stage included four mountains and Anderson belied his exhaustion and troubles of the previous two days by riding in the front third of the bunch all day. 'Once we were on the first Col I knew I was okay, but everyone else was suffering. Lots of riders were nervous as they fought to try and stay in the front,' says Anderson. In fact his only problem was an early puncture. Nearby was Bernaudeau who Anderson could have asked for his wheel, but amazingly, couldn't bring himself to and rode 5 km with a flat tyre before a team car came to change his wheel. '[Bernaudeau] was a good guy and trying to get back in the reckoning. He had lost his team leadership in the Pyrénées and some pride. So I didn't like to ask him to give me his wheel,' recalls Anderson.

Anderson rode into Paris and the finish, still in fifth place overall at 12 minutes 16 seconds to a victorious Hinault. De Muer was once again rubbing his hands in delight, and by all accounts so was Anderson. But it all came to nothing in the end. De Muer, as a victim of a purge within Peugeot, was ousted as *directeur-sportif*. And within twelve months, Anderson would himself face a ruptured association with Peugeot and its new team director, the former assistant *directeur-sportif*, Roland Berland.

Anderson had not paved the way for a smooth negotiation of his 1983 contract. He horrified Peugeot by bringing a solicitor with him to negotiations – something that had never before been done in cycling. Peugeot was willing to increase his salary from 6000 francs a month in the second year, but it was not to Anderson's liking or that of his legal advisers. 'They were offering me seven or eight thousand francs a month, but that was after all the races I had won, and having worn the yellow jersey for so long. It wasn't right,' recalls Anderson. 'I said I wanted a bit more, but they said I wasn't worth it. I couldn't read French and that was the language of the contract, so I turned up with a solicitor from Paris. But he read the contract and said it was a piece of shit, that it wasn't worth the paper it was written on.'

Anderson's solicitor had three concerns. 'There were no bonuses, it said Peugeot could fine me any time they wanted and that if I was sick for longer than a week, I could be thrown off the team. Looking back it was pretty funny, really – all these people around a table and me with my reps in suits fighting for a few extra dollars. But in reality, it was something the sport needed.' Anderson hit the headlines the next day after it was revealed that the firm he used to negotiate on his behalf was also used by Formula One racing drivers. 'The papers started saying that I wanted a Formula One driver's salary which was totally exaggerated.'

Anderson's spring campaign in 1983 marked the first stage of his eventual transition from a Tour to a one-day classic racer. The Tour was always his main objective, but after he finished second in Virginia's three-day Tour of America and returned to Europe to take third in the Liège–Bastogne–Liège classic and then win the Amstel Gold Race, a new direction became evident. Winning the Amstel Gold was a major breakthrough. It was his first classic win – a major hallmark in any racer's career – and the first for Peugeot since 1978. It also improved his self-confidence in the classics and inspired him throughout his career, especially after winning the Tour became virtually impossible. Victory in the one Dutch classic on the calendar also aroused interest from many Dutch teams. Unlike Peugeot which focused on the Tour, Dutch and Belgian teams often based their whole season on the classics. When Anderson fell out with Peugeot, it was no surprise that the Dutch Panasonic team snapped him up.

His win, however, did not shift his focus from that year's Tour. Anderson was set for undisputed team leadership, and as July approached, he justified the decision to his teammates by a second place to Roche and a stage win in the Tour de Romandie, and tenth in the Grand Prix of Frankfurt. It was in the hectic final lead-up to the Tour that Anderson's position suddenly became rocky.

It was the Dauphiné–Libéré stage race that opened Anderson's eyes to his very shaky future at Peugeot. After winning the prologue, he rode superbly to help Frenchman Pascal Simon win, and finished sixth overall. However, in a mandatory drug test, Anderson and Simon both tested positive. Simon had the victory taken away from him and handed to American, Greg LeMond, while Anderson was also relegated. Both riders explained that the substance had been in a mixture to treat hayfever and little was made of the scandal. It barely rated a paragragh in the French press, and to the best of my knowledge, was never reported in the English, American or Australian press. However, behind the scenes a fight erupted between Anderson and Peugeot. As Anderson recalls: 'It was kept pretty quiet that Simon and myself were both suffering from hayfever. The team doctor gave us something to help our breathing. Then three weeks later, we got a letter in the mail saying we were positive. It ended up that the doctor gave us something that had just been put on the list. It was all hush-hush, although there was a blurb in the paper. So I asked the doctor to come out and say that he administered something to us. But they [Peugeot] said they wouldn't do it. So it looked like Simon and I took the shit. Luckily it never got a lot of publicity, but still, it was there.'

Having won the final Tour run-up – the Tour de l'Aude – for the second time, Anderson was introduced as leader at the official pre-Tour team presentation. Roche, making his debut, was billed as a natural second-choice should Anderson find himself struggling in the mountains. In light of Hinault's absence due to a knee tendon injury, it was declared an 'open' Tour. 'Every team believes they have a winner in their ranks,' said Berland before the start. 'I have two: first, Phil Anderson who will be ready to go from the off; then there is Stephen Roche who will be looking for a surprise break.'

It seemed Anderson's status was secure as the Tour raced towards the Pyrénées with him nicely placed third overall. But no matter what argument was given later, Anderson labelled as treachery the incident on stage ten from Pau to Bagnères-de-Luchon. It had nothing to do with Millar brilliantly winning the stage. If anything, Anderson was pleased for his teammate. Rather, it was Pascal Simon's attack to take the yellow jersey. Anderson might have had an idea that something was up when he crashed earlier on the ascent of the Col d'Aubisque and lost his shoe. Not one teammate waited to bring him back and the energy used to rejoin the peloton proved costly when Simon went off.

According to Anderson, he was race leader on the road and would have taken the yellow jersey had Simon not attacked. But once Simon did go, Anderson was unable to do anything but watch him race away. Team ethics say you never chase down a teammate. But Anderson had no idea Simon, eighth overall at 2 minutes 45 seconds at the start, was racing for his yellow jersey. 'I was the protected leader. We had the last climb to go at the end of the day and I was going to get the yellow jersey because all the guys in front of me overall were dropped. I was leader on the road and working with Beat Breu, Johan van de Velde, Peter Winnen and Zoetemelk, but Simon was doing nothing. He was just sitting on. Then he attacked and I had to sit there,' says Anderson who then fell to tenth overall at 9 minutes 22 seconds.

After placing third in the stage, Simon crashed the next day and sustained a hairline fracture of his collarbone. For the next six days until he abandoned in the Alps, not a soul attacked. They knew he would never make it to Paris. Peugeot lapped up the publicity of having the yellow jersey. A French newcomer named Laurent Fignon, who was second overall, waited until Simon dropped out before taking the lead, and his first of two Tours. Anderson, on the other hand, was confined to domestique duties.

Opinions still vary as to who was right or wrong. Frenchmen like Peugeot teammate Roger Legeay – now *directeur-sportif* of Australian Stuart O'Grady's Crédit Agricole team – believe Simon would have won the Tour had he not broken his collarbone: 'If Phil had it, then he should have been able to stay up with Pascal. But where was he? No, Simon deserved to have the yellow jersey.' Nobody in the team thought differently. Although years later, Roche said Simon was wrong: 'When we finished that day and I said "Congratulations Pascal" I thought it was great at the time. But I found out later that he would do the same thing in other races. So looking back, it wasn't fair to Phil, really.'

Anderson took it as a betrayal. 'There was nothing said but I think Simon knew I was pissed off because he knew I was going to be in the yellow jersey. Nobody said anything to me about it, nobody. But still I don't think I would have won the Tour then anyway,' says Anderson. Today however, he is more compassionate towards Simon. Time heals, and he admits that in hindsight, the Frenchman's claim to the yellow jersey may have only been as opportunistic as his own in 1981 when Peugeot not only had Bernaudeau as a leader, but Dutchman Hennie Kuiper who had finished second in 1980. 'I don't want to be spiteful about it. If I didn't take the opportunity when I was in that first year with Hennie, if I had stayed with him, I would be just another rider in the back with all the other masses, just another number in the field. You've got to take those opportunities. Maybe if Simon didn't break his collarbone, he would have become a real winner. Sometimes you only need a couple of lucky breaks – or not!'

At the time though, Anderson sensed that he and Peugeot were heading for a split. Anderson was not offered a new contract, and he didn't ask for one. 'You can tell when a team doesn't want you,' he says. A few days after the Tour, it was announced that he would join the powerful Dutch Panasonic team for 1984.

The Australian bided the rest of his time with Peugeot by racing the City Centre criterium series in Great Britain. It was preparation for the world road championships at Altenrhein in Switzerland, but he still won two of the five events and finished second overall in the series. Then in the world title he placed ninth at 1 minute 36 seconds to his friend, twenty-two-year-old Greg LeMond. However, Anderson was the key aggressor in the race, having led an eight-man break for five laps before it was caught with two to go – a move that certainly helped LeMond's later attack. Anderson's career at Peugeot may have ended as a disappointment, but at the world titles he certainly showed that he had not lost his fighting punch.

1984 – The honeymoon is over

Anderson did more than reassure the Panasonic management they had made a sound investment in him leading up to the 1984 Tour. He began with a marathon 3-hour solo break in the Milan–San Remo one-day classic in Italy. He won the Henninger Turm race in Frankfurt, Germany, and took second place in the Liège–Bastogne–Liège classic in Belgium. In stage races he placed fifth in Paris–Nice, seventh at the Dauphiné–Libéré, and fifth again in the Tour of Switzerland before heading to Montreuil for the start of the Tour.

However, if the 1984 Tour is to be remembered for the growing number of non-Europeans, it was not the Australian who stood out. On this occasion, such an honour was left to LeMond who was the first American to finish on the Tour podium (third) in Paris; and Colombian, Luis Herrera, whose victory at l'Alpe d'Huez was the first by a South American in a Tour stage. Anderson's souvenir after reaching Paris in tenth place overall was one he could have done without. This was the most painful moment of his career – a broken sternum due to a high-speed crash in the Alps on the fifteenth stage to Grenoble.

No other day in Anderson's entire fourteen-year professional career hurt as much as the one 48 hours after the crash. He was trying to defend his well-earned top-five overall place and hoped he had recovered enough in the two days after the crash to hang on; but as he dragged himself up each climb on the 151 km seventeenth stage from Grenoble to l'Alpe d'Huez, his chest felt as if it was being wrenched apart with every pedal-stroke. 'It was as if I was already at the morgue and someone had dug a crow bar in my chest to pry me open.' Lesser men would have quit there and then, but there was no such option for Anderson, having come into the Panasonic team as a highly paid and rated leader and within a shot of winning the world's greatest and toughest race. 'It was near the end of the Tour. I was still placed highly and the team had already put so much effort into riding for me. I simply had to continue. I still remember the pain though. We were riding mountain over mountain. The pace was just winding up on each climb and every time I pulled on the handlebars as I pedalled, it just felt like I was ripping apart. Some of the guys even had to help push me up. They were urging me on. Saying: "Come on, Phil . . . come on." It was as if their whole Tour depended on me getting to the finish.'

Anderson still made it to l'Alpe d'Huez and with six days to the finish, persevered to reach Paris in tenth place, 29 minutes 16 seconds behind Frenchman Fignon who had won on his Tour debut the year before. Anderson would have normally regarded his result as disappointing, but given the circumstances, it was considered a victory. Anderson's true Tour prospects became clearer in 1985 – his greatest ever season with sixteen wins. Among his principal victories before the Tour were wins in the Dauphiné–Libéré, the Tour of Switzerland and the Mediterranean Tour. His all-round skills also led him to second place in the Tour of Flanders where teammate Eric Vanderaerden won, and again in the Ghent–Wevelgem one-day race in Belgium where Anderson should have won, but botched up the sprint to see Vanderaerden win again despite Vanderaerden almost braking on the line to let Anderson through.

However, the highlight was again the Tour where Anderson finished an incredible fifth overall. It was also during this Tour that his smouldering rivalry with Hinault was once again ignited. The Frenchman accused Anderson of pushing him off his bike in the bunch sprint to the finish of stage fourteen at Saint Etienne. The pile-up with less than 1 km to go left Hinault, who was wearing the yellow jersey, with a bloody and broken nose. The image of him walking defiantly across the line covered in blood shocked the millions who were watching the Tour live on television. Most of them being French, they wanted answers, and quick. Who could they blame? Hinault, his rage at boiling point, was quick to point his finger: it was Anderson's fault, he said. Despite Anderson declaring his innocence, a black-eyed Hinault repeated the accusation the next morning at the start of stage fifteen to Aurillac when he angrily warned a startled Anderson to stay away: 'He said, "You did that purposely." I said, "What are you talking about? If I would have put you down, I would have made sure you wouldn't have got up." '

Hinault rode on to win the Tour for his fifth and last time, while Anderson sailed through to finish fifth. Their rift never really healed, even though they now share pleasantries when crossing paths on the Tour. In 1987, during a visit to Australia on a promotional trip for a sponsor, Hinault revisited the incident at a press conference in Sydney. This upset Anderson more than the original accusations. 'I still don't know why he blamed me. It wasn't my fault. What upset me the most, though, was that he still blamed me later when he came to Australia and I didn't get the chance to respond.'

Nevertheless, conflict was not new to Anderson. In a sport with rural working-class roots where survival was tested daily, it was inevitable that 'knives' would be drawn on and off the bike. And Anderson certainly wasn't afraid to take a stand. By 1985, he was adding revolutionary dimensions to professional cycling. He pushed for higher wages and had already 'Americanised' contractual deals while at Peugeot. His reputation for driving a hard bargain was renowned and he openly criticised the system that he felt ripped-off riders. 'A lot of the team directors are pocketing money that should be going to the riders. The riders have no rights. There are no unions – well there are, but they are corrupt anyway. What the unions should do is set up a system to help the riders, such as a manager's representative, lawyers and an insurance system. All riders should have representatives when they sign contracts so that they aren't taken for a ride by the teams.'

At Panasonic, Anderson created another uproar by demanding his own personal doctor instead of relying on the team's medical staff. After his doping scandal at Peugeot, he was wary of allowing those he didn't know or trust to administer to him. 'In the beginning you are a little green. You don't know exactly what is going on all the time. You don't know who to trust, but you don't have a choice. After a while you get a little wiser and you see that you do have a choice and can buck the system if you want. And when I didn't abide by the system I was ostracised. I wasn't thrown off the team but I thought I had certain rights,' he says. 'I always felt it was important to come out of the sport healthy. Others wanted to live for the moment. They wanted to risk their lives, and be famous. I wanted to know exactly what the *soigneurs* (masseurs) were giving us. But they said, 'No, that's a *soigneur's* secret. That's why they are paid so much.' It was my body and I wanted to look after it the way I wanted. So I wanted *my* doctor, someone I could feel confident with.'

It was following the 1985 Tour that the first physical cracks appeared in Anderson's armour. After re-signing with Panasonic for the 1986 season, he was struck down by a hereditary rheumatic back ailment – sacroiliitis. The condition plagued his post-Tour season. While still leading the year-long Super Prestige series (since replaced by the World Cup series) that had him ranked as the world's number one rider, the pain grew so bad that he could not start the one-day Tour of Lombardy in Italy in October. Anderson's 'scratching' opened the way for a victorious Sean Kelly to win the Super Prestige crown.

Anderson was never the same. His back troubles caused him to miss the first half of 1986 and race the Tour 'only for training'. Then he appeared to come back to his best with season closing wins in the Créteil–Chaville one-day classic in France, the New York Cititour and a stage of the Nissan Classic in Ireland. He was also third overall in the Coors Classic behind Hinault and Greg LeMond. But in 1987, poor form and the rigours of a divorce with his former wife in late 1986 saw his career slide again. Panasonic boss, Peter Post, didn't hold much mercy, and capriciously changed his public view on Anderson.

After 1985, Post had praised Anderson for leading Panasonic down the winning trail with his sixteen season wins, acclaiming him as the greatest professional he had ever seen. But by the end of the 80 km time-trial in the 1987 Tour, he was dumping all and sundry on Anderson, claiming he rode the stage like a 'retarded human being'. Post tried to cut Anderson's salary, apparently bitter about recruiting such a big name rider only to see his career compromised by his condition. Unsurprisingly, Anderson left the team.

However, his subsequent spell in the Dutch TVM team from 1988 to 1990 was equally troublesome. On the bike, there were glimpses of the Anderson of old – even if he did sport the new look of a ponytail. He won seven races in 1988, although this was not enough to secure TVM its place in the Tour. There was more fortune in 1989 when, despite a disappointing Tour, Anderson won a stage and overall classification of the Tour de Romandie, as well as stages in the Tour of Italy, Tour of Britain and Nissan Classic. He was also third in Liège–Bastogne–Liège. But personal differences with *directeur-sportif,* Cees Priem, obstructed a long career with TVM. The crux of their many arguments was the presence of American *soigneuse,* Shelly Verses, on the team. She was Anderson's girlfriend and it was part of his contract that she work on the team. Although Verses was one of the best in her field, Priem was always against having her. He wanted to dispose of her and Anderson knew it.

It didn't help that in 1989 Anderson was in dispute with Priem over the selection of TVM's team for the Tour. With TVM's entry hingeing on a wild-card invitation from organisers, there was already a fair amount of tension in the lead-up. But that was nothing compared to the tension that festered after TVM was granted its start. Breaking-point came when Priem reneged on the selection of one of Anderson's trusted domestiques, Jan Siemons, before the start in Luxembourg. Anderson was furious and even threatened to boycott the Tour unless Siemons was re-instated. The team called Anderson's bluff, but was caught out when he telephoned Tour race director, Jean-Marie Leblanc, to discuss the issue and his position. The defiant Anderson was heartened when Leblanc readily took his side – the reason being that TVM's wild-card entry was based on Anderson riding the Tour. 'I asked if I don't do the Tour, would the team do it, and [Leblanc] said, "No, the only reason your team is doing the Tour de France is because you are part of the team." So I called up Cees and said, "Listen, if you don't keep Siemons on the team then I'm not going to go to the Tour either, and that means the team will not go to it." He started stuttering and, finally, Siemons got on the team.'

Morale in the TVM dropped to a low. Anderson, sensing the problem, called an urgent meeting of riders and staff in the team bus at 3 pm the day before the prologue in Luxembourg. 'I said,

"Listen, I want unity in the team, I'm pissed off with coach Priem because he tried to drop this bloke who helped me a lot. I don't like being blackmailed, and I didn't like having to do these sort of things. If anybody has anything against something say it now before the Tour because I want to go into this race with everybody being positive and I think we can get some results." I was just trying to boost everybody's morale and spirit because the team was starting to bicker.'

Despite his efforts, TVM failed to deliver during a Tour that was best remembered for LeMond's stunning 8-second victory over Fignon. Sadly for Anderson, it was remembered more for two spectacular crashes within three days. The first crash was midway on the thirteenth stage to Marseille when a feed-bag jammed in his wheel. He was sent flying from his bike and onto his face. With a black eye and severe cuts to his arms, face and legs, he then came a cropper in the Alps on stage sixteen from Gap to Briançon when one of his tyres rolled on a high-speed mountain descent. Besides receiving more abrasions, he was also severely burnt on the leg from the hot tyre.

Inevitably, the relationship between Anderson and Priem deteriorated and by mid-1990, Anderson felt he had no choice but to leave. It was a sad split considering the 1990 season looked like being a successful one for both parties. It was a year highlighted by Anderson's brilliant Giro d'Italia: he won a stage and the blue-jersey Inter Giro category, which was the second-most lucrative classification after the overall competition. On top of that, he finished second to Italy's overall winner, Gianni Bugno, in the points category and spent four days in the green jersey as best climber. Anderson's aggression was another reminder that he still had the fighting spirit that nine years earlier had once scared Hinault and so impressed Post. But it disappeared soon after the Giro.

Anderson spent most of the 1990 Tour in dispute with the TVM management and pondering his future rather than racing at his aggressive best. He finished without a stage win in 71st overall at 1 hour 30 minutes 1 second to LeMond. Anderson knew it was a risk to leave TVM without having signed elsewhere.

But by the end of the season, he felt he had little choice and left Europe for his post-season break in the United States and Australia without a team to go back for in 1991. His concern grew as the weeks passed well into the break with no prospect of a deal. Finally, on December 24, Anderson settled a new contract with the American Motorola team, swearing, 'I'll never let that happen again.'

To clinch the deal, Anderson had to take a big pay-cut, but it included a lucrative bonus scheme. It worked, as he stormed through the 1991 season to win twelve races – his best season record since 1985. The most important of those 1991 wins came in the 3900 km Tour de France, on the tenth stage from Rennes to the Breton town of Quimper. To win, he out-sprinted three other breakaways – Dane Brian Holm and Belgians Michel Dernies and Nico Emonds – bringing to an end a frustrating ten-year drought of stage wins in the event. After crossing the finish with his arms raised in a 'V' for victory, Anderson had no doubt which of the two stages he appreciated the most: 'My win in 1982 was great, but then I still had ten years ahead of me. Here, this win couldn't have come at a better time, especially after the recent years where I haven't had such good results. I would have to say it is a better one considering that, if not one of the best wins of my career.'

Anderson's win was indeed brilliant. When the break formed with 30 km to go in the 207.5 km stage, it went unchallenged by teams such as the French Z team of the defending Tour champion LeMond. With no riders in the break vying for the overall classification, it posed no serious threat to them; but the breakaway riders still had to fend off a strong chase led by the sprinters' teams wanting a bunch finish. Despite the leaders working together, they only milked a maximum lead of 1 minute 30 seconds with 20 km to go and from there knew that every pedal-stroke of effort counted, as Anderson recalls, 'I was worried with 20 km to go that the main group would catch us. We had to work together because it has happened so often that in the finale everyone starts looking at each other and then suddenly the group catches you. But once we got close I knew we would be okay.'

The sight of the pack closing in didn't dull Anderson's tactical senses. Allowing Holm to lead-out the sprint, he blasted from behind the Dane's rear wheel and passed him with 150 m to go – his left pedal clipping Holm's front wheel in the process. Anderson's sheer force and guile paid off as he crossed the line 6 seconds ahead of the pack: 'I knew the guys in the break well and they wanted the stage as much as I did. I followed Holm's wheel and he was forced to lead-out. But as I came past, my pedal clipped his front wheel. It gave us both a bit of a fright even though it has happened to me tons of times.'

For Anderson the win could not have been better timed. It reassured his team bosses and fellow riders that he was still a winner. It also gave the team's new sponsor, Motorola, reassurance that it was backing a winning team.

The only thing distracting the media from Anderson's win was the stunning withdrawal from the Tour of the entire star-studded Dutch PDM team during and after the stage. Initial reports said the team pulled out because of a bacterial infection from contaminated food, but the incident quickly lead to suspicions of a drug scandal that the team denied. Later, the team claimed it was due to PDM medico, Dr Wim Sanders, having administered the riders with a contaminated batch of Intralipid – a natural lecithin-based product that contains concentrated carbohydrates and proteins to aid recovery – that had either been left in the boot of a car or was out of date. The incident would continue to be debated and investigated well into the mid-1990s when doping accusations became more apparent. Whatever the cause, PDM's exit left the Tour without its first-placed team and three of its big-name riders who were then already placed in the top-ten overall – Dutchman Erik Breukink (third), Ireland's Sean Kelly (sixth) and Mexican Raul Alcala (ninth). The void had an indisputable bearing on the overall outcome of the Tour by its finish in Paris.

If the PDM controversy clouded media attention over Anderson's win, it did not dampen the spirit of locals from Quimper who wanted to celebrate 'their' winners the next day, rather than join the speculation about a suspected doping controversy. Before stage eleven, Quimper's elder farmers presented LeMond with a prize cow. Meanwhile, Anderson – as the stage winner – was given a haul of fresh vegetables from a local farmer's daughter who represented the young farming association. The moment offered some welcome comic relief when Anderson, more accustomed to receiving a bouquet for his wins, was unable to make the customary gesture of thanks by giving her a hand-picked flower in return. Instead, he simply improvised – handing the young woman a fresh carrot!

Without Anderson's stage win, the Motorola team's Tour may have been remembered for embarrassment. As the race moved into the mountains, the team came under official fire for allowing Swiss rider, Urs Zimmermann, a climber and former top-three finisher in the Tour, to make the transfer from Brittany to Pau by car rather than by plane. Tour rules require riders to make scheduled transfers together. Zimmermann, who took a car because he thought the air pressure would aggravate a recent eardrum complaint, was only caught when Tour organisers saw a photo of him in a French newspaper eating in a restaurant en-route to Pau. Zimmermann was disqualified from the race and Motorola's *directeur-sportif*, Jim Ochowicz, was suspended for stage twelve. However, Zimmermann's penalty was overturned when the riders collectively refused to start the stage from Pau to Jaca in Spain unless he was reinstated. Anderson was outspoken about the issue, his opinion shared by many. 'Okay, a mistake was made. Zimmi should have been on the plane, the organisation should have been told or asked if he could travel by car instead. But to eliminate him from the race is just too severe. What happens when a rider is found positive for drugs? They give him a 10-minute penalty and, if he is good enough, he can still win the Tour. But for not taking the chartered flight for a transfer and a car instead? Does that deserve elimination? No way. Where is the justice in that? The riders have to do something against it as a matter of principle.'

While Zimmermann was allowed back in the race, the Tour organisers' change of heart did not extend to Ochowicz. He was made to serve his ban after a heated 90-minute discussion between the organisers and the Motorola team management in the press centre at Pau. But the supposedly closed meeting led to further embarrassment for the Tour chiefs when they realised the media could witness every minute of it. The door of the meeting room was shut, but through its glass walls, every angry gesticulation was executed in full view of those watching from outside.

For Anderson, the rest of the 1991 Tour was a series of frustrations. On stage fifteen, a 235 km leg from Albi to Alès, he crashed for the second time. On a tough course that included five third category climbs and made harder by the 38 degree celsius temperature, he fell at 166 km with three others, including teammate Sean Yates who was Anderson's lead-out man for the stage finish. It took Anderson 20 leg-sapping kilometres to rejoin the pack, too long to have any strength left for the finish. His task was not helped by Yates who had severed an artery in his arm during the crash and therefore failed to catch the main bunch.

The following day was another case of 'if only' for Anderson when he went on the attack again in the 215 km sixteenth stage from Alès to Gap. He and seven others – including LeMond – got away with 15 km to go. It was the presence of LeMond, a close friend of Anderson, that became the Australian's undoing. When LeMond attacked on a descent with 10 km to go and was soon joined by Italian Marco Lietti, Anderson felt he had no choice but to let them go: 'I wasn't going to chase because we are friends. You don't do that,' said Anderson after finishing sixth and 21 seconds behind a victorious Lietti and second-placed LeMond who was to see his Tour crown pass to Spain's Miguel Indurain.

As the Tour ventured further into the Alps on stage eighteen from Bourg-d'Oisans to Morzine, Indurain continued to dominate, beginning a reign that would last five years. Anderson's concern was not for winning, but for recovering in readiness for the final flatter stages. However, recovery soon became a secondary priority to survival on a stage that saw heavy rain make the Alpine roads dangerously slippery. Respected as one of the fastest and most daring of descenders, Anderson rode as if he was possessed down the steep, 10 km-long drop from the Col de Joux Plane summit towards Morzine, despite being 7 minutes off the stage-winning pace. But when he reached the flat section to the finish with 5 km to go, he missed a turn and rode into a barbed wire fence. It was his third crash for the Tour. A bloodied and cut Anderson eventually finished 53rd at 7 minutes to French stage winner, Thierry Claveyrolat.

Anderson did survive the Tour and reached Paris in 45th place overall at 1 hour 8 minutes 13 seconds to the victorious Indurain. He may have been disappointed about his three crashes and lost chances for a second stage win, but in time he became more appreciative of the win he did get. The satisfaction was consolidated in the years to come as Anderson rode and finished three more Tours with varying fortunes. For mess-ups, nothing beat the stage seven blunder to Châlon-sur-Marne in the 1993 Tour when Anderson and two Motorola riders – including their then sprinter Max Sciandri – were in the winning seven-man break but somehow failed to win. Their only consolation after seeing Dane Bjarne Rijs outsprint Sciandri was that they had won 65 dozen bottles of champagne at intermediate sprints along the way to swill away their disappointment. For near-misses, nothing beat Motorola's second place in the team time-trial of the 1994 Tour.

It was during the 1994 Tour – Anderson's last – that he achieved his next-best individual stage finish: a fourth place on the final stage to the Champs Elysées. Fittingly, he had already told the Motorola team that he would retire at the year's end.

Chapter 7

The slave trade
ALLAN PEIPER
AND NEIL STEPHENS

It is arguably the most thankless of jobs. It is definitely one of the hardest in a road cycling team. But the domestique – a virtual servant to the protected team leader – is the most valued commodity of any team. Without them, winners wouldn't be winners. Their purpose is to ensure 'winners' reach the most crucial part of every stage as fresh and well-positioned as possible to strike with greatest effect. It is a mark of the collective strength of Lance Armstrong's US Postal Service teammates that after they helped him win the Tour for a fourth successive year in 2002, his score of solo efforts in attack or in defence in road stages, not including individual time-trials, came to only 23 km of the 3462 km route – less than one per cent of the race!

The duties of a Tour domestique are numerous. They range from collecting drinks, food and clothes for their leader to swapping wheels or bikes when he has mechanical problems; propping him up while riding when he needs to pee, pacing him back to the bunch after he stops, chasing down attacks or setting blistering tempos at the front so that the rival leader wouldn't find the speed or strength to attack to cycling next to or in front of their leader to protect him from the wind. Occasionally the domestique gets to enjoy a slice of personal victory, but for most, the closest he will ever get to winning is knowing that the rider he has flogged himself for has finally stepped up to the podium.

Australia has produced some of the finest domestiques. Fighting spirit and a self-sacrificing commitment to the greater cause has long been a recognised trait of the Australian Tour rider. They have so often held to the task bound by the same spirit that fuelled the Australian forces in the two world wars, or the Australian people during the Great Depression. Whether poised for victory or racing against the odds, the Australian domestique has always fought to the end, and the Europeans have been eager to use him.

It has been the case since 1914 when Don Kirkham and Iddo 'Snowy' Munro – Australia's first riders in the Tour – were recruited to help Frenchman, Georges Passerieu. In 1928 and 1931 Sir Hubert Opperman brought his own domestiques – Percy Osborne (1928), Ernest Bainbridge (1928), Frankie Thomas (1931), Richard Lamb (1931) and Ossie Nicholson (1931). But when Russell Mockridge raced the Tour in 1955, he did so to help Luxembourg's Charly Gaul finish second overall. Helping another win was Don Allan's goal – in his case as a key lead-out man for Dutchman Theo Smit, who won two stages in 1975. Then in the 1980s and 1990s came Allan Peiper and Neil Stephens who were so highly regarded in the job, they became known as 'super-domestiques' – a position that on many occasion also saw them promoted to the respected role of team captain or tactician on the road.

In that time, many other Australians became noted Tour domestiques – some of them classy riders who had leadership roles in one-day races or shorter stage events, but whose strengths in a three-week race like the Tour were more valued for a supporting role. In this category, Michael Wilson, Stephen Hodge, Patrick Jonker, Scott Sunderland and Henk Vogels come to mind – and not without their own moments of glory. In the 1989 Tour, Wilson, who won a stage of the Vuelta a España in 1983 and Giro d'Italia in 1982 was in the winning break in his second of two Tours on the ninth stage to Pau, which was won by Irishman Martin Earley. In 1990, Peiper rode to victory at Futuroscope in the team time-trial with Panasonic; and in 1987, on the seventh stage to Troyes, came close to pulling off a winning attack with 13 km to go before being swept up by the bunch 5 km short of the line. In 1994, Hodge, who rode six Tours and was a regular teammate of Stephens, also finished third in a stage, the tenth to Cahors. Then when Miguel Indurain's five-year reign as champion came to an end in 1996, Jonker gave hope for greater things with his twelfth place overall – the best since Anderson's fifth in 1985. Another hope for the future was Vogels, a strong sprinter and time-trialist who, in the first of two Tour starts for Gan in 1997, placed third on the final stage in Paris. Sunderland, a strong climber, raced one Tour in 1996 and probably would have ridden more had his career not been interrupted by injury, the worst being a near-fatal crash in the 1996 Amstel Gold Race when he was run into by TDM *directeur-sportif*, Cees Priem. Sunderland sustained a blood clot that was only detected when his wife Sabine suspected he was not fully recovered after being released from a Dutch hospital.

Allan Peiper

When Allan Peiper first arrived in Belgium in 1977 as a seventeen-year-old wanting to race as an amateur, the Tour de France was not on his mind. Sure, he dreamed of the Tour – every cyclist does. But he had been told the road ahead would be long and hard. He had read about the Tour in old cycling magazines from his home in Melbourne, where he lived with his single mother in the working-class suburb of Alexandra.

Having arrived in Ghent in the cold of midnight, Peiper's priority was not the Tour but finding the address of his arranged accommodation – a butcher's shop where he and twenty riders were to share a freezing and damp basement. 'At night it was so cold. I had brought a beach towel with me, so I used that as a second blanket. In the day it became a towel again.'

However, it wasn't too long before Peiper's talent as a cyclist was noticed; nor did it take too long for his living conditions to improve. He befriended another Belgian star-in-the-making, Eddy Planckaert, whose family – a cycling dynasty in Belgium – invited him to live with them.

Peiper and Planckaert dominated the domestic junior circuit, with Planckaert, being the local hero, desperate to take as many wins as possible. This didn't worry Peiper. With barely a penny to his name, he was happy to earn extra money by setting up Planckaert for the win in attacks and sprints, taking second place himself and the money on offer at any intermediate sprints during their races together. Peiper's horizons expanded when other riders lucky enough to be with him in breakaways began asking for his services, and in time an obliging Peiper became a valued asset – so valued that riders directly asked him to let them win.

Not that he was as blindly giving as he may have appeared at the time. Often, after agreeing to let them win, Peiper would still have a go himself, knowing that his street talk had placed him in a win-win situation: 'If I lost they paid me. And if I won, it was hard luck for them. I was a professional junior. I had to be hard. Money meant food and tyres.'

Peiper may have always carried an innocent appearance – his smile and neatly groomed black hair projected a boyish trade-mark for most of his career. But from the beginning of his cycling career, it was apparent to most that he was blessed with the atypical mindset of a seasoned professional, rather than an amateur rookie. He relished the culture of Belgian cycling and seemed destined for greatness. But at the end of 1979, his body surrendered: he was struck down by hepatitis after his third season and returned to Australia. As he says, 'I had aged ten years mentally and didn't feel young anymore.'

However, Peiper soon recovered in health and spirit, and after winning the 1981 Dulux Tour of New Zealand, was given the chance to return to Europe in 1982 – this time to follow the path ridden by many English-speaking riders. His victory in New Zealand earned him an invitation to join the high-profile French amateur team, Athletic Club de Boulogne-Billaincourt (ACBB), a feeder team in Paris for the French professional Peugeot squad.

The ACBB was *the* team of French amateur cycling and boasted a number of other English-speaking graduates who had gone on to be recruited by Peugeot, including Australian Phil Anderson. The 1982 season ended with Peiper winning fourteen races for ACBB – including the amateur Grand Prix des Nations. It was obvious that his penchant for hard work and time-trialing ability made him an attractive recruit for Peugeot who signed him in 1983 on a contract worth 6000 French francs a month.

As a first-year professional, Peiper never expected to be selected for the Tour, and he was happy to focus on smaller events, forging his reputation as a strong domestique. It was a hard life though, so hard that during an end-of-season trip back to Australia, Peiper had a nightmare about *directeur-sportif* Roland Berland: 'I dreamt I was begging Berland to let me go home and quit. People think it's all roses over there but it isn't.'

At least Peiper's reluctant return to Europe was rewarded with some fortune. He raced well in the early season, particularly in prologue time-trials and in criteriums – inner-city races held on short and fast circuits with many corners. His time-trialling ability, strength over the short distance and good bike-handling skills were all vital ingredients for this type of racing. Peiper also gave every indication that in shorter stage races he could become a handy rider for Peugeot for the overall classification. He lead the Tour Mediterranean for a day before stopping with tendinitis, and then recovered to win the Tour de l'Oise, a victory he put down to his win in the 3.1 km prologue time-trial and help from English teammate, Sean Yates. Peiper tasted more success in the pro-am post Giro Tour in Sweden, an eight-day stage race. He won that with another time-trial success, this time in the last stage over 16.2 km and again with the help of Yates. For Peiper, so long accustomed to working for someone else, being a team leader was a new and difficult experience to accept: 'When you've been conserving your energy all week, which I had to do as team leader, it's negative riding and I don't like that. But you have to, and in the time-trial be positive and somehow explode. It's difficult.'

Nevertheless, his consistent performances – which included four prologue wins that spring – were enough to earn Peiper selection for the 1984 Tour de France. He quickly repaid Peugeot's faith with a third place in the 5.4 km prologue at Noisy-le-Sec. Adding credibility to his performance was the calibre of the two French riders ahead of him – Bernard Hinault who then had four of his five Tour wins to his name, and Laurent Fignon, the defending Tour champion who would go on to win the 1984 edition.

But Peiper didn't stop there. After finishing third on stage one from Bondy to Saint Denis, he was suddenly on the brink of repeating Phil Anderson's yellow jersey feats of 1982 and 1983. Going into stage two from Bobigny to Louvroil, he was third overall at 8 seconds to the Belgian race leader, Ludo Peeters. The prospect of a yellow jersey excited the Peugeot management. At their pre-race team meeting, they pencilled in Peiper to bridge the gap by winning bonus seconds on the intermediate sprints. Yates, who had so far proven to be a terrific lead-out man, was appointed as the man to get him into position. But then the plan went awry as Peiper couldn't hold Yates's wheel and messed up the very first intermediate sprint: 'His lead-outs being what they are, I lost the wheel, and when I finished fifth or sixth he said disgustedly: "I'm not leading you out anymore." '

Peiper finished his first Tour 95th from 124 survivors, 2 hours 31 minutes 28 seconds behind Fignon – a long way from the 6 seconds that separated them at Noisy-le-Sec. However, he had easily done enough to raise interest elsewhere. The Italian Carrera team offered Peiper a contract, but he remained with Peugeot who raised his salary to 15,000 francs a month – a decision he later questioned when the team fell apart due to infighting, bickering and disillusionment with Roland Berland. Peiper still finished his second Tour in 86th place, 1 hour 56 minutes 54 seconds to Hinault who won the race for a fifth time after a sensational duel with his American teammate, Greg LeMond.

But seeing his old Peugeot teammate Anderson – then with Panasonic and enjoying the season of his life after a terrific year with the Dutch – only fed Peiper's desire to leave Peugeot, and importantly, join Panasonic.

At Panasonic, Peiper's appetite for riding hard at the front of the pack, being part of a powerful chase or leading out sprinters was more than adequately satisfied. In the one-day classics, his name became synonymous with many great victories by Panasonic riders, so much so that winning opportunities for him became very scarce. However, it must be said that he failed to capitalise on those opportunities when they *did* eventuate, thereby undermining his claims for a future chance. Panasonic *directeur-sportif*, Peter Post, very rarely gave riders second chances, and Peiper's career with Panasonic began to slide as soon as he allowed three such winning occasions to slip through his fingers.

The first was in the 1987 season-opening 295 km Milan–San Remo one-day classic in Italy. Peiper was the only rider with the eventual winner, Eric Maechler of Switzerland, before being dropped early on the last climb of the day, the Poggio, with only 8 km to go. Then in the 1988 world road championship in Ronse, Belgium, he placed tenth after leading out the sprint for the bronze medal but was caught with 75 m to go. Then finally in the 1989 Tour of Flanders, Peiper was in the seven-man break and placed seventh – a result that one week later, after the Schelde Prijs mid-week race in Belgium, led to an argument in front of about forty fans between him and Post over whether he was meant to have worked in the break or not.

Peiper earned selection for the Tour with Panasonic on only two occasions: 1987 and 1990. It was a hard team to get into, and Peiper's spritely size compared to the strapping Dutch and Belgians in the team brought into question his ability to endure a three-week race. Still, he appeared to be holding his own when he got a start in 1987. He rode strongly in the 40.5 km stage two team time-trial at West Berlin where Panasonic placed third. Then on the seventh stage from Epinal to Troyes in northern France, Peiper launched his own brave attack in a bid to win – or more probably in Post's mind, to prompt the sprinters' teams to chase him down – by setting off alone in the 211 km stage with 13 km to go.

Peiper's move came after the race had seen a rally of attacks test the main bunch of 97 riders. It was hoped his bold attack would be the one to break them. However, despite riding head down and digging into all his reserves on every pedal-stroke, Peiper was caught with 5 km to go. His arrest by the chasing pack marked the end of the final break for the day and signalled a bunch sprint for which he had nothing to give. Despite his efforts being in vain, Peiper recovered, but sadly only enough to last until the twenty-first of twenty-five stages when fatigue forced him to withdraw from the Tour, which was won by Irishman, Stephen Roche.

When Peiper got the nod for his next Tour start in 1990, his selection came at the last minute and was due only to the unavailability of his Dutch teammate, Gert-Jan Theunisse. Theunisse, the Tour's 1989 King of the Mountains champion, had been slapped a six-month suspension for recording an excessive level of testosterone for the second time in two years. His ban opened the door for a replacement, and it was only after Peiper's strong performance in the Giro d'Italia that Post put his name down for the position. It was a surprise considering Peiper had already told Panasonic that he would be leaving at the end of the season to join a new Dutch team, Tulip. *Directeur-sportifs* rarely select riders who declare their intent to leave, because it is thought that doing so only augments the rider's negotiating clout with another, rival team.

However, on this occasion Post did the unexpected and selected Peiper. Not even he could argue that Peiper was short on form after seeing him win the fourteenth stage of the Giro. Peiper's victory at the lakeside town of Klagenfurt in Austria was the greatest individual win of his career. The image of him crossing the line, arms thrust into the air and mouth wide open, was almost a look of shock, rather than joy. Either way, it was a finale that saw Peiper fight fiercely to reap the desired result – a place on the Panasonic team. This time, he knew he could ill-afford to repeat any of the 'mistakes' that Post had perceived in his racing in the past.

Panasonic lost nothing by calling up Peiper for the 3145 km Tour de France that started a few weeks later at the space-age theme park of Futuroscope, near Poitiers. His form in the Giro where he placed 144th overall was still on the boil when the race began. Most importantly, his strength was there for the team time-trial on stage two which Panasonic won. Held on a windswept, rolling and technically difficult 44.5 km course that passed through seven villages in the first 20 km, Panasonic beat the Dutch PDM and Spanish ONCE teams. It was a result so satisfying to the Panasonic camp that even Post was brought to tears.

In the Tour, victory in the team time-trial is one of the most sought-after successes of any major squad. It is not only important for the time gain it gives its leader. Coming as it usually does in the first week, it is also an important phase of a team's bonding and provides a chance for the strong teams to show collective might and establish an aura of strength within the pack. The psychological gain is immense. Little wonder that it is also one of the trickiest disciplines to master. Every nine-man team needs to ride together for as long as possible, and with finishing times taken on the first four riders in each squad, teams are only as strong as their weakest riders. Slipstreaming each other and taking scheduled turns at the front position is the basic tactic, but any excessive acceleration from the stronger riders can often lead to time-wasting detachments of the weaker ones. And ultimately, the price in lost or gained time could win or lose a Tour.

Unfortunately for Panasonic and Peiper, their stunning team time-trial victory failed to develop into the rolling snowball of success they had hoped for. Peiper failed to finish the Tour, withdrawing after numerous disputes with Post over his change of teams before stage eight from Epinal to Besçancon. According to Peiper, many of these arguments happened in front of his teammates at the dinner table and caused him to become depressed. Meanwhile, Panasonic savoured only one more win after the team time-trial – on the day Peiper quit at Besçancon, when former East German, Olaf Ludwig, won in a sprint between thirteen breakaways and became the first eastern European to win a Tour stage. There was as much relief as joy in the Panasonic bunker when Ludwig won, after all the work his team had done – in vain – to set him up in earlier stages. With their help, Ludwig rode on to win the sprinters' green points jersey at the finish in Paris. But for a team as ambitious as Panasonic, there

was no hiding the fact that their highest-placed rider overall –
the 1988 runner-up, Dutchman Steven Rooks – had placed as
low as 33rd at 43 minutes seconds to the American winner, Greg
LeMond.

Peiper's problems with Post were the core of his troubled spell
at Panasonic. A former Six Day track star and champion road
cyclist (who no longer owns a team), Post was a hard-nosed boss.
According to Peiper, he quashed every ounce of love and passion
the Australian had for the team, and very nearly destroyed his
love of the sport. An unapologetically open man who doesn't
hide his emotions, Peiper felt Post thought less of him than the
other riders, and spent most of his time at Panasonic trying to
match his expectations, only to feel he failed.

However, Peiper was certainly not alone in his feelings for
Post. Many riders were emotionally stirred up by Post's order of
rule – including stars like Anderson. Peiper had crises of confidence with his riding and needed a lot of reassurance, which Post
simply would not give. In the end, Peiper simply decided he had
had enough.

After pulling out of the 1990 Tour, he rode out the season with
Panasonic and soon signed with Tulip for 1991. There were
certainly no flowers growing at the Tulip camp though. His two
years there were unproductive: the team was riddled with
conflicts, lacked professionalism and a competitive spirit. In
1991, the team wasn't even selected for the Tour.

However, it did get invited in 1992, giving Peiper one last
chance to test himself in the greatest race of them all. He didn't
go out with the bang he had in 1984, but judging by Peiper's
smile in a photo of him standing next to a victorious Miguel
Indurain (after placing 126th from 130 finishers at 3 hours
40 minutes 21 seconds) this was the last of his worries.

Today, Peiper still lives in Belgium with his wife, Christine,
and son, Zane. Cycling is no longer his life, but rest assured that
whenever a major classic or tour comes past, he walks out to
watch . . . and reflect.

Neil Stephens

The victory list that runs beneath Neil Stephens' name belies the struggle he endured as a cyclist. Throughout his fourteen-year career as a professional racer, the nuggetty, blond Australian was in centre ring, facing Lady Luck as she threw him challenge after challenge – so many, he could have easily retired to live a comfortable life in Australia rather than punish himself for virtually every day of the fourteen years he raced in Europe. But it was Stephens' unwillingness to give in that made him such a resolute force as a domestique, especially for teams wanting to win the Tour de France.

It would be easy to brush off Stephens' career with the dirty cloth of the Festina doping scandal that rocked the Tour in 1998. It cannot be ignored that he rode on the controversial French team and, after he and his teammates were expelled from the Tour for 'systematic doping', he later admitted to unknowingly being administered drugs like erythropoietin (EPO). While never punished or declared guilty by the Union Cycliste Internationale or Cycling Australia, it is still an episode that dogs him. But there is far more to the Stephens' story than a drugs' controversy.

Despite his many feats on the bike – foremost being his stage win in the 1997 Tour – there was arguably more angst in Stephens' career than joy. Not that many who saw the blond-locked Stephens at races could have guessed. No matter how tough a day, Stephens was always the first person smiling. Short and stocky he may have been in frame, but he was a giant when it came to heart. And he needed plenty of heart to pick himself up from the woes that beset him. There were many: from the day he arrived in Belgium in 1988 to find his sponsor had already pulled out; to his abandonment of the 1993 Tour due to illness, the same year his highly fancied Spanish ONCE team suffered one of their worst-ever races; to the 1995 Tour when he drew the classy Dane Rolf Sorensen in a winning two-man break in stage fourteen and was accused by his team *directeur-sportif*, Manolo Saiz, of giving up; to his crash in the final kilometres of the fifteenth stage in the

1996 Tour as he was trying to join the eventual winner, Italian Massimo Podenzana; and ultimately, to the 1998 Festina scandal after which he raced one more time, in the Commonwealth Games in Kuala Lumpur before retiring. And this is not including the many career-threatening injuries from crashes and overuse along the way. The list includes seven broken collarbones, torn shoulder tendons in both sides, two cracked ribs, three hernia operations, one cracked femur, one fractured knee, one arthroscope of the knee, two sheath tendon extractions, three tendon operations in the last twelve months of his career, too many cuts and abrasions to count, and a broken nose sustained in a fight with Mexican rider, Raul Alcala, during the sixteenth stage of the 1994 Tour which could have seen Stephens expelled from the race had officials witnessed the incident.

If Stephens, who now lives in the Basque village of Orliatzun with his wife Amaiia and two children, were a prizefighter, life would be the centre ring. It was for his combative instinct as much as for his cycling prowess that he was such a sought-after domestique. It is a mark of the value placed on him that in 1992, Stephens was even picked by ONCE to race in all three major three-week tours of Spain, Italy and France. At that time it was a feat only a handful of leaders could pull off, let alone a domestique who rode his guts out from the first stage to the last. Such a tough schedule today would leave most professional racers laughing, believing it was a joke.

Stephens may have come from a cycling family – his father, Fin, and two brothers were also racers – but his introduction to the sport was far from conventional. His father, a truck-driver who owned a haulage business, was worried about his teenage son's wayward ways – Stephens loved the booze, smoked cigarettes, the odd the joint, a party and supporting the Canberra Raiders rugby league team – and believed cycling would instil discipline. The trouble was getting Stephens to ride; that is, until his brother Brian found a way. After once more earning Fin's wrath for coming home at 4.30 am one Saturday, Brian appeased his father by telling him Neil was sorry and wanted to enter the local club 16 km handicap race in Canberra that afternoon. Only, the idea had not even been mentioned to Neil who will never forget that first race: 'I got flogged but got drunk afterwards and thought, "This is great." Then the next week I raced again and had a big handicap. But this time I won and still got drunk after, so I thought, "Wow, this *is* great." '

So began the cycling career of Neil Stephens. He didn't waste time making it his living, and turned professional on the Australian domestic circuit at age seventeen after which he made his first racing trip to England in 1984 where he raced with the local ANC team for a season with Australian, Gary Sutton. But then, just before he was due to return to England in March 1985 after a spell at home, Stephens' career was put on hold with the sudden death of his father from a heart attack. 'We were at a race and I saw him fall over. I thought he had tripped but no, he died right there,' Stephens recalls.

Stephens stopped cycling to run his father's business until selling it in time to race the 1985 *Sun* Tour (now *Herald Sun* Tour) of Victoria. His fourth place overall and win in the climbers' category gave Stephens the credentials to earn – via the lobbying of former professional and current race promoter, John Trevorrow – a place on the Italian Santini team for the 1986 Giro d'Italia. At that stage, Stephens still didn't harbour any ambition to race professionally in Europe, and didn't think more of it after finishing the Giro in 78th place at 1 hour 59 minutes 46 seconds to Italian winner, Roberto Visentini. It still wasn't his plan after he returned to Australia to win the 1986 *Sun* Tour, and break the world indoor hour and 20 km track record at Launceston in 1987 before winning the Australian King of the Mountains title which offered a trip back to Europe.

His plans began to change while in England where he was racing with the local Eveready team and training for the world road titles at Villach, Austria. A representative of the small Belgian team, Eurotop, approached Stephens with an offer for the 1988 season. 'I still didn't want to race over on the Continent, but someone told me the best way out of it without losing face was to ask for a lot of money and expect them not to meet your offer. I did all that but they came back and said, "Okay".' However, the team unintentionally came up with another bailout option: it disbanded before the season began.

Having made the trip to Belgium, Stephens had nothing to lose by supporting a plan by the jobless Eurotop riders to create their own squad. And because they had no sponsor, they named it 'Zero Boys'. After registering with the Dutch Federation, the guilder-less team sold space on their white jerseys at pay-per-race rates. 'We had no money, and the worst bikes, clothing and back-up,' recalls Stephens. Financially, it was hardly a fruitful exercise. However, by fulfilling the promise to sponsors to be in the lead breakaway when television coverage began, they achieved a dual purpose: while providing their sponsor publicity, they could also attract the attention of other teams – in Stephens' case, the Spanish Caja Rural squad of top Dutch sprinter, Mathieu Hermans.

For Stephens, the offer to join Caja Rural for the 1989 season as Hermans' domestique was the first major break – even though his contract was for only £4000 a year. The team disbanded after the 1989 season and Stephens confronted a frustrating series of injuries – beginning with a fractured kneecap in the 1989 Milan–San Remo classic. But he did enough in 1990 and 1991 as leader with the small Artiach team (known as Paternina in the second year) to impress other big Spanish teams like Seur, Clas, Amaya and ONCE. For 1992 he opted to join ONCE, a winning squad backed by Spain's national blind society who sold lottery tickets to raise funds.

Stephens lined up for five of his seven Tour starts with ONCE, riding for such champions as Spaniards Marino Lejarreta and Melchor Mauri, Switzerland's Alex Zulle, Dutchman Erik Breukink, and Frenchman Laurent Jalabert. Whenever they won or raced well, Stephens was always a contributing factor.

Stephens' popularity with his teammates was shown by their concern for him when things weren't going well – such as when he abandoned the 1993 Tour. His grey, pale and drawn look at the start of the thirteenth stage from Marseille to the Mediterranean seaside city of Montpellier read: 'Abandon.' It was as clear as the blue skies above that all the energy he had mustered to overcome the headaches, nausea and weakness of mind and body in the back-breaking Alps was at its lowest ebb. And it was even clearer several minutes after the stage start when Radio Tour announced that Stephens was in trouble and dropping off the pack – in the neutralised zone. One by one, teammates came back to encourage him. One by one, they worried for his state, yet were impressed by his dogged refusal to stop – until there was simply no option. A couple of hours later when he did abandon as the race laboured through a day of searing heat, the one consolation for his teammates, supporters and himself was that Stephens' misery was over as quick as the second it took for a race *commissaire* to strip off his race number.

Despite having no choice but to abandon, Stephens hated having to do so, such was his loyalty to the ONCE team. His commitment never really waned despite the appearance of a few cracks later on.

The first came in the 1994 Tour when Saiz bizarrely gave Stephens a serve for losing to Sorensen in a two-up sprint for the fourteenth stage from Castres to Montpellier. Saiz's frustration over ONCE's inability to rattle the glory-run of Indurain – who rode on to win the fourth of his five Tours – was understandable. ONCE had not won a stage (nor would they) and their best-placed rider overall would be Zulle in eighth at 20 minutes 35 seconds to Indurain. In hindsight, Stephens says Saiz's remarks were probably to the point. But at the time, upon hearing Saiz vent his frustration on the hard-working domestique – who was hardly fancied to win the stage – his treatment appeared harsh.

It was felt by some that Stephens' services were taken for granted by Saiz, especially when it came to contractual re-negotiation. In the 1995 Tour, Stephens rode brilliantly to help Zulle finish second overall, Jalabert fourth, and Mauri sixth. He also helped Jalabert win the sprinters' green points jersey. It is hard to pick one day of that Tour which stands as the finest example of Stephens' impact in that Tour. But no one would refute the twelfth stage from Saint Etienne to Mende as one of the best.

Under sweltering heat and over a 222 km stage, Stephens and Mauri joined Jalabert in an epic six-man 200 km break with three rival Italians. Stephens and Mauri rode themselves into the ground to help the French leader claim a magnificent stage win, fittingly on Bastille Day. Tour history records the win as one of the top two exploits of that race – the other being Italian Marco Pantani's stage wins at l'Alpe d'Huez in the Alps and Guzet-Neige in the Pyrénées.

Stephens was as committed to ONCE in the 1996 Tour. That year Indurain's bid for a record sixth win fell apart as shockingly as ONCE's hopes of a win faded with the abandonment of Zulle and Jalabert. Also as loyal in deed was Jonker, another Australian ONCE rider who came to help Zulle in the mountains and, after finding all his work for the Swiss to be in vain, capitalised on the opportunity to finish twelfth and became ONCE's best-placed rider overall. His result was secured in the 154 km eighteenth stage from Pamplona to the Atlantic beachfront of Hendaye by joining a break that escaped on the second-last climb of the Tour, the Col d'Ispeguy (672 m), with 88 km to go. He finished 17 minutes ahead of the main group.

Stephens was unlucky not to have won three days earlier in the 176 km fifteenth stage from Brive-la-Gaillarde to Villeneuve-sur-Lot. He would surely have caught eventual stage winner, Podenzana, had he not crashed when a tyre rolled off his wheel at a roundabout 4 km from the finish. His odds against Poden-zana were better than against Sorensen the previous year. And his anger at not getting the chance to try became obvious later. After finishing sixth at 1 minute 41 seconds down, Stephens revealed the cause in a television interview. His explanation shed poor light on the ONCE mechanic's professionalism, but Stephens wasn't sorry for having upset the mechanic. As he said: 'I did roll a tyre, mate. I wasn't going to lie about it. Besides, I am the one standing here bleeding.'

Stephens had something to show for his effort two days later after the seventeenth stage through the Pyrénées from Argèles-Gazost to Pamplona near Indurain's hometown of Villava. He led the stage for the first 100 km and picked up a 20,000 French franc (Aus $5000) *prime* (bonus) for taking first at the summit of the Col d'Aubisque (1709 m). 'I was feeling so rough, I felt I had to win something before I was caught and tailed off,' he said.

However, by the end of 1996, Stephens needed a change –
and the chance to earn better money before retiring. Saiz
wanted to keep Stephens, but said he should look elsewhere
because he didn't have the budget to give him a payrise.
Whether for good or bad, Stephens' destiny was with the
Festina team. It seemed the natural path to take. Stephen Hodge
had also signed with the team and saw out the rest of his career
there until retiring at the end of 1995. It was also a winning
team led by Tour contender Richard Virenque, then the most
popular rider in France. When Stephens told Saiz of his
decision, there was no counter-bid to keep him. Joining Festina
on a two-year contract worth $US250,000 a year seemed to be
the perfect option.

The switch looked like an ideal union come the 1997 Tour.
Festina was the number one team in the world. Virenque may
not have won overall, but he was second to Jan Ullrich and first
in the King of the Mountains competition for the fifth of five
times. Festina also won three stages – among the winners were
Virenque, Didier Rous and Stephens who by now was recognised
as one of the sport's premier super-domestiques. So often was
Stephens' gritted jaw and blond locks seen at the front of the
pack on television screens that commentators were forced to
speak endlessly of his work and the example he set for young
amateur riders. Little wonder his stage win on the seventeenth
stage from Fribourg in Switzerland through the Berne and Jura
hills to Colmar was championed so passionately.

Stephens' victory was a rarity not just because he was an
Australian rider. It also symbolised a victory for all domestiques
as *l'Équipe* expressed in its page-one headline the day after:
'*Stephens au nom des équipiers*' (Stephens in the name of domestiques). Stephens also added his own touch to the spectacle as he
finished 3 seconds ahead of twelve other breakaway riders. With
a smile beaming from ear-to-ear, he gave a rock-the-baby motion
with his arms. It was a belated dedication to his daughter,
Maaielen, born the year before in March: 'After she was born I
said I would dedicate my next win to her . . . it's just taken this
long to win a race.'

To see Stephens win, you could have thought he did it all the time. He was at the centre of all the action from start to finish. He started the break after 60 km on the slopes of the third category Col de Pierre-Pertuis and was soon joined by the twelve others. The group, representing thirteen teams, got a maximum lead of 7 minutes before the Telekom and Gan teams began to chase them down to 3 minutes with 24 km to go. But this late in the Tour, with Telekom assured of the yellow jersey for Ullrich who was in the bunch, the odds of catching the stage leaders were simply too great.

For Stephens, the orange light for his imminent attack came with 5 km to go, as a barrage of attacks began, one of them coming from Stephens to test his rivals' measure. But Stephens waited for the right moment to execute his winning strike – when it was close enough to the finish to pull off a triumphant attack, yet still far enough away to cause the group to hesitate as they look to one another to do the job of reining him in. That moment came with 3.5 km to go on the sinewy entry into the town of Colmar. Darting off to the right of the road, Stephens pedalled head down as if he was leading out the bunch for a sprint finish, only this time there was no bunch or rider on his wheel. Stephens was alone, heading for a great victory.

After he won, the accolades came flooding in. Riders from all teams yelled 'bravo Neil' as they crossed the line after him – from the group he was in to the main bunch that followed 3 minutes 58 seconds later who saw him on the podium. Festina team *directeur-sportif,* Bruno Roussel, was all praise for Stephens: 'If it is necessary to control the race, he will control it. If it is necessary to attack, he will attack. He is always there, his nose on the handlebars, stuck to the [wheels] of all the good riders. He is a clairvoyant. He sees everything happening. He feels danger as if he is feeling the wind.'

Sadly, there was one danger he did not feel – that being the Festina doping scandal a year later. After such a great Tour in 1997 and the 1998 race edging towards an anticipated fairytale end to Stephens' career, this was a danger of the worst kind. It came at the Tour start in Dublin with news of a Festina *soigneur,*

Willy Voet, being caught by customs on the Belgian–French border with a stash of 400 phials of illegal drugs, including EPO and human growth hormones. The story spread as quickly as a summer bushfire, only this time it would be reputation, careers and lives ruined by the accusation and drama that followed.

Every Festina rider – Stephens included – was targeted by the police investigation that began. The team tried to defend itself during the Irish leg of the Tour that included the prologue time-trial and two stages. It continued to plead innocence even after returning to France via Roscoff for stage three where French police soon took in Roussel for questioning.

Meanwhile, back in Australia, South Australia's Stuart O'Grady was hitting the headlines with his three-day spell in the yellow jersey which he claimed on stage four to Chôlet, rather than Stephens and the problems in the Festina team. For them the pressure was still mounting, especially after Roussel and team medico, Dr Eric Ryckaert, were kicked off the race at Chôlet when the UCI withdrew their licences because of their implication in the controversy.

It seemed inevitable that the whole Festina team would be expelled when Voet, during police questioning, accused Roussel of ordering the use of drugs within the team. The axe finally fell after stage six to Brive-la-Gaillarde when, at 11.15 pm, Tour race director Jean-Marie Leblanc convened a press conference to formally announce the expulsion of the Festina team from the Tour for systematic doping, adding that the decision was prompted by Roussel's incrimination of the riders. Stephens, who had maintained his innocence since Dublin, had never felt worse: 'My morale has been really low. Continuing has been hard. I wish I never came on the Tour.'

If Festina's expulsion sent shockwaves through the race, so too did the reaction from six of their nine riders. The six, not including Stephens, pledged to defy the expulsion and start the 57 km seventh stage time-trial from Meryignac-l'Église to Corrèze. It was embarrassing for Tour organisers, especially since Corrèze is the hometown of President Jacques Chirac's wife who was to attend the stage. One weekend, President Chirac was celebrating France's

World Cup victory, the next his wife was 'hosting' the Tour at her own home, only to discover it to be the scene of one of the biggest drug scandals in world sport. Fortunately, the stand-off was averted thanks to a meeting in the back room of the Chez Guilloz café in Corrèze. On one side of the table sat Leblanc, while on the other were the 'Festina Six' who were led by Virenque. Finally, Virenque and his henchmen agreed to leave as ordered – albeit in a pathetic shower of tears.

Stephens, meanwhile, had already left. When the order came for the Festina riders to leave their hotel and go to the stage start, he remained in his room. As his teammates drove off, he waited several minutes for his brother Brian to arrive. Soon after, the pair began the drive back home to Spain, hoping that the nightmare was well and truly over.

Nothing could have been further from the truth. On the morning of stage ten, claims from Dr Ryckaert's lawyer were published in the French daily *Aujourd'hui* – one being that Festina riders had paid money into a slush fund to finance the purchase of the drugs. Stephens maintained, 'All I know is that we put money into a fund for vitamins. What people may have done – or not – with that fund is news to me.' Then two days later, Stephens and the Festina riders heeded a summons from French police to go to their headquarters in Lyon for questioning. They believed they would only have to make a witness statement and leave the same day. But upon their arrival, they were treated otherwise.

Each rider was placed *en garde a vue* (in remand) and under French law, could be incarcerated for up to 72 hours. During the first night, three riders – Laurent Brochard, Christophe Moreau and Arman Meier – were released after confessing to using EPO, as was Virenque early the next morning even though he did not confess for another two years. Stephens, at this point, was still being held alone under lock and key and probed for answers. Meanwhile, back in the Tour, as the race resumed for the twelfth stage to Cap d'Agde, the released Festina riders went public over their treatment by police, Meier being the first. 'We were treated like animals. I was stripped. They took my belt, my money, my car keys, as if I was a criminal,' he said in a broken voice on radio. 'Then I was thrown in a cell which had a wooden bed. I stayed there for about five hours.' Meier's comments shocked everyone, especially the riders who led the first of two mass protests against the police action by refusing to race until their discontent was formally heard on Radio Tour.

Stephens was the last Festina rider released. He was let go on the Friday, after 36 hours of detention during which police interviewed him for a total of 16 hours, in 90-minute spells between short sleeps in a small, soiled and permanently lighted concrete cell. All he had to eat was a stale croissant and a small cup of black coffee. And like his Festina teammates, he made similar allegations of police mistreatment. It was a full day after his return to Spain before he felt comfortable enough to speak about his shocking experience. He told me: 'I was stripped and given a full body search – told to bend over. The whole thing was pretty horrific. They took all my clothes, put me in a cell with a wooden bed, a pillow and no blanket. I was given back my pants and socks to sleep in, but when I went for a pee they wouldn't give me my shoes. I had to stand there in my socks, over one of those holes in the floor.' It was humiliation like he had never before experienced.

After being presented with police evidence, Stephens admitted he had been administered illegal drugs, but maintained he did not know it at the time. He testified that Dr Ryckaert informed him that the substances he was given were vitamin C and E. Stephens was cleared of criminal charges. Part of his defence was that any rider who signed with Roussel's company, ProSport, was contracted to abide by the team's medical charter run by Dr Ryckaert. As Stephens explains, 'There was a clause in the contract that said if we did not agree to the medical philosophy of the team then our contacts could be made null and void. At the same time, there was a clause in the contract between Festina and ProSport that in the event of a drug scandal, their contract could be torn up too.'

At the time, Stephens was still unsure of how his cycling career would be affected by the scandal – especially due to his place on the Australian road cycling team in the Commonwealth Games in Malaysia. He knew that a suspension and hostile reactions from the media and the public were possible ramifications.

Meanwhile, the Tour continued to stumble its way to Paris amidst a series of police raids, media leaks of evidence and the second of the two rider protests against police treatment. A mood of disillusionment swept the entire race – so much so that the Tour came very close to stopping altogether. Some commentators even proposed the Tour be suspended for a year and given time to cleanse itself from the drugs problem and the sour taste it had left on everyone's palate.

Stephens, meanwhile, was left to get on with his life. Cycling Australia (CA) – backed by the Australian Olympic Committee and Australian Commonwealth Games Association – officially cleared him of any guilt, declaring that he had still never failed a drugs test, neither in his career nor throughout the controversy. Stephens raced the Commonwealth Games with his usual dogged commitment and helped Australian Jay Sweet to a gold medal ride in the road race. Then he retired to live with his family in Orliatzun where he has tried his hand at many jobs since. He first worked as representative for the sports sunglass manufacturer, Oakley, before taking up position as *directeur-sportif* with the British Linda McCartney team until it disbanded in 2001. He is now CA's rider liaison for European-based Australian riders and assists the Australian road team when it races in Europe. He also conducts occasional bike tours to the Tour.

As has always been the case since Stephens first rode a bike, despite all the bad that happened, he still thinks of what he can do for the best – and in most cases, for someone else. As a kid, he first raced to make his dad happy; then as a professional he lived and breathed the sport motivated by the sole aim of helping others win. Today, all his time in cycling is invested in helping others – whether they be riders or fans.

Chapter 8

Yellow fever

STUART O'GRADY

Stuart O'Grady was preparing for another lung-bursting dash to the line in the 2002 Tour de France. Suddenly his heart began pounding 220–235 beats per minute. With 55 km to go in the 174.5 km third stage from Metz to the champagne city of Reims and no sign of his heartbeat easing, he dropped off the bunch in search of Tour medico, Dr Gérard Porte. O'Grady knew he had had a tachycardia attack. News of his distress sent other heart-rates rocketing in concern as Porte leaned from his open-roofed white Fiat to assess the rider's condition. The scene was repeated three times over the next 45 km before O'Grady finally settled back into the pack with 10 km to go. He still managed to finish tenth in the stage which was won by Australian, Robbie McEwen.

The drama worried most people – fellow riders, the media, race officials and anyone who was following the race live. Incredibly, the one person who *wasn't* that shocked was O'Grady who, despite his obvious discomfort, was at relative ease with it all. It was a condition from which he had suffered before, at the 1996 Olympic Games and in other smaller races. He also knew it was one that could be controlled and it was just bad timing that this latest attack happened during the biggest race in the world with millions of people watching. 'It was obviously a little difficult to breathe. I felt light-headed, so I stayed down the back of the bunch and the guys kept me in there. I think they were freaking out about it more than I was. I have had it a few times, but not for a couple of years now,' said O'Grady who underwent tests at the hospital in Reims and was declared fit to race on.

That night O'Grady ate and slept as well as he always did. He had more heart tests the next morning before stage four, the 67 km team time-trial from Épernay to Château-Thierry. During the stage, an ambulance followed O'Grady and his Crédit Agricole team, but O'Grady rode strongly, taking all his scheduled turns at the front. Their eleventh place – against their stunning victory in the team time-trial in 2001 – was in no way a reflection of his performance. O'Grady also attempted to water down continuing concern for his health, adding that of the two forms of tachycardia, he had 'the good one' which, even without an operation or medication, is not life-threatening.

Not everyone was convinced though. The Union Cycliste Internationale ordered O'Grady to undergo and pass one more battery of heart tests four days later – on the rest day at Bordeaux – if he was to be allowed to continue racing. O'Grady did pass, and he 'celebrated' the next day by placing third in the decisive four-man breakaway group on the tenth stage from Bazas to Pau at the foot of the Pyrénées. This would be his best result for the Tour.

When O'Grady reached the finish in Paris, he was third in the points competition behind a victorious McEwen and Erik Zabel, had seven top-ten stage placings to his name and was 77th overall at 2 hours 7 minutes 2 seconds to the American winner, Lance Armstrong. While disappointed over his 'moderate' race, all was not lost. O'Grady was just starting to hit his straps and find form when the Tour finished. One week later he won the Commonwealth Games road race gold medal in Manchester, England.

For O'Grady, the 2002 Tour reminded him of the fluctuating fortunes the event presents to those who live for it. His career as a cyclist began at age ten in Adelaide, albeit not well. He lost his first race – a handicap – to a girl who raced away from him as he looked down to reach for his drink bottle.

But in the twenty years since, he has forged a career that includes a string of feats that would make any professional rider proud, despite the frustrating problems O'Grady has had to overcome along the way. Examples are not in short supply. There was O'Grady's near-fatal end-of-season mugging in 1999 that fractured his skull and left him with a 5 cm blood clot in the brain. Then came his broken collarbone sustained on stage six of the 2000 Tour from which he was forced to withdraw, compromising his Olympic Games preparation. And after another successful recovery and Tour in 2001, O'Grady was struck down again in March 2002. This time it was due to an iliac arterial operation to clear a blood clot in his leg, leaving him very unprepared for the Tour in which he suffered his tachycardia attack.

However, when judging O'Grady's impact on Australia's history in the Tour, success rather than misfortune stands out; in particular, his claim to the yellow jersey in the fourth stage of the 1998 Tour from Plouay to Chôlet which made him the first Australian to lead the Tour since Phil Anderson in 1981 and 1982. It could be argued that this feat alone signifies more than his other successes put together, including the 1993 and 1995 world team pursuit titles, two victories in the Tour Down Under in South Australia and the 2002 Commonwealth Games gold medal.

O'Grady's yellow jersey coup that year was not his last. Nor was it necessarily his hardest fought. In 2001 he took it again, this time for six days in the far more difficult scenario of being one of the pre-Tour favourites as an early race leader. But his first spell in yellow will be best remembered because of the ramifications, foremost being to set in motion the wave of success Australians riders now enjoy in the Tour. Unlike Anderson's era when there were very few Australian riders coming through the ranks, in 1998 there was a growing depth of Australian road talent in Europe. In the 1998 Tour there were three other Australians racing: Neil Stephens, Robbie McEwen and Patrick

Jonker. In trade teams around Europe, Australian riders were a growing presence. Seeing O'Grady succeed helped them to realise that they could too. It ignited the belief that success in the Tour was not out of their reach.

American cycling learned this lesson when Californian-born Greg LeMond won the Tour in 1986, 1989 and 1990; furthermore, the 7-Eleven and Motorola teams were making long and very successful campaigns. But in Australia – a nation further away from European cycling geographically and culturally – there was still a lack of belief that Aussie riders could win. This changed when O'Grady slipped on the yellow jersey, and backed it up by winning the fourteenth stage to Grenoble in a brilliant sprint over five other breakaway riders.

O'Grady's rise to stardom wasn't quick nor easy. It didn't take long for him to understand that life as a professional cyclist was far from glamorous, despite the exotic travel destinations and the glitzy image of the Tour. Today the O'Grady most Australians see is the pin-up hero from Adelaide, a sports-car loving, happy-go-lucky bloke wearing trendy clothes and gold jewellery. But O'Grady suffered to get to where he is today.

The transition from Australian track star to professional rookie on a French team was challenging. He signed with the Gan team (Crédit Agricole today) shortly after the world track championships in Sicily at the end of 1994. He was offered a two-year contract which allowed him to still race on the track for six months a year until after the 1996 Olympics. But within a month of the 1995 season, O'Grady was already finding the going tough; he abandoned one of his first road events, the five-day Mediterranean Tour in the south of France.

After turning professional with so much promise, he was devastated – physically and morally – when we met one night at l'Auberge Provençal, a quaint restaurant in Antibes which has long been a favourite amongst many cycling greats. His tired and boyish face – not the hardened chiselled regard he wears today – was torn with guilt, despite his withdrawal being due to a knee injury. He felt he should have been with his teammates at their hotel planning the next day's tactics – the chases, the attacks and the lead-outs for sprints – rather than planning what he would eat from an *à la carte* menu.

O'Grady can be his hardest critic. When things go wrong, he likes to be alone, and certainly not answerable to the media. Approaching him can be perilous when results don't go his way. That night in 1995, he was being characteristically severe on himself. He knew first impressions counted and the prospect of a six-week break to recover from injury was not the start he needed, especially for a new foreign rider on a French team. All he had was a burning desire to get back on the saddle and show he was as good as he had been touted.

As O'Grady sat before me in Antibes, he seemed not to notice the jerseys that hung on the walls around us of the many cycling greats who had eaten there – from past Tour de France stars like Eddy Merckx to Bernard Hinault, Laurent Fignon, Greg LeMond, Stephen Roche and Phil Anderson. 'Maybe I will have one of yours one day,' said the smiling owner, Andy Martin, to O'Grady who allowed his eyes to look at the signed cycling memorabilia. The way he was feeling that night, such fortunes seemed unreachable. There he was, a rookie humbled and limping after quitting one of his first races, surrounded by the richest history of cycling greatness.

But seven years on, the contrast between him and that greatness is far diminished. O'Grady has never won the Tour de France overall, but he has worn the yellow and green jerseys, and either would hang beautifully on Martin's restaurant wall.

1998 – Three days in yellow

When O'Grady first put on the yellow jersey on July 15, 1998, he famously dubbed the feat 'not bad for a freckly red-headed bastard from Adelaide'. As he stepped down from the podium that afternoon at Chôlet, he still couldn't hide his joy over fulfilling a childhood dream: 'It's bloody awesome. All I have ever dreamed of since I was a kid was wearing the yellow jersey. I don't care for how long I've got it. Even if it's only for one hour, it's mine for the rest of my life.'

At his hotel that night, O'Grady and his teammates celebrated. Overnight, he also received the now-customary fax of congratulations from Prime Minister John Howard in Canberra. His family back home at Ingle Farm, a suburb north of Adelaide, was also inundated with well-wishing calls and visits. His mother Fay first thought the news of her son's success was a prank. His father Brian, himself a former racing cyclist and a Commonwealth car chauffeur for politicians, became the target of media interest. The day after his son's triumph, he was driving former Opposition leader Kim Beazley when he was forced to stop before a pack of media and television crews. To his great surprise, it was him they were after, not the politician.

The news of O'Grady in the yellow jersey made both the front and back pages in Australia. It should have been an opportunity for cycling to raise its profile in Australia, but the timing of O'Grady's achievement dampened the chances of that. For it happened in a Tour that became better (or worse) known for the drug scandal that destroyed the French Festina team, one of the biggest teams in the race. While O'Grady was unassociated with the scandal, it dominated the media and O'Grady didn't get much recognition in France for his spell wearing the yellow jersey.

Gan team director, Roger Legeay, was outraged at O'Grady's lack of publicity – if not for O'Grady himself then for his sponsor who was getting minimal exposure in return for its multi-million-dollar investment. Legeay called it a national disgrace. But nothing could push the Festina affair off the front page. So, as quietly as O'Grady's three-day reign in yellow began at Chôlet, it came to the same end in the 58 km individual time-trial at Corrèze when the Festina riders stole the headlines again by threatening to protest their expulsion by defying it.

However, O'Grady didn't give up the jersey without a fantastic fight. In stinking hot conditions, he finished fifteenth and 3 minutes 7 seconds to Ullrich, an astonishingly small deficit against one of the greatest time-triallists in the world. It was also a credit to O'Grady that he publicly remained unworried about his low profile in France, saying, 'This is my yellow jersey, no one can take that away from me,' whenever asked. When he did relinquish the jersey, it was clear the psychological and physical pressures of defending it had taken much from him, although he knew the experience would serve him well for the future. As he said, 'I'm a bit relieved, to be honest. These three days have definitely given me new objectives in my life. It has given me new perspectives on what I can expect as a professional and of myself. Now I need a few days' recovery.'

That O'Grady found himself in the yellow jersey in the first place was not surprising to those who had seen him progress through the junior and amateur ranks. Former Australian Institute of Sport track teammates with whom he won the team pursuit gold medals in the 1993 and 1995 world titles, and bronze in the 1996 Olympics, will recall his immense strength and endurance, especially during their annual month-long high-altitude training camps at Tolluca, Mexico, in February. In camps that would see riders tally 4000 km in the month at lung-bursting altitudes reaching 4000 m above sea level, it was not uncommon for O'Grady to cycle off alone during 300 km-plus rides. The smoothness of his pedal stroke on a massive gear belied O'Grady's strength. After riding away, he would often be showered, dressed and waiting at the team hotel when his teammates arrived 40 minutes later.

In his first full season as a road racing professional, O'Grady was often on the attack. It was a popular joke that in his first season, he learned little about etiquette in the peloton. Why? Because he had spent so much time out of it. He now races with more rat-cunning than brazen gusto. Although, he would beg to differ that the task is any easier – as he did after twelve of the twenty stages in the 2001 Tour which saw him spend eighteen days in either the yellow or green jersey. With barely half of the 3462 km race over and Armstrong poised to win his third title, O'Grady was on the brink of physical ruin. He even wondered if he would finish the Tour, after finishing 112th in the stage eleven mountain time-trial from Grenoble to Chamrousse: 'The body takes an absolute hiding. You wake up each morning feeling worse and worse,' said O'Grady, whose consolation was that most in the race felt the same after dealing with a variety of ailments caused by the accumulated effect of racing such as fever; diarrhoea; nausea; dehydration; bronchial, urinal and stomach infections; insomnia; saddle sores; and weight and appetite loss. On the road to l'Alpe d'Huez, O'Grady lost three kilograms in fluids and, as on every day, had trouble consuming enough calories to maintain energy levels. He felt as if his body was eating his muscle away. His heartbeat couldn't rise when pushed. On the start-line to l'Alpe d'Huez, it was still only 35 beats per minute, and hours later could not rise above 140 bpm. 'When that happens, I know I'm in trouble because my heart is tired. It's a muscle and just doesn't want to work. I'm climbing at 140 bpm when it should be around 170 bpm-plus.'

With the aggressive way he races, O'Grady is the atypical first-week contender for the yellow jersey. He indicated as much on his first Tour in 1997 when he regularly finished near the leaders in the flatter stages, as did West Australian teammate Henk Vogels whose best finish in two Tours was a third on the final stage to Paris. O'Grady's top result on debut came on stage five when he took second place after figuring in a breakaway with French teammate, Cedric Vasseur. Were it not for team instructions designating Vasseur as the team's protected rider, it could easily have been O'Grady on the podium.

O'Grady also has a calculative knack for reading a race, especially the mathematical challenge of counting time bonuses and figuring out how many seconds and minutes are between him and his closest rivals. He is a rider who will always be fancied to go for the time bonuses at intermediate sprints that count for overall time, regardless of whether he is in a breakaway or the bunch. That he is not a good climber and is always likely to lose the Tour lead also helps, for he will never be a threat and is unlikely to ever be challenged by those hoping to win in Paris.

It is little wonder that each year, O'Grady's strategy on the Tour is the same. He attacks. He sprints. Attacks. And he sprints and sprints. It seems he races as if the Tour were only one-week long, seemingly oblivious to the two more weeks of leg-sapping racing, most of which happens in the mountains of the Alps and Pyrénées. To be true, there are many riders like O'Grady who race the same way. They all know too well the contractual value – to themselves and their team and sponsor – of wearing the yellow jersey. It is also no secret that such a strategy augurs well for O'Grady's continual hopes for the green jersey. But as O'Grady said on the eve of his feted 1998 Tour after winning the Pru Tour of Britain and two stages of the Tour of Luxembourg: 'I was criticised by so many for wasting my energy, but I believed it would pay off.'

Unsurprisingly, after both of O'Grady's spells in the yellow jersey – for three days in 1998 and six in 2001 – and two in the green jersey – for three days in 1999 and twelve in 2001 – his French team offered him new two-year contracts with a hefty pay-rise; and deservedly so considering his successes came when the team's own tally of wins was lean and continued sponsorship looked dicey. In an era when team switches are frequent, O'Grady's loyalty is refreshing, especially since he had been offered lucrative deals by other teams, one being the powerful Spanish ONCE team.

But what looked like a bright future for O'Grady suddenly turned bad. Two months after signing with Crédit Agricole, he not only saw the end to his season, but almost his career – if not his life – after being mugged by three men outside a restaurant in Toulouse. The attack left O'Grady with a fractured skull and a blood clot in the brain. Also victims were his former girlfriend Jamie Grey, Henk Vogels and Scottish rider, David Millar. In the attack, which occurred on the night before he and Vogels were to leave for the Tour of Poland, O'Grady was hit on the head and Grey on the hand with a windscreen wiper; Vogels and Millar were punched in the face. O'Grady's $300 gold neck chain and Vogels' watch were stolen. 'We were walking after leaving the restaurant and back to the car. Then three guys bumped into us. I said, "What did you do that for?" And one guy grabbed my neck chain and another grabbed Henk's watch. I knew which one grabbed my chain and pushed him onto the car. Then Jamie came over to try and calm everything down. He hit her over the arm and she fell to the ground. Then he smashed me over the head. If the guy had a knife it could have been a lot worse. When you stop and think about it, it's pretty scary.'

Due to his recovery period, O'Grady missed that year's world road championships in Verona, Italy. But even after being given the green light to train, O'Grady provoked a major scare back in Australia when he suddenly collapsed 10 minutes before the start of a criterium race in Noosa Heads, Queensland. It was later diagnosed as a focal seizure, which also caused temporary paralysis of his right arm. O'Grady had not taken his medication to treat the clot in his brain that scans revealed to be 1.7 cm in size. 'I remember most of [my collapse]. I had just ridden down from the hotel to the race and had just started trying to pin my number onto my jersey. Then I started getting a black blotch in my vision. I thought, "This will go away, take a few slow deep breaths and it'll be back to normal." But it just got worse and, in the end, I couldn't see anyone in front of me. I was sitting down. Then I had the seizure. My body started jittering and my head started thrashing about. I lost movement in my right arm and couldn't see it or feel it.' The danger of further seizures was very real. O'Grady underwent more tests on his return to Adelaide, but results indicated that, provided he continue taking his medication rather than forget it as had been the case, the clot would disappear – which it did.

O'Grady made a full recovery for 2000. But all his good work came to nought. In the Tour, he began well even though any chance of winning the yellow jersey quickly eluded him. But a stage win appeared to be on the cards when he nudged close to victory on the 194 km second stage from Futuroscope to Loudun. He finished second to Tom Steels in the sprint finish, but ahead of Zabel. However, it was all to no avail. On stage six he crashed with nine riders at 60 kmh, soon before the village of Chevire-le-Rouge and 110 km into the 195 km race from Vitré to Tours. O'Grady knew he had broken his collarbone, but hoped for the best. He instinctively remounted his bike and bravely rode the final 85 km to the finish. With blood oozing from his shredded green-and-white team jersey, O'Grady reached Tours in a group of ten riders, 22 minutes 26 seconds behind Dutch winner, Leon Van Bon.

It was later announced that O'Grady would not start the next day, but this was expected after the sight of him soft-pedalling across the line directly to the Crédit Agricole team van. All he could do when he dismounted was wince in pain, clutch his shoulder and hobble past his worried parents and a legion of media and fans before being whisked to hospital. Later, while lying in a hospital bed, O'Grady recalled the pile-up that was caused by a rider mistaking the sound of a beating drum for a crash up ahead. When he braked, other riders – including O'Grady – concertinaed into the back of him: 'One dickhead panicked and shoved the brakes on and went down. I jumped over him and thought I was okay. But I nose-dived and landed on my head. Deep down I knew [my collarbone] was broken but I rode to the finish praying it wasn't. In truth, the further I went the more trouble I was in.'

2001 – So close, but . . .

In 2001, O'Grady came as close as anyone to winning the green jersey. He wore it for twelve days, only to see Zabel take it from him in the last stage. Some thought his undoing was due to the energy he had expended to claim and defend the yellow jersey, which he wore for six days. But O'Grady, whose sheer speed in the bunch sprints is inferior to Zabel, had no choice but to chase the bonus seconds and points on offer at the intermediate sprints and stage finishes. For O'Grady, racing for the yellow and green requires the same tactic. His only course of action was to be up front and near the action all day. Even had he not worn the yellow jersey and was focusing only on the green one, he would still have had to race as hard from the moment the Tour began.

O'Grady was arguably in his best-ever form in the 2001 Tour. When he arrived at the start in the North Sea port city of Dunkirk, he was still without a win since the Tour Down Under back home in January. But O'Grady made it clear he was ready to have a serious crack at claiming the green and yellow jerseys. Confirmation came with his eighth place in the prologue time-trial – 13 seconds behind the winner, French time-trial specialist,

Christophe Moreau, who had finished fourth overall in the previous year's Tour.

It seemed that O'Grady's run for the yellow jersey was then just a matter of time. That is, until the 220.5 km second stage from Calais to Europe's diamond capital of Antwerp in Belgium. When the day began it was expected the jersey would be O'Grady's by night. But at nightfall, the only colour he had was the red of embarrassment and anger. With a little more than a kilometre of the stage to go and as one of eighteen riders (including three of his Crédit Agricole teammates) in the lead group, O'Grady was in the box seat to snare an extremely rare Tour treble: the yellow jersey, green jersey and a stage victory. But by the time Belgian Marc Wauters had claimed victory, all O'Grady had to show for it were two words: 'If only . . . '

O'Grady's woes began when Wauters attacked with 1 km to go, and managed to fend off the breakaway group. With the stage win surrendered, fifth-placed O'Grady then endured an agonising wait as officials calculated the overall times to determine the yellow jersey. But that too went to Wauters. Finally, after officials beckoned O'Grady to the podium to claim the green jersey, they had to turn him around just as he arrived at the dais because a re-count determined it should go to Estonian, Jaan Kirsipuu.

The Crédit Agricole team was stunned, especially O'Grady and his teammates in the break – American Bobby Julich, Frenchman Anthony Morin and German Jens Voigt – who had flogged themselves to control the break for its last 20 km, but incredibly forgot to consider the danger posed by Wauters. 'I have never screamed at my teammates so much in my life,' said O'Grady, admitting he erred by working too hard in the group when he should have been resting for the sprint finish where two more points would have secured him the green jersey. Those 'lost' points, it later proved, would also have been invaluable come the finish in Paris.

The odds of O'Grady making up for the botched finish the following day were slim. Stage three was a tough 198.5 km run from Antwerp in Flanders to Seraing in the hilly Ardennes of

Belgium. O'Grady was still second overall and 12 seconds behind Wauters, but with 65 riders within a minute of Wauters on overall time, and all vying for the yellow jersey, the task was suddenly much harder for one team or rider to pull off.

But then fate took a liking to O'Grady. On the last of three climbs with 12 km to go, Wauters – who had celebrated his glory by leading the Tour into his hometown of Lummen earlier that day where he stopped to hug his wife and family – was dropped by the front group that included O'Grady, who was also tiring on the steep hill. But when told of Wauters' demise via radio link with his team car, O'Grady immediately dug deep to stay with the leaders. They didn't make the task any easier as several Tour favourites like Armstrong and Ullrich began testing each other with sporadic attacks. But O'Grady, sensing he had a rare second chance to avenge the disappointment of the day before, seized the opportunity: 'I had to just hang in there and give it everything.' What O'Grady gave he got in return. Zabel won in an uphill sprint between 102 riders. But importantly for 31st placed O'Grady, Wauters came in 6 minutes 36 seconds behind – easily enough to move O'Grady to first place overall with 17 seconds on Moreau. O'Grady was also third in the points competition and well-positioned to challenge Zabel for leadership when his reign in yellow came to an end.

It had taken one of O'Grady's most defiant rides to achieve what many – O'Grady included – had thought was nearly impossible 24 hours before. He also revealed how badly he felt about his botched finish at Antwerp: 'It was devastating. I felt like the guy who had missed the [match winning] penalty in the World Cup soccer final. It was such a blow to the team and me. It was probably the most disappointing day of my life on the bike.'

Not that anyone in the pack had any sympathy for O'Grady. On his tail were several riders who wanted to end his race leadership there and then. Had he forgotten how hard it was to defend the jersey, he was reminded of it on the fourth stage from Huy in the Belgian Ardennes to Verdun in France. For O'Grady it was 'a day from hell'. He came under fire throughout the

215 km stage, the most dangerous being an attack with 35 km to go from three riders, including French hero, Laurent Jalabert.

When Jalabert's group drew out their lead to two minutes, O'Grady's yellow jersey was in danger. But his team found handy allies in the Bonjour team of Frenchman François Simon, a sparrow of a man who was vying with Jalabert to take the yellow jersey. But by helping Crédit Agricole chase Jalabert's group, Bonjour's aim was not to help O'Grady earn one more day in yellow but help Simon get it himself. Jalabert still won the stage after attacking again with 3 km to go. The win also meant he earned a 35-second time bonus, but it was not enough to overtake a relieved O'Grady who was eighth on the stage and moved to second in the points competition.

'Jalabert's attack was about the last straw,' said an exhausted O'Grady that night. It was a lot of work to defend a jersey whose significance is belied by the mere $500 a rider wins for wearing it each day. It's true value, though, is shown through the contractual ramifications. In O'Grady's case, it helped to renew his deal with the team, then believed to be about Aus $600,000 a year and now reportedly Aus $1 million. It also guaranteed him lucrative invitations to the traditional post-Tour criteriums or exhibition races. As a yellow jersey wearer, O'Grady could command $20,000 to $30,000 for every two-hour race, of which he could start fifteen in a two-week period.

It was the day after Jalabert's stage win that O'Grady and his team rose to the occasion and raced at their arguable best by winning, against all the odds, the stage five 67 km team time-trial from Verdun to Bar-le-Duc. No one expected Crédit Agricole to win. At best, they had targeted a top-five finish on a day that saw a torrential downpour and winds that tested the best of bike-handling skills.

For O'Grady it was sheer pain from start to finish: 'It was a total test of courage. But every time it started hurting, I just looked down and saw the yellow jersey on my sleeve.' Observers walked away in disbelief as Crédit Agricole defeated the fancied teams of ONCE, Festina and the US Postal Service squad of the defending champion, Armstrong. Their win from twenty-one teams was the first major upset of the Tour, astonishing even O'Grady and his teammates. 'It has been a big surprise for everyone,' he said, admitting such a ride seemed beyond him when he woke up that morning to take a 90-minute training ride with his team. 'I didn't want to get out of bed. I was sceptical because my legs felt like lead. As it turned out, it was a good decision.' A bonus for Crédit Agricole was that the win also gave the team a buffer for any immediate challenge to O'Grady's yellow jersey. Teammates Voigt and Julich moved into second and third places at 26 and 27 seconds respectively, leaving them in an ideal position to go with any breakaway, sit with it and try to win the jersey should the attack stay away.

By emulating his yellow jersey feat of 1998 – when he was less known and unmarked by his peers – O'Grady established himself as a truly talented rider. The accolades flooded in from some of the best riders in the world. Among them was Miguel Indurain, the five-times Tour champion from Spain who retired after losing his bid for a record sixth win in 1996. 'He is a great rider who has made a great adaptation to European cycling. O'Grady is very, very strong. He also has great endurance and a lot of speed for the sprints. That is his key to winning races, especially the yellow jersey. His success shows cycling is a world sport. So far, that is his biggest legacy,' said Indurain the night before O'Grady began a third day in yellow on the 162.5 km seventh stage from Strasbourg to Colmar.

Another Spanish Tour champion, Pedro Delgado, who won the race in 1988, put O'Grady's success down to a toughness derived from his mugging in 1999 and his broken collarbone in the 2000 Tour. His comeback, said Delgado, had developed O'Grady into a better rider: 'He is stronger, mentally and physically. He is a very good cyclist, and he has not only shown that this year, he has done it in other years. But I am very happy for him after the difficult year he had [in 2000] and all he has gone through.'

It mattered little to O'Grady that he lost the yellow jersey the next day. By passing it onto the shoulders of his loyal teammate,

Voigt, he saw it as fair compensation for the German who had ridden so hard to help him. In any case, it was a short-lived break, for O'Grady incredibly took the yellow jersey back from Voigt on stage eight, the day before the Tour reached the Alps. Furthermore, by placing fifth and figuring in the winning thirteen-man break that reached the finish in Pontarlier with a massive lead of nearly 36 minutes, O'Grady also took the green jersey from his German nemesis, Zabel.

O'Grady knew his renewed reign as race leader would not last for long though, and that the half-hour gained on the stage would count for little come the finish in Paris. O'Grady was also aware he had only 4 minutes 32 seconds on the Frenchman, Simon – a far better climber who had openly pledged to put an end to O'Grady's lead on the tenth stage to l'Alpe d'Huez. In fact, few people gave O'Grady a chance of surviving longer than one more day. Irish legend, Sean Kelly, also dismissed suggestions that O'Grady would be helped by any extra self-confidence garnered from Crédit Agricole's team time-trial win. 'The confidence he got won't help. That got him here,' said the forthright Kelly.

The death-knell on O'Grady's lead sounded the next day, a 185 km stage from Pontarlier to Aix-les-Bains. That he had managed to keep a grasp on the race lead was a feat driven by sheer will, rather than form. He placed third in the bunch sprint and sixth on the stage that saw another Australian, Brad McGee – making a brilliant Tour debut – figure in the winning break to take third place. But O'Grady made no secret of the fact that the huge effort sapped any possible strength he would have for the first dreaded day in the Alps 24 hours later. 'If I didn't have the yellow jersey, I probably wouldn't have finished in that [main] group. On the last climb [at 145 km], it was the fact that I was in yellow that got me over. But I think it is *au revoir maillot jaune* for now.'

In fact, it was *au revoir* for good. Closing O'Grady's reign in yellow after six days was Simon, who took it on the 209 km tenth stage from Aix-les-Bains to l'Alpe d'Huez. He had no need to win, only to surpass O'Grady's overnight lead of 4 minutes

32 seconds with the best margin. It was also a day when the over-all main contenders came to the fore, the biggest name being Armstrong who brilliantly won the stage and consolidated his authority. O'Grady was doomed on a course that included four climbs – three being giant passes in the last 100 km. He struggled from the first pedal-stroke and lost touch with Simon's group after 114 km, 7 km up the 24 km-long Col de la Madelaine. O'Grady rode on to finish the stage 33 minutes 2 seconds down on Armstrong, and conceded the jersey to the popular Simon who still suffered terribly to place nineteenth at 10 minutes 29 seconds.

With the yellow jersey and all its responsibilities now in his sight, Armstrong provided a short but cutting insight into the pressures that O'Grady would have experienced: 'It's a very heavy jersey.'

Again, O'Grady seemed to be happy to be relieved of it. 'I never believed I would have got this far in yellow,' said O'Grady after finishing. However, whatever pressure he had cast off was soon replaced by the pressure of another sort – defending the other jersey he really wanted – the green jersey. As it turned out, it was a defence to last all the way to the finish-line in Paris.

Armstrong powered away to Paris to claim his third Tour victory, passing over the Alps and then the Pyrénées – where he took the yellow jersey on stage thirteen. Attempts by Ullrich and Spaniard, Joseba Beloki, to foil his bid were futile. As each day passed, the inevitability of another Armstrong victory only firmed. Some unfairly said the Tour had become boring and begged for some drama. This came in the nail-biting showdown between O'Grady and Zabel for the green jersey.

No Australian had ever won the green jersey. After having already finished second twice, O'Grady needed no reminding of this fact. He also knew that this was his best chance of setting the record straight, which hinged on maximising every remaining sprint – hence his bold solo attack early in the first day into the Pyrénées – stage twelve, a 166.5 km race from Perpignan to Aix-les-Thermes. The aim was to win the first intermediate sprint after 40 km, on the approach to the first of five climbs, the first category Col de Jau. It was a mission accomplished, but even with the Pyrénées behind him and the green jersey clinched, O'Grady knew the fight would go down to Paris.

On the eve of the Tour's longest stage – the 233 km fifteenth stage from Pau to Lavaur – O'Grady's lead on Zabel was only thirteen points. It was a day which offered his last respite from the pressures as the route passed through his home village of Labarthe-sur-Leze after 164 km. Following cycling tradition, he and two of his teammates who live in the small village, peeled off from the pack and visited waiting family and friends in a local café where the chef was serving giant yellow cake in O'Grady's honour.

In the back of his mind, O'Grady sensed the bungled stage finishes and intermediate sprints of the first week would come back to haunt him. He estimated as many as 40 points were left begging in that first week: 'There are points out there that I know I could have got. Now every point from here to Paris will count.' And how they started counting. By the time the Tour had covered seventeen stages, the margin was down to eleven points in O'Grady's favour and then only two points after the nine-teenth stage to Evry. As predicted, the green jersey would be won or lost on the final stage from Corbeil to Paris – and probably on the final 400 m cobblestone stretch to the finish on the Champs Elysées.

The last days were not kind to O'Grady. During the 61 km stage eighteen time-trial from Montluçon to Saint Amand-Montrond, he was stung by a bee and started the nineteenth stage from Orléans to Evry with his swollen face untreated. O'Grady feared the medicine would contain illegal products – as was the case for his American teammate, Jonathan Vaughters, who had no choice but to quit the Tour earlier after informing the UCI that he had taken medication for a wasp sting that made his face swell up like a balloon, only to be told he would not be exempted.

In the nineteenth stage, the problems resumed with O'Grady losing four points to Zabel in intermediate sprints. He then fell victim to mechanical trouble: his brake cable snapped with only

20 km to go. Then after rejoining the pack and saving his green jersey by coming second to Zabel in a very tight finish, he faced the threat of a possible protest for an allegedly irregular sprint in Evry. During the final crucial dash, O'Grady had pushed through a seemingly non-existent gap just metres from the line on the inside of Latvian world champion, Romans Vainsteins. Had Vainsteins beaten O'Grady, the green jersey would have gone to the victorious Zabel who was a clear winner. Asked afterwards about his tactics, O'Grady was quick to justify his actions, pointing the finger at Vainsteins: 'Guys like that are pretty dangerous in the sprint. He knew Zabel and I have a full-on rivalry going for the green jersey. He is interrupting it and making it dangerous.'

With only two points separating him and Zabel, O'Grady was remarkably calm about the final stage the next day: 'I just can't stress about it. I feel most comfortable when I am out there on the bike. The worst part of it is waiting and waiting.'

Which is what O'Grady, Zabel and everyone following the Tour did right up to the last pedal-stroke. Zabel began the stage to Paris with an overnight deficit of two points, but turned the screws on O'Grady by winning intermediate sprints at Breux-Jouy and Chatenay-Malabry to add twelve points to his score. With O'Grady only managing to finish second and third at those same sprints for six points, Zabel was catapulted into the competition lead, with a four-point advantage.

The odds of victory were stacked heavily against O'Grady. With Zabel's superior top-end speed, O'Grady was not favoured to beat him in a sprint on the wide, cobblestone finish straight in Paris. Furthermore, O'Grady didn't have the team support that Zabel's Telekom henchmen could provide for the lead-out. Both had six teammates at hand, but man-to-man, not only was Crédit Agricole's firepower weaker when the Tour began, by the time it neared Paris, it was almost expended.

However, O'Grady still had his options. The simplest yet most unsporting and unlikely one was for Zabel to crash and not finish, and for O'Grady to place at least twenty-first and win the points needed to take back the lead. Otherwise, on points differentiation according to stage placings, O'Grady had to either: win the stage, knowing the 35 points on offer would overhaul Zabel's final score by one point; place at least second with Zabel finishing worse than third; finish third with Zabel placing worse than fourth; or finish fourth with Zabel worse than sixth; and so on . . .

Unfortunately for O'Grady, neither option prevailed on a stage won by the Czech rider, Jan Svorada, from Zabel and O'Grady in that order, leaving the two green jersey combatants with respective final scores of 252 and 244 points. As the pack sped past the finish-line and up into the summer haze that smothered the Arc du Triomphe, they were the last to stop. Every other rider had already come to a halt and turned their bikes to ride back to the finish by the time O'Grady and Zabel slowed 500 m down the straight. One had just ridden up the Champs Elysées wearing the green jersey but having lost it; the other was about to ride back down the famous avenue without it, but having won it.

Zabel, who had won the jersey for a record sixth time, summed up the emotion and importance of their tight contest which saved the Tour from the predictability of another Armstrong win: 'There is no loser in this battle,' he said. O'Grady was brave in defeat, sensing that if anything, the bold struggle against Zabel showed the world that he is not just a first-week opportunist. 'When I get time to sit back and reflect on the last three weeks, I'll see it has been a huge emotional roller-coaster. It has been stress from the prologue to right now,' he said.

But as O'Grady knows too well, when is it otherwise?

O'Grady is no longer the 'red-headed freckly bastard' he was in 1998 – if not for any reason than he often dyes his hair bleach-white. Now 29, he is reaching the latter years of his professional racing career. However, his ambition to win the green jersey is as strong as it ever was. Adding to the frustration, McEwen, who was second to Zabel in 2000, beat O'Grady to the post in 2002 by becoming the first Australian to win the jersey. To achieve his goal,

O'Grady's challenge will no longer be to outwit and outsprint Zabel, but also McEwen and another Australian, up-and-coming Victorian Baden Cooke who showed his potential as a serious candidate by placing fourth in the green jersey competition in his debut in 2002.

Chapter 9

Winning Lotto

ROBBIE MCEWEN

Sitting inside the Lotto-Adecco team van before stage eight of the 2002 Tour de France, the rider was quietly sticking his race number onto the jersey spread out on his lap. In a zone of concentration clearly marked, 'Do not disturb,' he was making sure that every air bubble was squeezed out from his number so everyone could see that No. 147, Robbie McEwen, was wearing the green-and-gold-hooped white jersey. 'I am really proud of this jersey,' said the Australian road champion, who wanted to look perfect for the long day on the saddle from Saint-Martin-de Landelles to Plouay in Brittany. 'It is awesome. It is great to be riding around [in it]. It stands out like anything.'

McEwen's infectious smile made you believe he had just won the jersey. In fact, he had been wearing it for seven months, ever since he won the Australian road title the previous December. But McEwen had hardly needed a national champion's jersey to stand out from the pack. In the six months before the Tour, the then 30-year-old Queenslander had already amassed numerous victories – including two stages of the Giro d'Italia – vaulting him from 100th in the Union Cycliste Internationale world rankings to tenth. Once the Tour got underway, he added a win on the third stage to

Reims. Then he began a gripping battle with Telekom's Erik Zabel for the green points jersey. It was a struggle McEwen won in the final stage onto the Champs-Elysées in which he also took first place, repeating his 1999 win and becoming only the third rider to do so after five-times Tour champion, Frenchman Bernard Hinault (1979, 1982) and Uzbekistan's Djamolidin Abdujaparov (1993, 1995), otherwise known as the 'Tashkent TGV.'

McEwen's run of success didn't end there. By season's end, he had nineteen wins in UCI classified races – the most of any rider in the peloton – and a silver medal behind Italian star, Mario Cipollini, in the world road race championship in Zolder, Belgium. He was also voted the Australian Cyclist of the Year, a clear winner despite a stellar season that saw thirty Australians become world champions across all disciplines.

With a world ranking of fourth and 1927 points at the end of 2002, the question I put to McEwen on that morning before the Tour's eighth stage was not all that far-fetched, despite his modest denial. When asked if he had thoughts about deposing Zabel from the top spot, the usually confident Queenslander chose his words carefully: 'That's a bit too much,' said McEwen, who ended 2001 with 462 UCI points. 'Last year, Zabel had 2500 points. That's a hell of a lot. That's [from] winning World Cup races, Tour stages, one-day races and the World Cup overall. But I said at the beginning of the season that my goal was to finish in the top twenty-five. The way it is, with the points scored now, I will already finish in the top ten.'

McEwen is fast. But his rise from being a former BMX racer and native of the surfing town of Burleigh Heads to the top of the world sprinting ranks has not been sudden. It has been a steady progression that began in 1996 when he turned professional with the Dutch Rabobank team. 'I have a lot more experience,' he said. 'It has been a build-up. Finally, things are just going right. I haven't had any big problems. I've reached a level this season that I feel is my level, a level where I really belong.'

McEwen's seesaw battle with Zabel for the green jersey was one of the highlights of the 2002 Tour – a welcome one too, considering the race for the yellow jersey was once again dominated by

American, Lance Armstrong, who clinched his fourth successive title. Adding a little extra spice to the Tour, McEwen and Armstrong – while vying for different jerseys – entertained with some of their own verbal jousting.

The two haven't seen eye-to-eye since McEwen broke an unwritten law and attacked during an early season race in 2001 when Armstrong had stopped to relieve himself. He then allegedly brushed off the American's open anger with a response that certainly didn't include an apology. On the Tour, their brewing feud became public in the second week when McEwen's off-the-record remarks about Armstrong were reported on the Cyclingnews.com website. The rift widened when Armstrong read the report. By the time McEwen's comments were retracted from the site, the fuse was already burning and the controversy making headlines around the world. At the centre of Armstrong's wrath was McEwen's alleged threat to punch Armstrong in the face after the Texan was said to have mocked him when he rode off the road in a narrow section early in the twelfth stage to Plateau de Beille. Both riders tried to dismiss the issue, refusing to elaborate on what words were really shared. But other riders confirmed their exchanges were anything but cordial.

For McEwen, the issue became a potential hazard to his green jersey ambitions as Armstrong is known to seek payback from those who cross him. McEwen tried to defuse the problem by approaching the Texan during the thirteenth stage from Lavelanet to Béziers. He said after the stage, 'I wouldn't say it is totally cleared up. He is obviously not happy about it. So he shouldn't be.'

Armstrong said he was focused on winning the yellow jersey and not interested in wasting energy trying to destabilise McEwen. Experienced Tour journalists speculated on the options that were available to him should he wish to cause problems for McEwen. However unsporting it may have been, Armstrong could have easily ruined McEwen's race. The Texan could have ordered his US Postal Service team to help Zabel's teammates lead him out in any remaining sprint offering points. He could have told them to block McEwen and open the door to Zabel for a much clearer run in claiming the points he needed. Or, should

McEwen catch Zabel on the hop and jump away from the pack near a sprint – as he successfully did in the second-last intermediate sprint on the final 144 km stage from Melun to Paris – Armstrong could have dispatched his teammates to chase down the Australian.

Neither scenario eventuated, but if anyone believed Armstrong had forgotten the affair, they were left thinking otherwise when he rode up alongside Zabel just after McEwen had won the penultimate sprint on the outskirts of Paris to extend his lead of one point. Armstrong, clearly preferring to share the podium with Zabel rather than McEwen, had some advice for the German who was now looking down the barrel of his first green jersey defeat in seven years. He reportedly told Zabel he should not contest the second sprint with 63 km to go, but save himself for the final which offered more points, not to mention the chance of victory in one of the Tour's most prestigious stages.

However, the ever-vigilant McEwen, flawless in his attention to check Zabel's every move, overheard Armstrong's words.

McEwen was happy to let his duel with Zabel come down to the final burst to the finish line, confident he had the speed to beat him in the stage finish and win the green jersey. But even had McEwen wished to grab extra points in the final intermediate sprint on the Champs Elysées, his hopes were quickly snuffed. Whether it was to prevent McEwen from winning points, parade his triumphant team down the world-famous boulevard, or both, Armstrong ordered his US Postal Service teammates to take the first nine positions in the pack and set a tempo that made it impossible to pass.

However, come the stage finish, McEwen was the impossible one to pass as he outsprinted Australian Baden Cooke and Frenchman Damian Nazon to repeat his 1999 Champs Elysées stage win. In his wake he left a strung out and exhausted bunch that included seventh-placed Zabel who lost his race by misjudging the final right-hand corner. McEwen thereby clinched his green jersey, finishing with a final points tally of 280 to the German's 261. After three second places by O'Grady and one by

McEwen, Australia could finally celebrate its first green jersey victory and second of *any* colour since Phil Anderson took the white of best young rider in 1982.

That McEwen managed to cope with his rift with Armstrong, win the green jersey and the final stage into Paris proved that when it comes to handling pressure, he is one of the best. But as strong as McEwen is under that pressure, he admits that fighting for the Tour's second-most prestigious jersey can be a burden. 'It is kind of stressful,' he said of the points competition, which is as much a game of mind as of speed. 'You have to be concentrating all day and know where the sprints are – if they are downhill, uphill or flat. Even if it is for eighth or twelfth place, you have to sprint.'

The rewards of McEwen's success have been plentiful. He has tremendous contractual clout, which leveraged him a new and far more lucrative deal with his team, Domo-Lotto. He also has a greater say in choosing teammates – one of his first demands was that Australian Nick Gates be signed up from the lowly-ranked German team, Agro Adler to race for him. McEwen also became one of the most sought-after stars for the post-Tour criteriums – in which he could demand an estimated $20,000 to $30,000 in appearance fees for each race. Importantly, his success has also made him a name in Australia. In the week McEwen won his first stage at Reims, the Tour was the most mentioned item in all media back home, according to a survey by Media Monitors Australia which was published in the *Australian*.

When the 2002 Tour came to a close, many Europeans were swept off their feet by the emergence of Australian riders. Brad McGee confirmed the potential he showed in 2001 with a stage win, Tour debutant Baden Cooke emerged as a green jersey contender and Stuart O'Grady – while short of major success – proved his courage by claiming seven top-ten places and finishing third in the points competition after having recovered from an iliac arterial operation. But with McEwen, many were left wondering at his transformation at age 30 from an occasional winner to a regular one, and heir apparent to the king of sprints, Cipollini.

Putting his brain to work along with his legs has helped McEwen take that next giant step forward. He has definitely matured. It is no secret within Australian cycling that McEwen has had differences with many of his fellow riders. Accusations of selfishness stem from his amateur racing days with the Australian Institute of Sport road racing team, then coached by former East German, Heiko Salzwedel. But for McEwen, who turned professional with the Dutch team Rabobank after winning a stage of the 1996 Tour de L'Avenir, his problems with the Australians hit a new low in the mid to late 1990s as they all rose to prominence and battled amongst themselves for recognition. Disputes also flared with McEwen over race tactics in several end-of-season races in Australia, foremost being a conflict with West Australian, Henk Vogels, in the 1997 Perth criterium series.

These days, McEwen carries himself far better. To some observers, he is the consummate professional, arguably the best from Australia. He has certainly come a far way from the fresh-faced, relatively unknown professional I saw outside a 1996 cycling exhibition in Queensland, trying to sell bags of his unused trade team clothing to earn a few extra dollars. Today, with O'Grady, Brad McGee and a growing number of Australian riders, McEwen is a heavily courted and recognised guest at many formal functions who realises that people within and outside cycling may act according to his word or deed. Nevertheless, he is the first to admit to his mistakes, and in an era where professional athletes often call on agents or managers to attend to the barrage of fans' requests, McEwen's willingness to sign cycling memorabilia and to acknowledge their interest and support is refreshing.

Some reckon McEwen's greater maturity comes with being a father – McEwen's Belgian wife, Angelique, gave birth to their son Ewen on the eve of the 2002 Giro d'Italia. He admits fatherhood has helped make him more responsible, but rejects claims that it has had much effect on his cycling performance: 'People say it makes you settle down and that you feel more responsibility. You feel more responsibility in life generally, but as far as affecting your riding, I don't think so. It is great having a little boy.

But to do well on the bike you have to be concentrating on what you are doing on the bike.' What did make the difference in 2002 was McEwen's extra work in the gym and more training sessions in the hills at Geraardsbergen, near his home in Flanders.

While he once confined gym work to the off-season, in 2002 McEwen included two four-week weight-training blocks during the racing season. The first block was in April after the early part of McEwen's season. During that block, he also had a ten-day spell off the bike. It was the first of two breaks before the Tour; the second coming after he quit the Giro d'Italia halfway in May. The second weight-training block came after the Tour in August as preparation for the autumn classics and world titles.

Weight-training has made a difference to McEwen who, at 171 cm, has an optimum race weight of 66 kg. 'In the racing season you get a lot of muscle breakdown, and you have to get that back up. It is especially important for a sprinter. You have to have that explosive power. And there is only one place to get it – the gym. [The weight-training block] has to be three to four weeks . . . If you start a gym program from nothing it takes three weeks to get any result. When you are already trained in racing, after two weeks you start to get some benefit, then after three weeks you get really strong. I can feel it myself after a couple of weeks. I get stronger and start pushing bigger weights. You need that strength to go day after day.' In the gym, McEwen focuses on doing leg presses. In a workout, he will push six sets of twenty-six repetitions with the weights set at 200 kg: 'I have to be careful with my knees. It is not excessively heavy. I know I can push 320 kilos, which I have done before, but I do repetitions for strength and endurance.'

Little wonder McEwen is no longer regarded as the cheeky, pint-sized sprinter who first arrived on the Tour as the runt of the litter, fighting for gaps like a puppy would scraps. Now, he is as fast as he once was daring, and far more powerful at top-end speed. He is also close to becoming the king of the sprinters, given his ascendancy over Zabel and Cipollini's retirement, whenever that may be. Asked if he already commands authority in the bunch, McEwen, who has beaten both rivals in key sprints, gives an unequivocal thumbs-up. 'Yeah, I do,' he said. 'Whereas before I was hoping I could get a gap, now I deserve to start up the front.'

1999 – 'Second is second'

It wasn't that long ago that McEwen found just getting to the front of a bunch sprint a leg-breaking effort. He could do it in one-day races, but in the Tour where riders have to overcome accumulated fatigue, the task became harder as each day passed. McEwen still remembers the first two of his five Tours, in 1997 and 1998, when his Rabobank team refused to lead him out, forcing him to fight the lead-out trains towing Zabel and Cipollini alone. His ability to get as close to the front as he did was a tribute to his daring bike-handling skills, developed in his pre-teen years as a BMX racer. But even when McEwen got to the front in a Tour sprint, racing into the wind was like crashing into a wall. 'In my first year on the Tour, I was basically doing it on my own,' said McEwen. 'I was trying to move myself up in the wind, then starting to sprint and be completely stuffed in the last kilometre. I would be trying to set myself up and would be starting to sprint from eighth position and finishing fourth.'

In the 1997 Tour, McEwen garnered six top-ten places, including one fourth and fifth place; in 1998 he claimed one second and several top-five places. But if these results are a testimony to his natural speed and courage, his trademark wheelie at the top of mountain finishes was also indicative of his guile. For McEwen, like most sprinters unsuited to the giant climbs of the Tour, the wheelie was his expression of joy for having finished a mountain stage. In some conservative circles, however, it was deemed as cheek. Either way, McEwen's combination of class, courage and confidence was in ample supply for his third Tour in 1999.

In terms of rivals that year, McEwen had plenty. Among them were Zabel, Cipollini, Estonian Jaan Kirsipuu, Belgian Tom Steels and Australian Stuart O'Grady – one of four Australians to start, the others being teammate Patrick Jonker who finished twelfth overall in the 1996 Tour, sprinter Jay Sweet who was a

Tour debutant and O'Grady's teammate Henk Vogels, a rider blessed with a handy sprint when in a small group and tireless on attack.

McEwen started the Tour full of belief that he could pull off a win. He came into the race with stage victories in the Tour of Luxembourg and Route du Sud, declaring, 'I know I can beat them all on a good day.' He also had the experience of two Tours behind him. But unlike O'Grady who – helped by the ever-dogged Vogels – was earning top placings from the beginning and making a solid start in his bid to win the green jersey, it took several days for McEwen to make his presence felt in the sprints. A seventh place on stage three and sixth on stage five were his best results before he and the other sprinters fell into obscurity with the arrival of the Alps.

The 'break' of twelve days in the Alps and then the Pyrénées did McEwen good. By placing second to Steels on the seventeenth stage from Pau to Bordeaux, he showed he is a rider who can survive the mountains and be stronger for it. The sprint finish was a rough affair, marred by O'Grady's crash with 1 km to go as he and five other riders – including McEwen – jostled for position between Zabel and Steels. However, McEwen was far from happy with the outcome: 'I did well, but second is second. It's not a win. This was a day I hoped I could do it, but hoping is not enough. You have to get across the line first. At least I am up there. I cruised past Zabel.'

McEwen's major problem was the reluctance of his Rabobank team to set him up in the sprint finishes. Earning team support in cycling is not easy; riders have to be reassured that their work for another's victory will pay dividends. Despite several good results, it seemed that McEwen was still left to fight out the bunch sprint finishes without anyone in the Rabobank team leading him out. He finally went public with his frustration. After first telling Australian journalists of his angst, he then told the Dutch media – the news damaging his relations with Rabobank *directeur-sportif*, Theo De Rooy, even more.

De Rooy denied McEwen's claim, expressed anger about McEwen going to the media with his complaint rather than to him, and then admitted that McEwen's future with the team was in doubt because he had not produced the results they had expected, saying, 'Robbie has not proven in three years that he's one of the best sprinters in the world. We have not said to him that he has to leave the team but . . .'

If ever McEwen's career was on the line, it was on the eve of the final and twentieth stage from Arpajon to Paris. He had no contract for the next season and seemed to have isolated himself from any support for his last roll of the dice for some Tour glory. His attempt to calm the issue by explaining to De Rooy that the Dutch media had misquoted him failed: 'I was quoted as saying I don't give a stuff about Rabobank, that Rabobank knows nothing about tactics. I wouldn't say things like that. Then the directors chose to believe everything they read in the press. The point I was trying to get across was that morale in the team during the race seemed so low that our guys were beaten before they started.'

McEwen vented his own fury in the most positive way: he recovered from a crash after only 20 km into the 143 km final stage to emphatically win it by three lengths, beating Zabel, Italian Silvio Martinello and O'Grady. His victory was labeled by *l'Équipe* as *le coup du kangourou* (the kangaroo's coup) and was arguably the most convincing sprint finish of the Tour. The result made McEwen the fourth Australian to win a Tour stage after Anderson (1982, 1991), Neil Stephens (1997) and O'Grady (1998).

Interestingly, McEwen's breakthrough coincided with another breakthrough, arguably the most significant in world sport – Armstrong won his first Tour after a miraculous recovery from cancer that at its worst gave him a meagre twenty percent chance of living. Like many, McEwen paid tribute to Armstrong in his stage winner's press conference. However, just before his conference broke he could not resist the temptation of blasting the Dutch media for their reports of his rift with Rabobank.

Watching McEwen as he sat beside his gold stage-winner's trophy, it seemed he had yet to realise the enormity of his feat. When pressed for his emotions several days later, the memory of his best friend Darren Smith came to mind. He joked that his extra three-length burst at the finish in Paris may well have been thanks to an invisible handsling from the deceased former Australian road cyclist. Smith, who raced with McEwen in BMX when they were kids, was touted as one of Australia's finest road prospects until he was killed in 1992 by a passing truck while training on the Gold Coast of Queensland. McEwen has since ridden in spirit with Smith, who shared with McEwen a deep belief that self-confidence will reign supreme over the doubts of others.

Finding a new team for 2000 may have been easy, but finding one that could provide him with the support he needed in the Tour was not. McEwen joined the Dutch Farm Frites team and started the season strongly, but even before a pedal-stroke had been made, things went awry in the Tour. One of McEwen's key lead-out men, Sergei Ivanov, the Russian champion and a contender for the best young rider, was one of three riders who failed blood tests on the eve of the race. Because their blood levels recorded a haematocrit level higher than the permitted maximum of 50 percent, Ivanov, Italian Rossano Brasi and Slovenian Andreij Hauptman were kicked off the race and placed on a two-week suspension.

That three riders still failed blood tests when every rider had been warned about them was a major embarrassment for the Tour which was still trying to resurrect its image after the 1998 scandal. To race director, Jean-Marie Leblanc, the riders' high blood readings were a betrayal of his call for riders to abide by the blood laws. Compounding the issue was that Leblanc had refused entry to the Farm Frites and Vini Caldirola (Hauptman) teams in 1999 because of their implication in doping scandals. Farm Frites (then TVM and without McEwen) was excluded as pay-back for quitting the 1998 Tour over police treatment of riders and their involvement in a separate doping investigation before the Tour. Worse for Farm Frites was that Ivanov's offence was the second such breach by one of its riders for the year.

McEwen, who passed his blood test at 7 am – nine hours before the Tour's opening 16.5 km prologue time-trial in Futuroscope, near Poitiers – was philosophical about the loss of one of his strongest riders. 'It's a shame for our team. I am going to miss him. He is a great helping hand for the finish. It's a setback but the race goes on.'

And it did, albeit with a couple more obstacles along the way. A spectator struck McEwen in the arm as he was hitting top-end speed in the finish of stage one, before coming seventh. Then, after surviving the Pyrénées and Alps, McEwen's legs surrendered on stage seventeen just as it seemed he was going to set himself up for the win on the stage from Evian-les-Bains to Lausanne in Switzerland. He was dropped on a small urban hill, 7 km from the picturesque stage finish alongside Lac Léman. McEwen miraculously rejoined the pack, but the effort sapped the energy needed for the sprint finish which saw 'the flying Dutchman,' Erik Dekker, claim his third victory in the Tour.

McEwen sensed the winning opportunities were running dry and was already looking ahead to the 2000 Olympic Games in Sydney. He was selected for the Australian road race team and by the time the Tour reached the finish in Paris where he took a disappointing eighth place, Sydney was firmly on his mind.

However, success at the Games eluded McEwen and the rest of the Australian team, prompting hopes for a better year ahead.

But the next season brought no fortune for McEwen who joined the Belgian Domo team in 2001. He soon fell into conflict with *directeur-sportif,* Patrick Lefévère, their differences hitting the worst patch when McEwen was omitted from Domo's Tour team. His place went to the reigning world road champion, Romans Vainsteins, around whom Lefévère planned to build his team. When Lefévère took the great Belgian one-day classic star, Johan Museeuw, to the Tour, McEwen's chances of going as a back-up sprinter were thwarted. It was a clear message to McEwen that he didn't figure in Lefévère's plans, the only option being for him to leave and race elsewhere.

2002 – 'Today I am the best'

McEwen returned to Australia at the end of 2001 without a contract for the next season. It was a nervous period, one similar to what Anderson experienced at the end of 1990 when he quit the Dutch TVM team. But like Anderson, who was recruited by Motorola, McEwen's employment changed when Lotto-Adecco approached him with an offer. The two parties eventually worked out an acceptable contract. It was modest in salary – below what McEwen had asked for – but rich in performance-based incentive bonuses. And there was another angle to the deal. Lotto-Adecco guaranteed McEwen every bit of help to win races. Finally, he would have teammates to lead him out for sprints. 'Now I have a good team around me that can position me. Now I am starting [the sprint] in second or third, and winning,' he said during the 2002 Tour.

McEwen's strong start to the 2002 Tour was not a surprise. He trained more than most riders in the off-season, tallying 3300 km in December 2001. His string of early season successes flickered like a warning signal for any challenger. Throughout the season, he followed to the letter a well-planned racing and training regime which allowed for specific peaks like the Tour, as well as lows. And significantly, McEwen remained largely injury- and illness-free. His only real concern during the Tour was a pinched nerve in the back sustained during the prologue time-trial at Luxembourg. McEwen received urgent osteopathic treatment which continued up to three times a day in the Tour. You couldn't have guessed seeing him race, but as he said, 'I had a lot of pain, so much so that I couldn't put my shoes on.'

The form, however, was still there. In fact, McEwen's ride towards the top of the podium became a virtual procession. Despite the backache, he still finished third on the first stage, 192.5 km out and back from Luxembourg behind Zabel and the little-known Italian-Swiss, Rubens Bertogliati, who jumped away and surprised everyone to win. The next day, on stage two from Luxembourg to the industrial and university city of Saarbruck in Germany, McEwen took second place behind the two-times Spanish world road champion, Oscar Freire, and ahead of a very frustrated local hero, Zabel, who was expected to pep up for the Tour's arrival in Germany, win the stage and take the yellow jersey. But if anyone was taking note of Zabel's defeat,

McEwen was not among them after Freire snuck past his right next to the barriers: 'I don't care if I beat someone for second. I want to win. The signs are there that I can win.'

With the Tour in its infancy and most riders still fully fuelled on form and ambition, the permutations of who would succeed and fail in the first week were numerous. Bertogliati had profited from his anonymity. Zabel had disappointed with his fame, but was determined to win soon. McEwen was hitting his straps, but so too were others, two of whom were the Victorian Tour rookie, Cooke (fourth) and the 2001 green jersey runner-up, O'Grady (tenth). Form and fortune was made all the more precarious by the danger of an estimated one million-plus spectators lining the route in Germany. 'It's great having lots of people, but they were standing all over the road, not leaving enough room for the bunch to pass,' said McEwen who was not alone in nearly being hit by fans leaning out to see the race.

But if McEwen was growing frustrated with his near-misses, his angst was soothed 24 hours later with a magnificent victory in the third stage, the 174.5 km leg from Metz to Reims. It was the second Tour stage win of his career, but one he called his finest, a *grande cru* of sorts: 'The one on the Champs Elysées [in 1999] was less expected. This one was [harder] because people expected me to win here. There was a lot more pressure on me.' McEwen's win over Zabel and a rapidly improving Cooke also prompted many to suggest he could declare himself the world's greatest sprinter, no matter that Cipollini was a controversial absentee from the Tour because his Saeco team was refused entry. Wisely, McEwen didn't take the bait and played the diplomat when asked if he was the best sprinter in the sport: 'I wouldn't go around saying I am the best sprinter in the world. Whenever one sprinter wins, they are the best on that day.' But with a devilish smile, he hesitated before adding, 'Today I am the best.'

Much credit went to McEwen's Lotto-Adecco teammates who had been one hundred percent behind him, no matter that he fell short of wins on stages one and two, as team *directeur-sportif*, Claude Criquelion, said: 'There you are . . . recompensation for three days of work. On one side, having a sprinter uses the whole team. You make all your riders work for him alone, but we were confident [of McEwen] after his two wins in the Giro against Cipollini.' Criquelion also stood up for McEwen against claims from other teams that he was a difficult rider to work with: 'Certain directors have told us that he is not easy to live with. He hasn't yet created one problem. Before he came to us he rode for teams that weren't one hundred percent behind him in the sprints.' Then smiling and with tongue firmly planted in his cheek, Criquielion corrected himself, saying the only problem he had with McEwen was getting him out of bed in the morning: 'He adores his bed.'

But McEwen had a lot more to show for his daring 75 kmh sprint than his winner's smile, the trophies and a sniff of the yellow jersey (he was now second overall and eight seconds behind Zabel who took the lead from Bertogliati). His arm and neck were covered with deep red fingernail scratches from fans leaning over the barriers in the sprint. His face had also been hit by giant green placards given out to spectators by the French sports-betting agency PMU (sponsor of the green jersey). The next morning he had the bruises and swelling too.

McEwen, a rider who has a penchant for sprinting close to the barriers, had often complained of the hand-shaped giant placards. In 1998 at Neufchâtel and in 1999 at Bordeaux, he suffered the same problem. This time, however, he made his concern formal. Maybe it was a reflection of his new standing, or the increasing concern within the Société du Tour de France for on-course safety, but by the next day's stage four team time-trial from Épernay to Château-Thierry, race organisers had officially requested PMU to no longer distribute the green hands among fans in the last kilometre.

Having bagged a stage win, McEwen could now focus on the battle for the green jersey which since stage one had been on the shoulders of Zabel. Until then, McEwen had politely avoided discussing the points competition, saying he would see how it stood once he had won a stage. But one sensed all along that he had it in his sights. By the end of the fifth stage, McEwen had every reason to focus on the points competition and challenge Zabel who was showing his first sign of weakness.

After the 195 km stage from Soissons to Rouen, Zabel led the points competition with 113 points. But close on his wheel was McEwen (second – 111 points), Cooke (third – 80) and O'Grady (fifth – 74) who all beat him in the bunch gallop.

McEwen suspected that Zabel was not feeling strong. Had he been, the German – who explained he had heavy legs from the team time-trial – would have ordered his Telekom team to chase down the stage-winning break that still only finished 33 seconds ahead of the main bunch. 'He didn't feel that confident,' said McEwen. 'I heard he was back at the team car and the doctor's car not feeling that good.' O'Grady concurred, wondering if Zabel's confidence was shot.

It still took another two days of racing – including a face-saving win by Zabel on stage six and a brilliant win on stage seven by Australian Brad McGee – before McEwen publicly declared his intent to go for the green jersey. Not that anyone doubted he would, especially those who had looked inside his suitcase and found the supply of green shorts, arm warmers, gloves, shoe-covers and eyeglass-rims to match the sprinter's jersey.

It therefore came as no surprise that after the eighth stage from Saint-Martin-de-Landelles to Plouay, McEwen narrowed his deficit behind Zabel to two points. With no points on offer in the 52 km stage nine time-trial from Lanester to Lorient, the margin remained that way going into the 147 km tenth stage from Bordeaux to Pau – the final stage before the Pyrénées. 'I have to finish what I started, but Erik will fight all the way to Paris,' said McEwen who had 191 points to Zabel's 193, the pair edging away from Cooke (134 points) and O'Grady (119) who conceded defeat.

McEwen was given some handy advice from O'Grady who had been second to Zabel in the competition three times and rated the Queenslander's chances of going one better: 'He has the speed to hit out before Zabel. I advised Robbie on one of those first days. I said, "You have to jump before him. If you try to wait you are not going to make it." I am not the kind of sprinter that has the kick Robbie has. If anyone can do it, Robbie can.'

It was a prediction that McEwen set into motion on the road to Pau. His sixth place and second in the bunch sprint, 3 minutes 57 seconds behind behind a four-man winning break that included third-placed O'Grady, was enough to depose seventh-placed Zabel from the green jersey. The outcome left McEwen with a precarious tally of 210 points to Zabel's 209, but he felt the German was in greater strife than the narrow margin indicated. He said, 'I've beaten him in a number of situations. It is good for my confidence that I have been able to win [over Zabel] by coming from behind, next to him and from in front of him.'

However, while confident with ten days to go, McEwen was far from complacent heading into the mountain stages where each day he would be outclassed by those like Armstrong and Beloki who were vying for the yellow jersey. Because he would be dropped once the race hit the mountains, McEwen's one opportunity was to race for the first intermediate sprint before the first climb: 'It's not going to be an easy ten days. If I'm not suffering going up the hill, I will be sprinting my legs off to defend the jersey. The important thing will be to stay with Erik, make sure he doesn't get any points I don't. The first sprint before the first mountain will be important. We will be going full gas there. Then we'll have no legs left and will probably be the first two dropped when we hit the climb.'

His prediction was not exactly correct. The next day – a bad one for Australia as McGee crashed heavily on the descent of the Col d'Aubisque when in a potentially stage-winning position – McEwen was dropped before Zabel on the same 18 km climb with less than 90 km to go in the 158 km eleventh stage from Pau to La Mongie. Albeit, Zabel was dropped soon after, but unlike McEwen, he rejoined the main group and was able to win four points on the second intermediate sprint with 26 km to go.

For his effort, Zabel was able to take back the green jersey. McEwen, however, played down Zabel's move: 'If Erik wants to get points on the climbing stages that's fine by me. There are plenty more sprints to be won on the flat and a couple more flat stages. I just have to stick to my plan and take points in the sprints.'

McEwen retrieved the green jersey after two more days of racing – one in stage twelve where Armstrong won up the switch-backed ascent to Plateau de Beille and the other on stage thirteen from Lavelanet to Béziers. McEwen and Zabel were equal on 229 points after thirteen stages, but McEwen was awarded the green jersey on a count-back of placings. His claim went unchallenged in the fourteenth stage from Lodève to Mont Ventoux when Zabel finished well behind McEwen on the notoriously long and steep climb up the scree-sloped ascent to the finish. It may have been a day of emotion for most – especially Armstrong who was visibly upset about being booed by drunken fans up the last climb – but McEwen seemed to take one of the most-feared and hard-fought stages of the Tour in his stride. After finishing, he said cheekily, 'I just rode up easy, and came to the top to collect my jersey.'

McEwen and Zabel remained tied on 229 points through stages fifteen (to Les Deux Alpes), sixteen (La Plagne) and seventeen (Cluses), the first three of four stages in the Alps after which Armstrong secured the Tour with a 5 minute 6 seconds lead on Beloki.

By the time the last mountain was behind the Tour after stage eighteen to Bourg-en-Bresse, McEwen's point score was 239, but only one point separated him and Zabel. It was a margin that would not change in the stage nineteen time-trial from Régnié-Durette to Mâcon, and one that followed them right to the start of the final stage from Melun on the outskirts of Paris to the Champs Elysées, and finally all the way to the finish line 144 km later. This time, the balance of scales finally tipped in an Australian's favour.

Chapter 10

Rising to the top

BRAD MCGEE

When a fresh-faced cyclist from Sydney named Brad McGee put pen to paper on a professional contract in late 1999, it was predicted he would win the Tour de France in five years' time. Call it positive thinking by his new *directeur-sportif*, Marc Madiot, a wild prediction or maybe a hunch aimed at exciting his sponsor, the French lottery, La Française des Jeux. It said something about the calibre of McGee that his boss, himself a professional rider and regarded as a staunchly parochial Frenchman, could speak so well of his foreign rookie recruit.

But Madiot's faith was not out of the blue. He had courted McGee since the 1996 Olympics, urging him to consider turning professional and inspiring him to lift himself from a post-Olympic Games slump. By inviting him to watch the final stage of the 1999 Tour six months earlier, he gave McGee a sample of what awaited him.

It was clear that Madiot really wanted McGee. When he said he felt McGee could win the Tour, he meant it. He also sensed a charismatic personality in the dark-haired, frequently smiling, broad-shouldered former soccer player, cross-country runner and water-skier. McGee was seen as potentially the full package, the consummate professional cyclist. It may have been a heavy and arguably unfair burden for McGee to carry into the infancy of his professional career, but by all accounts, McGee was already a star. He had gone a long way to prove he was not just suited to the velodrome where he etched his reputation as an amateur, nor only good at flat time-trials rather than in a mass-started race. No, McGee was making great inroads into his predicted future as a serious Tour rider.

At 68 kg, McGee may not be a natural climber with the lightweight frame of Tour champions. But since the start of his professional racing career that includes finishing two Tours, one Giro d'Italia and numerous top category stage races, McGee is now viewed very differently by critics. It has not gone unnoticed that combined with his sheer strength, incredible endurance and a penchant for pursuing goals that many people suspect are beyond his ability, he may well develop into a successful Tour rider much the same as Spain's Miguel Indurain. This is not to say McGee will win five Tours like Indurain – or even one. But if Indurain and his hulking frame could develop from a back-of-the-packer to one of the greatest champions of all time, the potential for McGee to become a top-ten contender is a feasible prospect. Certainly, McGee – never shy of declaring his intent – is aiming that high.

McGee has always set himself lofty ambitions. The youngest and the former 'runt' of four cycling brothers, he joined the Australian Institute of Sport track endurance squad at the age of seventeen. Within three days of moving from his family home in the Sydney western suburb of Wentworthville to Adelaide where the track program was based, he found himself on a punishing 240 km training ride in the Adelaide Hills, then the longest ride of his life. In the years to come, he would ride up to 40,000 km a year under the guidance of former Australian track coach, Charlie Walsh.

McGee quickly produced results and found himself wearing the rainbow jersey of a world champion track racer. Before turning professional on the road, he won his first of three gold medals in a world junior championship competition in 1993 before winning one at the senior titles in 1995 for the team pursuit. Then after winning two bronzes for the individual and team pursuits at the 1996 Olympic Games in Atlanta, McGee signed to join the professional La Française des Jeux team, with a view to joining the professional ranks in September 1997. The next year in March he attempted cycling's hardest and most sought-after track record, the hour, which most professionals never consider trying until they are at the peak of their careers. At twenty-one, McGee still had a go, and on the Superdome in Adelaide, he set an Australian record of 50.52 km. However, he paid a hefty price for his effort. Coming during a post-Olympic hiatus when he was burning both ends of the candle – partying at night and racing by day – his body and mind surrendered and he wandered to thoughts of retirement. He didn't know it at the time, but he was soon diagnosed with glandular fever, the illness postponing his road career start to January 1998.

In the years that followed, Madiot resurrected McGee's love of cycling by dangling before him the Tour de France carrot. But he still continued to impress on the track. He won a bronze medal in the 4000 m individual pursuit event at the 2000 Olympics Games in Sydney, two weeks after breaking his collarbone in a training crash in Adelaide. In 2002, he won gold in the same event at the world titles and Commonwealth Games. The latter took his career tally of Commonwealth Games gold medals to five.

2001 – Experience in the bank

McGee had long pencilled in the 2001 Tour for his debut, but it was not until two months before the start that his team received confirmation it could even take part. Entry was dependent on whether his French La Française des Jeux team would be granted a wild-card entry by the race organisers. When the news came on May 2, an extremely relieved Madiot took the call. The future of the team's sponsorship hinged on a Tour entry.

McGee, who was longing to test himself on the Tour, was equally as relieved. As he said after hearing Madiot's news, 'This is what I have been aiming for. This is what every cyclist has been aiming for.'

A lot was expected from McGee when, late on a dark and windswept afternoon at Dunkirk on July 7, 2001, he took his place on the start-ramp of the 8.2 km prologue, mounted his bike and steadied himself while the time keeper counted down the last five seconds. Everyone's eyes were on the Australian who was an outside favourite to win the prologue and become the first wearer of the yellow jersey. He certainly had the results to support his billing, including a time-trial win in the Route du Sud stage race in France where he defeated the winner of the opening time-trial at the previous year's Tour, Scot David Millar.

If there was any obstacle to McGee's victory chances on the prologue, it was his lack of Tour experience. The demands of performing and coping with the Tour's pressures are enormous. In any smaller race, the prospect of a rider of McGee's calibre winning against the same opposition would be very real. But the Tour, with its high stakes, is another ball game. McGee virtually admitted as much after finishing a still credible twelfth and 15 seconds behind Frenchman, Christophe Moreau, who was fourth overall in the previous year's Tour.

The result brought McGee back to earth, as did the crash-filled first stage from Saint-Omer to Boulogne-sur-Mer when he came a cropper near the finish. Unafraid to try his hand, McGee had attacked into a roaring headwind along the final kilometres, to crash as soon as he was caught. But as happened time and time again whenever McGee's hopes were scuttled along the 3462 km route of that Tour, he came back smiling to say of the experience, 'It'll pay off some day.' For him the 2001 Tour was all about putting experience 'in the bank'.

As O'Grady rode on to claim headlining spells in the yellow and green jerseys, McGee knuckled down to some hard aggressive racing, and not without some reward. He bagged two top-three finishes in successful breaks on the ninth and sixteenth stages. In the first, the 185 km ninth stage from Pontarlier in the Doubs to Aix-les-Bains in the Savoie region at the foot of the Alps, McGee instigated the escape of the day at 36 km, 8 km after the first intermediate sprint: 'There was no way I was going to miss *the* [main] break,' he said then. 'I wanted to get up the road. I've been too far down the back when there has been a breakaway. I got into a couple of breaks early, but they didn't work. Then I said to Stuey [O'Grady], "You have to help me out here. I don't know how to get up the road. When is it [a break] going to go?" Stu just said, "Sit back, wait, wait, wait." Then he said, "I think it is going to go soon." Two minutes later we were up the road.'

Joining McGee in the 149 km escapade was the Spaniard, David Etxebarria. Then 24 km later, Russian Sergei Ivanov bridged across to join them on the approach to the Col des Rousses (1060 m) in the forested hills of the Jura. However, the peloton wasn't making life easy for McGee and his companions. The race covered 50.5 km in the first hour and the gap between McGee's group never passed beyond 1 minute 30 seconds, until after reaching the summit of the Rousses climb at 68 km. Using the long descent and sinewy tricky roads to their advantage – it is easier for a small group rather than a large one to gain time on such a route – the leaders extended their margin to 9 minutes at 110 km.

There was no relief for them, however, as their lead soon dropped. With 20 km to go, the pack was only 2 minutes 5 seconds behind and then only one minute with 13 km left. By now, McGee had been on the attack for the best part of three hours. But when Ivanov bolted away alone with 9 km left, he didn't have the energy to answer. Despite McGee's graceful bike position and smooth pedal cadence, with the peloton chasing hard it had been tough enough for him to maintain the speed they already had, let alone chase Ivanov down. Ivanov hung on to win the stage, followed at 16 seconds by second-placed Etxebarria, and McGee at third after cramping with 200 m to go. He crossed the finish with his face caked in dry saliva and on the brink of exhaustion. Hot on their tail 8 seconds later came the peloton led by German sprinter, Erik Zabel.

Typically, McGee saw the positive side of the result, saying, 'I'm not disappointed. Third is not bad. It was a good tactic.' It was also a tactic much appreciated by others. The next morning, just before the tenth stage to l'Alpe d'Huez in the Alps, McGee was presented the 'Most Aggressive' rider of the stage award, aptly sponsored by the French cheese producer, Coeur de Lion (Heart of the Lion).

Stage ten would normally have been McGee's first real climbing test. But after his efforts the previous day and with the mountain time-trial 24 hours away, it was natural for a tired McGee to cautiously ride the dramatic stage to l'Alpe d'Huez with the 'laughing bunch', the main group of non-climbers who ride together in steady tempo to finish in the time limit. But the next day, there was some curiosity over McGee's potential. In the 32 km stage eleven mountain time-trial from Grenoble to Chamrousse, he placed a modest twenty-fifth, just over 5 minutes behind Armstrong who won again. But he only rode hard to the foot of the final 18.4 km long mountain before pacing himself to the finish. 'I felt awesome,' said McGee on the finishing straight at Chamrousse. 'I never really felt like I was suffering . . .' Later many were wondering how close McGee might have been had he given it a shot.

There was some sense behind McGee's strategy though. As the Tour left the Alps, he said his body felt better than when he began the race, but he knew this could change overnight. 'I've got veins popping out everywhere now, from my stomach, my back, legs and arms,' said McGee whose body fat had dropped dangerously below six percent. Despite consuming 5000 calories a day, he was using up as many calories, as well as losing three kilograms a day in fluids, not to mention vital salts, nutrients, vitamins and minerals.

Still McGee pushed his body onwards to the Pyrénées. And significantly, it was in those final mountain stages that many contract offers came his way. Not that it was such a surprise that they did.

Before the Tour, McGee gave every indication that his climbing was better than what he had ever been given credit for. In the Tour de Romandie – a Swiss race he led for a day after finishing third in the prologue time-trial – he lost only 1 minute 49 seconds in the crucial stage four mountain leg before placing thirteenth overall. And he held his own in the Midi Libre and Dauphiné–Libéré stages races in France.

Some offers came in the most bizarre circumstances, one during the fourteenth stage from Tarbes to Luz-Ardiden, which arguably produced McGee's greatest ride. McGee was still with Armstrong's group 5 km from the summit of the 17 km Col du Tourmalet – at 2115 m, the highest pass of the Tour. There was still 40 km to go and McGee was riding tempo for his Swiss teammate, Sven Montgomery, until he finally succumbed to the incline. Montgomery went on to claim the 'Souvenir Jacques Goddet' prize as the first rider over the Tourmalet. McGee, meanwhile, settled into his own rhythm and prepared for the descent, not knowing what awaited him on the other side. 'I caught a bunch of riders, but there was no one from my team,' recalled McGee. 'I asked another team car for a *bidon*. As the director handed me the bottle he asked, "What are you up for next year?" It's getting crazy really, all these offers.' By the time the Tour left the Pyrénées, McGee's name had gone from being on the shopping list of five teams to ten.

With a week to go, McGee decided to deal with all the attention the simplest way: by putting a halt to all negotiations until after the Tour. Hence, he announced during the rest day in Pau, 'I just want to get on with the Tour. I have shut down all talks until after.'

As the mountains disappeared, McGee had every reason to be satisfied with his achievements: 'I have shown my strength in areas I hadn't shown before,' he said. 'It was a great feeling too, to finish the mountains on a good note.' Adding to his satisfaction in a race with tighter doping controls was seeing several Italian riders associated with past scandals now suffering as they struggled to keep up with the pace set in the 'laughing group'.

Over the final six stages to Paris, McGee tapped into his new self-confidence, as is proved by his Herculean breakaway effort on the 227 km sixteenth stage from Castellsarrasin to the small village of Sarran.

This time, in one of the most dramatic finishes of the 2001 Tour, McGee was in a two-man winning breakaway with German, Jens Voigt, when he rode himself into oxygen debt. Blacking out on the uphill finish after Voigt dropped him with

500 m to go, McGee collapsed on the finish-line after zigzagging up the final straight. Again, victory had eluded him during a day of searing temperatures and a course littered with testing hills. And again, after finishing second and 5 seconds behind Voigt, and gasping for oxygen from attending medical staff, McGee got up, brushed himself off and was smiling as he explained the upside to his agony. He was even able to joke. Asked if he felt the stage was his last chance for a stage win, he smiled again and quipped, 'What – there's another stage?' Seeing McGee ride himself into a state where he only saw black, you couldn't blame him if he wished there wasn't another stage. 'It was too long, too many hills, too hot and the German was too fast. If it was another kilometre I would have fallen off,' said McGee of the punishing stage which saw him come into the fray by following Madiot's order to chase down the original breakaway of seven riders that formed after 61 km. 'It was there and then, or nothing,' he explained his chase which began at the bottom of a hill near the town of Aujols in the Lot. 'The break had gone. I just belted my way to the front [of the pack], pushed a few guys out of the way, turned the corner and hit it. I knew that if I didn't get them by the top, then I wouldn't ever get onto them.' Within 7 km, McGee was with them, and he soon recovered and settled into a steady rhythm, knowing that there was still 159 km to go.

As the hours passed, McGee appeared to be riding smoothly and within himself, even when he followed Voigt when the German attacked with 23 km to go: 'I always planned to go with Jens. I was all right then. But with the intensity of the race you just don't know what is around the corner.' McGee soon found out when his previous efforts to join the break drained him of the energy to contribute whenever he took his turn at the front: 'Somewhere up there I tanked. I couldn't even come through [to do a turn at the front]. When I did, it was only when Jens stopped pedalling.'

McGee finally finished the Tour 83rd overall at 2 hours 5 minutes 52 seconds to Armstrong but he was still being talked of highly amongst management of many top-tier teams looking for future stars. Madiot was well aware of the interest in his young protégé, and when pressed to explain what he saw in McGee, he coyly smiled. If he was being evasive, it was too late. McGee had already received offers from twelve other teams, included invitations from Crédit Agricole, US Postal Service, iBanesto.com and Rabobank who McGee tentatively chose, before ultimately deciding to remain with Madiot. His decision was not just based on a payrise either, but on the commitment of his French sponsor to support the creation of a development team in Australia in association with the New South Wales Institute of Sport.

While enjoying a late-night drink several hours after finishing the Tour, McGee was still talking enthusiastically about the race, as if he couldn't wait for 2002 to come around. And when it did eleven months later, an even stronger McGee very quickly reminded us why he had been so looking forward to it.

2002 – A roller-coaster ride

With a solid Tour debut behind him, McGee started the 2002 race with tall ambitions: to win a stage, take his climbing ability a step higher and finish the Tour placed as high as possible overall. He also wanted to help the new young professional, his teammate and fellow Australian, Baden Cooke, cross the line first in one of the sprinters' stages. While a leader in his team – now called FDJeux.com – McGee aimed to show that leadership is not just about winning, but teamwork.

McGee was once again a favourite for the prologue in Luxembourg. Meanwhile, Cooke had delivered the goods to warrant support from McGee and the team for the bunch sprints, winning several races in the early season – as did the team's other sprinter, Frenchman Jimmy Casper. For stage wins, FDJeux.com also had the durable and ever-attacking French favourite, Jacky Durand. So when FDJeux.com finally got their call-up to start via another wild-card entry, Madiot expected a successful race.

McGee's second Tour started in similar fashion to his first: in the 7 km prologue, he was best-placed of the four Australians in eleventh at 13 seconds to a victorious Armstrong. He confirmed his strong form the next day, placing twelfth on the uphill sprint finish, but was disappointed by Cooke's twenty-first place. However, on stage two from Luxembourg to Saarbruck, their cohesion in the sprint was better and Cooke took fourth place behind Spanish world champion Oscar Freire, Robbie McEwen and Erik Zabel in that order. If Madiot needed extra reassurance, it came on stage three where McGee helped Cooke to third. The two Australians were steadily working closer to the front. But when being at the front really mattered – at the finish-line – McGee rose to the occasion.

His victory on the 176 km seventh stage from Bagnoles-de-l'Orne to Avranches on the Atlantic Coast was impressive, as he bolted from the front group with 200 m to go and at the top of a 1000 m-long climb where all that stood between him and the finish-line was Spaniard, Pedro Horrillo. McGee, his pursuing power unleashed like a wild stallion from its stable, miraculously swept past the unexpecting Horrillo in a 54 × 11 gear to win his first stage in the Tour. It was also only the seventh stage win by an Australian. The stunned Horrillo hung on to take second place, followed by Estonian, Jaan Kirsipuu. And in an unprecedented result, all four Australians were in the top-ten: McEwen, fourth; O'Grady, sixth; and Cooke, eighth.

However, there was more to the stage than its special final result. It had been a frenetic day's racing on a hilly and windswept course, which was marred by two crashes on the narrow rural backroads leading to Avranches. The first came with 5 km to go and involved about twelve riders when a gust of crosswind struck the Telekom-led pack, creating a touch of wheels and a pile-up that nearly took McGee down. The second crash with 3 km to go caused a minor scare for Armstrong: he was forced to stop after being caught behind it and lost an inconsequential 29 seconds. But to hear the hysteria when he put his foot to the ground, you could have thought he had crashed himself!

Adding to the drama was the revelation that McGee's FDJeux.com team had planned the finale – almost to the very victory salute he gave at the finish. 'Marc had spoken to friends who lived in the area,' said McGee. 'Word was that it was a hard finish and it would suit me more to lead out with 800 m to go.

Then we would have Baden up there on the wheels in case I got caught. He would profit from the other sprinters chasing me down. It is not often that plans go that well, but obviously this is what you have to do to win a stage of the Tour.'

McGee was quick to use his post-stage euphoria to add another victory of sorts: he won the media over as convincingly as he did the stage. His repartee in English and French – even translating for anyone who did not speak both languages – was by far the most entertaining press conference held so far. He also used the occasion to pay a public tribute to Madiot for halting his retirement after the 1996 Olympics: 'I wouldn't be here if it wasn't for Marc. I am not like every other cyclist, or most, who grow up wanting to ride the Tour or be a professional cyclist. I finished at Atlanta in 1996, went home and started drinking beer and having a good time. Then this guy Madiot kept calling. He wouldn't let it go, he insisted I look at a contract and start thinking about being a professional. It was through his insistence that I am celebrating this.'

With a stage win now his, and the combination between him and Cooke improving day by day, McGee was able to relax. In his second Tour he had already achieved what many riders strive towards in their entire careers. However, as the Pyrénées neared, McGee quickly set his sights on his next objective: to test himself as a potential climber with a view to the grand plan of challenging for overall victory in years to come. Because he is not the naturally gifted climber he will need to be to win the Tour, any hope of victory relies on long-term planning. In 2001, McGee showed signs of being able to hold his own in the mountains while helping his teammates, but in 2002 he was anxious to play a greater role during the climbing stages and this time for his own benefit.

In a bid to recover and be ready for the Pyrénées, McGee took a more discreet role in the next three stages as the Tour continued to head south from Normandy to Brittany and then to Lorient in the Morbihan, before transferring 500 km on the rest day to Bordeaux in readiness for the tenth stage from Bazas to the foot of the Pyrénées. It was at Bordeaux, shortly before he sat down to eat dinner with his teammates, that McGee explained in greater detail his bold plans for an assault in the mountains, and possibly a crack at reaching Paris with a high overall place.

At this point, the Spanish riders were expected to make good of their pre-Tour pledge to use the mountains – and the support of a home crowd on the Spanish border – to challenge Armstrong. With Spaniard, Igor Gonzalez de Galdeano – teammate of Armstrong's key rival, Joseba Beloki – still in the yellow leader's jersey, they had everything going for them. McGee, who would start the tenth stage placed 36th overall at 5 minutes 34 seconds, thought they would be a threat.

McGee's confident approach to the mountain stages was based on a new pedalling technique he had used while training for the Tour. He knew that a high top overall finish was dependent on a five to ten percent improvement in his climbing. Hence, McGee's excitement to trial his new technique in the 158 km eleventh stage from Pau to the ski resort of La Mongie (1715 m) which sits 4 km below the famed Tourmalet summit. According to McGee, the technique improves the efficiency of energy output and is similar to the fast-pedalling style used by Armstrong where his pedal cadence reaches up to 115 strokes per minute. Whereas once McGee would drop his ankle and heel during every stroke, he now pressed down on his toes and followed through by quickly lifting the heel and ankle. 'It maximises endurance and speed in the mountains. You have more momentum in your pedal-stroke.'

When the eleventh stage neared the summit of the first major mountain of the Tour, the 18 km-long Col d'Aubisque (1709 m), McGee's strategy appeared to be going perfectly. Meanwhile, leading the stage was French hero, Laurent Jalabert, who, 48 hours after announcing he would retire at the end of the year, was making a brave solo attack (one of many he would begin on what became his farewell lap of honour of France). McGee was still in the main group, even after Armstrong had ordered his US Postal Service teammates to ride tempo up the climb, sensing the vulnerability of the ONCE team of de Galdeano and Beloki. Jalabert still led the stage over the Aubisque summit, followed by

Spaniard, David Etxebarria; but as the main group went over the top, McGee flew out from the pack from second wheel and, like a bird plunging from its nest with prey in sight, darted down the barren and twisting slopes in pursuit of the two stage leaders. He soon joined Etxebarria, and felt he was about to catch Jalabert who was coming closer into view with every turn. With less than 90 km to go, McGee was set up for the race of his life. All he had to do after catching Jalabert (which was likely at his comparatively faster speed) was recover, ride tempo and then climb 14 km to the finish at La Mongie with everything he had.

However, it was all too simple. As the distant image of Jalabert grew closer, McGee suddenly heard a press motorbike behind him scrape the ground on a bend. He thought it had crashed and, in probably the worst decision of his two Tours, turned to see what had happened. Suddenly he was the one who was out of control and plummeting off the road into a barbed wire fence that shredded his back like a cheese grater. As catastrophic as it was for his stage-winning chances, McGee was lucky to be alive. He was checked for bone damage on-site after medicos untwisted him from the fence. In so much pain that he couldn't even look up to see Jalabert and Etxebarria ride off towards La Mongie, he nevertheless knew that he had to rejoin the pack as quick as possible and was soon calling to Madiot for a new bike.

Once back with the pack and after receiving more treatment on the saddle, McGee realised he could do nothing to change what had happened. Jalabert finally attacked the last climb alone and was caught and passed by Armstrong with only 4 km to go. But throughout the ride, McGee was haunted by what might have been. Had McGee joined Jalabert, would the pair have stayed away to the finish? Would McGee have dropped Jalabert and been allowed by Armstrong to ride off and win the stage because he was no threat overall? Would McGee have won the stage whether Armstrong chased or not and proved he was the strongest? McGee knew it was an opportunity lost: 'It wouldn't have taken more out of me to be up with Jalabert than sitting in the bunch. It would have been nice coming into that last climb with the legs I had on the Aubisque.'

McGee managed to finish the stage, crossing the line only 9 minutes 45 seconds after a victorious Armstrong. But as soon as his front wheel rolled over the line at La Mongie, he was swept up by attentive FDJeux.com personnel and rapidly pushed on his bike through a wall of crowds to – of all places – a surf shop. Because of the congestion at the finish, Madiot had already asked the shop's owners if he could 'borrow' their change-rooms for his riders. It was a savvy call. Amidst the chaos and searing heat outside, the calm, quiet and cool confines of the shop were a luxury.

While the shop was still open, it was made clear to 'outsiders' (such as the media) that the change-rooms were out of bounds. Finally, after 40 minutes, McGee hobbled out from behind the change-room curtain. 'I'm going to be very stiff. But I don't think anything is broken,' he said before Madiot stepped in to help him to the team car and take him to their hotel. Even as he left, McGee managed to smile between painful winces. Later that night, Madiot confirmed he would start the twelfth stage from Lannemazan to Plateau de Beille.

From this point, McGee's Tour took a dramatic change. While managing to start, the pain of his cuts, bruises and torn ligaments was excruciating. Embarking on a brutal mountain stage that included four major climbs and a mountain-top finish didn't help. Every bump, gear change, acceleration of the pedals and degree of rise in the melting bitumen roads provoked a hot jab of agony to his battered and aching body. McGee's priority now was to recover. And on his agenda were three goals: to help Cooke go for a stage win, finish the Tour, and still be fit enough for the Commonwealth Games at Manchester and the 4000 m individual pursuit track event three days after. It was a tall order for McGee.

But if he needed any incentive to push through the agony, Cooke gave it as the Tour left the Pyrénées the next day – on stage thirteen from Lavelanet to Béziers. The punchy sprinter won the bunch sprint for twelfth place. The result reassured McGee and his teammates that despite the battle between McEwen and Zabel for the green jersey, Cooke still had the top-end speed needed, and deserved their support.

The gruelling fourteenth stage from Lodève to Mont Ventoux didn't spare McGee. He struggled all day, was dropped by the main bunch several times and even feared he would lose contact altogether and be eliminated for not finishing in the time limit. But each time his body and mind gave way, McGee was helped back to the bunch by valiant teammate, Jimmy Casper. And after finally reaching the scree-sloped summit finish on Mont Ventoux in 155th position from 163 survivors (29 minutes 52 seconds behind the victorious Frenchman, Richard Virenque) his first words were of thanks to Casper, a rider who started the Tour as a protected rider for the sprints, but after failing to deliver was now proving invaluable as a domestique. No doubt surviving one of the toughest stages was a major feat for McGee: 'I'm in a bit of a mess with the crash. I was very worried this morning. But after getting through that, I think I am right now.'

With the rest day and Alps to come, there were two more chances for the FDJeux.com team to get Cooke across the line first – on stage eighteen, a 176.5 km leg from Cluses to Bourg-en-Bresse; and stage twenty, 140 km from Melun to Paris. McGee was committed to finishing (and performing), despite reports in Australia that he was on the verge of quitting the Tour. Even if his body had been battered and bruised, his spirits were very much intact.

There were still fears he would pull out from the Australian Commonwealth Games team to compete at Manchester in the week after the Tour, with McGee admitting that his participation was in doubt. But he allayed them as soon as the Tour bade farewell to the Alps on the eighteenth stage from Cluses to Bourg-en-Bresse. That night, McGee telephoned Australian head coach Shayne Bannon to talk about his condition, having deliberately left the call until the last minute. 'Talking with him about it during the Alps wouldn't have been a very positive conversation,' he confided. 'I am feeling a lot better. I have assured him I don't want to change a thing.'

The best sign that all was well with McGee – in mind and body – came the next day, in the 50 km stage nineteen time-trial from the Beaujolais wine town of Régnié-Durette to Mâcon. In 114th place, he was way out of contention for a high overall place and more than two and a half hours behind Armstrong. But the stage provided him with the perfect opportunity to use the twisting, hilly and then undulating and technically difficult route as a final test of his form (and recovery from injury) for the Commonwealth Games pursuit. Soon after McGee left the start ramp, it was obvious that he was riding within himself. But his relaxed posture and impressively smooth cadence were still producing good speed, enough to indicate he was back to his pre-crash strength.

McGee later confirmed he rode the time-trial conservatively, even though he still finished a solid fifteenth at 3 minutes 22 seconds to Armstrong. An analysis of McGee's time-trial splits later that night by veteran Tour journalist John Wilcockson indicated that over the final 6 km, McGee was on par for a 4 minute 30 second time for the 4000 m pursuit.

Three days later at the Commonwealth Games, McGee clocked the second-fastest qualifying time of 4 minutes 21 seconds before winning the gold medal in a Commonwealth record of 4 minutes 16.358 seconds.

McGee looked back on the 2002 tour as a 'roller-coaster' ride of fate and fortune: 'In the first week I was stomping. Then it was crash and burn for a week. But in the last few days I've been feeling better and am now back to strength.' As in 2001, after finishing 109th and 2 hours 39 minutes 2 seconds behind Armstrong, McGee left with plenty to be happy about – and full of anticipation for the following year's Tour.

McGee is a rider who should be approaching his best years, and he feels he has done his utmost to make sure that he can seize the opportunities when they arise. He has settled down, living in Nice with his wife, Sharnie, and baby daughter, Tahlia, who was born in 2001. By producing results, he has also established clout as a leader within his team and has ensured it is tapped into a vein of Australian talent. Baden Cooke and Matt Wilson are two Australians already on its roster, and others should follow from the New South Wales Institute of Sport/FDJeux.com development team. The only concern is whether McGee has – or will – allow himself to be distracted from his racing by his sense of responsibility to the various projects and plans in which he has immersed himself. At the end of the day, his career will be judged on his results as a bike racer not on his charisma.

Chapter 11

Reading the stars

BADEN COOKE AND CADEL EVANS

Ever since I moved to Europe in 1987 to cover the road cycling circuit, I have nurtured the hope that one day an Australian would win and I'd be there to report on the feat. On no occasion did I hope for it more than on the Tour.

Three questions have preoccupied me since recent successes: first, who are the riders to carry on what the generation led by O'Grady and McEwen has achieved? Second, of those Australians who find their name on a Tour start-list, will any of them ever win the world's most famous race? Third, what will it take for the Australian corporate world to back a team – as 2000 Olympics Games sponsor, AMP, reportedly almost did in 2001?

In 2001, the question of why there wasn't already an Australian trade team led many observers to believe in such a prospect. A year later when all four Australians in the 2002 Tour – McEwen, McGee, O'Grady and Cooke – finished the race and tallied three stage wins from nineteen top-ten places and first, third and fourth in the green jersey competition, I was still being asked the same question. Similarly, I was incredulous at the apathy of corporate Australia to support such a concept.

It could be argued that the recent spate of drug scandals in the sport has scared potential sponsors away as it did the sponsors of some already existing teams. And there have been worldwide economic ramifications due to the September 11 terrorist attacks on the United States in 2001. But research has shown that professional road cycling provides one of the greatest values for the sponsorship dollar – especially in Europe where cycling is a major sport with live coverage of virtually every road race.

It can't be argued that Australians are indifferent to the Tour. In the week of McEwen's win on stage three in the 2002 Tour, the race was the most-mentioned item of news, according to a survey by Media Monitors. And each night, SBS shows 30-minute high-light packages as well as live broadcasts. Nor can it be claimed that Australia does not have the talent. The core of an experienced and formidable Australian team already exists. Supplemented with a top-ranking Tour rider or two and several up-and-coming Australian riders, we have the makings of a terrific division-one team. However, to convince an Australian business to sponsor a trade team, the 'promise' of value can't be sold on present stocks of talent, but rather on future prospects. As with the US, the only race that would attract an Australian sponsor is the Tour since it is the only major three-week race that is covered by Australian television. Despite the prestige of the one-day classics and other races, the Tour is cycling's global face.

For an Australian team to qualify for the Tour, it needs riders who can win: whether it be stages, or the yellow, green and red-and-white polka-dot jerseys. So, who are the Australian riders who can inspire corporate Australia to sponsor a team? Following the likes of O'Grady and McEwen, the new generation has already made giant inroads. McGee is leading the charge, with his brilliant Tour debut in 2001 and stage win in 2002. But close on his wheel are many Australians who are expected to shortly emerge as major stars of the Tour, foremost being Cadel Evans who is considered a serious prospect for the Tour's overall crown; and Cooke, already a legitimate green jersey contender.

One Australian rider who should have etched his name as a Tour rider by now is Matt White. Were he on another team he would already have secured Tours to his name. But after bring courted and recruited by Armstrong's powerful US Postal Service team, until 2003 White has been unable to make its nine-man squad because of the strong competition to be selected. This, despite the fact that Armstrong was so determined to have White, he telephoned Neil Stephens for advice on how to recruit the Australian at 6 am the day after exploding on the mountain finish to Hautacam during the 2000 Tour.

A seasoned European professional, White has styled his career on the work ethic of Australian super-domestiques, Allan Peiper and Stephens. He missed the 2000 Tour when his former team, the Italian Vini Caldirola team, was refused entry by race organisers because one of its riders, Sergei Honchar, failed a blood test in the Tour of Switzerland. After being headhunted by US Postal Service, he ultimately missed selection in Armstrong's 2001 and 2002 line-ups when preference was given to climbers, rather than strong riders for the flat.

Other Australians tipped to soon step up to the Tour include established professionals like Michael Rogers who sees himself as a potential all-rounder; Graham Brown, who is one of the fastest and fiercest sprinters in the world; and the attacking Matt Wilson – all of them already proven winners in other races around Europe. Close behind them is a tier that includes Mat Hayman and up-and-coming stage racer, Allan Davis. Then further behind is the growing pool of talent from the Italian-based Australian Under-23 squad coached by Shayne Bannon, already the source of much speculation.

Baden Cooke – Hard and fast

He has one Tour de France finish to his credit, but Baden Cooke's debut in 2002 gives a strong indication of what we can expect from him. His sprinting prowess already rates him as the biggest name on the rise, but it is not just in a high-speed bunch sprint of 180 riders that Cooke will show what he is made of. Give him half a chance and he will display his aggressive flair in an attack.

From the country town of Benalla in Victoria, Cooke may be as rebellious as Ned Kelly, the famous Australian bushranger who came from the nearby town of Glenrowan. He has regularly been seen sporting punk-styled blond hair and playing up the image of the party boy, but come the Tour de France or any other major event, Cooke will prepare and race it with all his heart – plus some.

Today, he is one the finest assets to the French FDJeux.com team. It is hard not to imagine Cooke's punch, lightning top-end speed and brazen bravado bringing him the green jersey one year. He showed every indication of this possibility in the 2002 Tour where he finished fourth overall in the sprinters' competition after reaching the finish in Paris with a second place on the final stage. He is also a rider whose strength and aggressive style could see him develop into the mould of Belgian, Johan Museeuw, one of the greatest one-day classic riders.

Like teammate Brad McGee, Cooke is a former track racer. Starting the sport at age eleven, between 1996 and 1998 he was a member of the Australian Institute of Sport track endurance squad, representing Australia in both the pursuit and points races. However, since focusing on the road, he has never looked back. After taking a year off from cycling in 1999 due to an Achilles tendon injury, he started his professional road career half-way through 2000 with the American Mercury team for whom he won twenty-five races – including a stage of the 2000 Tour de l'Avenir (Tour of the Future), a ten-day French stage race run by the Tour de France organisers and known to unveil many future stars.

Cooke's career with FDJeux.com began in 2002, a move prompted by his stage win and sixth place overall in the Tour de l'Avenir. After setting up base in Nice on the French Riviera where McGee and another Australian, FDJeux.com teammate Matt Wilson also live, it wasn't long before he started winning. Before the Tour, Cooke won several races, including the Across Flanders one-day race in Belgium and stages in both the Circuit des Mines and Midi Libre races in France. After the Tour, he won a silver medal (behind Australian Stuart O'Grady) in the

Commonwealth Games road race in Manchester before ending the year with a formidable overall victory at home in the *Herald Sun* Tour of Victoria – also the first such win in the race by an Australian rider since Neil Stephens' 1986 win.

In the Tour, Cooke failed to bag the stage win he sought, but his performance did much to establish his name as a rider destined for greatness. Within a week of the Tour getting underway from Luxembourg, Cooke had already been labelled as *the* revelation of the event by Germany's six-times green jersey winner, Erik Zabel. After a disappointing twenty-first in the first stage at Luxembourg, Cooke showed that the poor start was an aberration by placing fourth in the 181 km second stage to Saar-bruck in Germany. Cooke may be a rider only satisfied with first, but his neck-and-neck finishes with the likes of Spanish world champion Oscar Freire, McEwen and Zabel showed his winning prospects were not as far-fetched as some critics claimed. With McGee's help, Cooke proved himself again on stage three to Reims with a third place behind McEwen and Zabel; and once more on stage five to Rouen by placing second in the bunch sprint for fourth place, beaten by McEwen but impressively finishing ahead of a frustrated Zabel.

Cooke's improved finishes raised many eyebrows, but none more so than those of Australian Formula 1 car-racing driver, Mark Webber, who was impressed by Cooke's bike-handling skills. While used to 350 kmh high-speed accelerations on four wheels rather than 75 kmh ones on two wheels, Webber followed the 195 km stage to Rouen in the FDJeux.com team car. An avid amateur cyclist who rides about 300 km a week, Webber was blown away by the sight of Cooke darting and weaving on McGee's wheel, between seemingly non-existent gaps. 'It's interesting to see when and how they find room to pass and the phenomenal power put through the bikes when they do it,' said Webber who saw similarities in the gain for bicycle and cars from slipstreaming. 'It is a lot more effective to sit behind someone and save your energy. It's the same in a F1 car. If you sit behind someone at 350 kmh, it's going to make a big difference to your car.'

Cooke will never get the chance to experience a 350 kmh tow in a bunch sprint, but McGee's horsepower is not to be dismissed. Cooke was reminded of this when McGee was given leave of his lead-out duties and ordered to try and win the seventh stage to Avranches. This he achieved, much to the delight of Cooke who finished eighth, close enough to catch sight of McGee raising his arms in a victory salute. With morale high in the FDJeux.com team, Cooke toiled away over the next days as riders from break-away groups won the stages. After stage eight, his placing in the bunch finishes still positioned him third in the green jersey point competition behind Zabel and McEwen.

However, with the Pyrénées approaching, stage-winning opportunities were passing fast. Cooke realised he needed to reassure his FDJeux.com team that he had the speed to beat the sprinters – the Zabels, McEwens and O'Gradys. For once the mountains were behind them, Cooke would need every pedal-stroke of their help. Thus, his win in the bunch sprint for fifth place during the tenth stage to Pau did much to strengthen his cause.

Cooke survived the Pyrénées well by coming out the other end feeling stronger than his sprinting peers. He won another bunch sprint from McEwen, O'Grady and Zabel, this time on the thir-teenth stage to Béziers and for twelfth place behind a lead group of eleven riders. There was still one more week of racing – including the Alps – but Cooke was doing the groundwork to further secure his teammates' faith in him for an all-out winning bid on the last stage to Paris. 'It has been real important that I win these bunch sprints when there are breakaways to get the confidence of the team. They set me up real well today. Now they are all ready to lead me out in Paris,' said Cooke, adding that he also hoped to capitalise on the brewing contest between McEwen and Zabel for the green jersey. 'They are slowing because they have been racing each other so hard. Hopefully, they will be busy watching each other and that will leave an opportunity for me.'

However, the third and final week of the Tour produced an unexpected hiccup for Cooke as it journeyed through Provence and into the Alps before heading north-west to Paris. As McGee was still recovering from his lacerated back from his crash in the Pyrénées, Cooke began to notice his backside becoming more sensitive with every bump. It didn't take much time to realise he had the worst of cycling ailments: a saddle sore. Simple to diagnose, they are hazardous to the most well-executed race plans. Sean Kelly, the great Irish cyclist and one of the toughest men in the sport, will agree. While leading the three-week Vuelta a España in 1987, with one day to go, Kelly had to quit the race due to an excruciating saddle sore on his backside.

For Cooke, the cyst was the size of a golf ball by the time the Tour reached the Alps. The pain was so bad, he had to cut a hole in the left-hand side of his saddle to allow him to sit down without the infected area being pinched. When Cooke finally reached the finish of the 179.5 km sixteenth stage to the ski station of La Plagne (1970 m), he was wincing not so much from the pain in his legs but from his cyst. 'I had to do a fair bit of work on it before the stage,' explained Cooke, pointing to his hacked saddle as he dismounted. 'I tried it out, did some more. I did it again during the stage. I reckon I'll need to do it more for the next stage.'

With Paris so close and after all the work he had done to earn FDJeux.com's support for the final stage, Cooke never doubted he would finish. He doggedly pedalled, winced, then pedalled and winced some more over the final tough stages for his rendezvous on the Champs Elysées. At this end of the Tour, it is often the strongest rider who wins in Paris, rather than the fastest and Cooke felt he was both. Trouble is, McEwen felt the same and, bolstered by his ambition to win the green jersey, the Queenslander was unbeatable. But it was a measure of Cooke's ability that McEwen had to pull off one of his best ever sprints to win. It was also a measure of the second-placed Victorian's desire to win that his face showed nothing but disappointment for not having repaid his team with the win he had so desired. But as one teammate quipped later that night as beer and wine relaxed every aching limb, 'It could be a good thing really. To win on your first Tour would have been too easy. He's going to win so much anyway.'

Cadel Evans – Is he the man?

Cadel Evans embarked on his first full season as a professional road cyclist with the Italian Mapei team in 2002. His background as a mountain biker made him the butt of jokes when he first started. Like many mountain bikers who switch to the road, Evans found it would take time to earn the respect of road racers who traditionally look down on mountain bikers. Often, he would receive taunts about his ability to ride on skinny tyres after having spent so much time competing on fat ones. Sometimes, he and his fellow former mountain bikers were the victims of suspect pushes as 'roadies' darted around them in tightly packed bunches.

But all this changed five months down the road in 2002 when, at age twenty-five while racing high in the Dolomites mountains of northern Italy, Evans became the first Australian to ever claim the pink jersey – or *maglia rosa* – as leader of the three-week Giro d'Italia, regarded by most as the world's biggest race after the Tour de France.

With one mountain stage and four days to go in the 3393 km Giro, Evans had the cycling world amazed at his turn of fortune after having spent the best part of two-and-a-half weeks riding himself into the ground in aid of Italian teammate, Stefano Garzelli – until Garzelli was kicked off the race for testing positive for the drug probenecid. To be fair, Evans' riding had already been impressive, having placed third overall in the mountainous Tour de Romandie in Switzerland. Once Garzelli left the race after stage nine, Evans seized the opportunity to steadily move up from fourteenth place. He had his share of problems though. Fatigued and disillusioned with a number of doping controversies that marred the Giro, he had considered pulling out before the thirteenth stage to San Giacomo in central Italy's Appenine mountains. But he was urged to continue and eventually took second place on the stage behind Mexican, Julio Perez. The result convinced the Mapei team that Evans could be a dark horse Giro winner.

To race so strongly in the mountains after all the work he had done, and move into second overall behind Jens Heppner also boosted Evans' confidence. Three days later, on stage sixteen – a tough 163 km leg from Conegliano over the Passo Pordoi (2239 m) and the Passo di Campolongo (1875 m) before a downhill run to the finish in Corvara – Evans placed seventh to take the pink jersey from Heppner. But it wasn't long before the reality of the challenge Evans faced struck home. The next five riders behind him on the overall classification were within 48 seconds: Italian Dario Frigo (at 16 seconds), American Tyler Hamilton (18), Spain's Aitor Gonzalez (24), followed by Italians, Pietro Caucchioli (32) and Paolo Salvoldelli (48). As thrilled as he was, Evans acted remarkably calm under the pressure despite being in with a real chance to win the Giro on his first attempt, and becoming the first non-European champion since American Andy Hampsten in 1988. 'It's my first three-week race. If someone said I was going to do well I would have told them they're dreaming,' said Evans that night, as he rested to defend his jersey in the 222 km seventeenth stage from Corvara-in-Badia to Folgaria.

But Evans lost the lead the next day – on the last 9 km of the last but certainly not hardest mountain of the Giro. Watching him blow up after surviving most of the steepest pitch of the 19 km-long Passo Coe was painful. Until then Evans had appeared to be in control as he sat on the wheels of teammates Andrea Noe and Dario Cioni (another ex-mountain biker). But then Evans appeared to labour and suffered a moment's lapse of concentration while trying to listen to the team radio in his earpiece. It did not go unnoticed by Hamilton who was on Evans' wheel and immediately launched the attack that snuffed the Australian's chances of victory in Milan. Not that the move helped Hamilton who was unknowingly carrying a broken shoulder from an earlier fall and could not match the counter-attack by Salvoldelli who won the stage and took an unbeatable lead of the race. Evans was shattered as he reached the finish 15 minutes after Salvoldelli and fell into the arms of his *soigneur*. He later said it was the hardest day in his life on the bike, and rejected suggestions he did not eat enough. After a cycling career spent racing two-hour mountain bike events,

Evans had long ridden his body into the unknown. 'On the last climb I was feeling very good, feeling fine,' he told the American journal *VeloNews*. 'As soon as the pace started to change – boom – there was nothing I could do. After the previous day and the final week of a three-week tour, it was a new experience for my body. My entire body just shut down.'

As painful as the loss was – physically as much as emotionally – the best sign of Evans' potential as a tour racer was his tirelessly devoted work for Garzelli; his handling of the sudden attention that swamped him once he took the race lead; and his very credible fourteenth place overall.

But the Giro was always going to be an apprenticeship for Evans. He came to learn and help Garzelli with a view to learning as much as possible for when his time came to win a major tour. 'It is not just physically taxing but mentally,' said Evans of the step up from leading two-hour events to a three-week race. 'You have to concentrate for hours on end, even on the stages where it may not be that hard. You still have to stay near the front in case it [the pack] splits from a cross wind or something out of the ordinary like a crash. There are so many factors in getting there, putting them all together is something else.'

Soon after the Giro, Evans said he wanted to race the Italian tour again before tackling the Tour de France for the first time, but plans for the French race were fast-tracked by two events: Mapei's decision to withdraw its backing after the 2002 season followed by Evans' eventual decision to join the German Telekom team. Evans was recruited as a leader for Telekom, but so too were the German team's two other new faces: Salvoldelli and Colombian, Santiago Botero. While each believes he is the key leader, the question of who will take priority will be answered in the best possible arena – the Tour. Take note of Evans though, who before signing with Telekom made clear his intention to leave his mark on the Tour: 'When I do the Tour I plan to do it well not just to start.'

Evans' potential as Australia's first ever Tour winner was the subject of discussion long before his spectacular debut in the

Giro, and he has never shied away from accepting a challenge. A former two-times World Cup mountain bike champion, he has always openly expressed high ambitions and never regretted it, even when falling short of winning, as he did in the 1995 world championships when he punctured within sight of the finish and in the lead. One of the constants of his mountain biking career was the pressure of being the pre-race favourite. On no occasion did he feel this more strongly than at the 2000 Olympic Games in Sydney where he placed seventh. 'To go to the Olympics in Australia as one of the favourites was a real pressure situation. To lead the Giro was easier to handle,' he told the Australian magazine *RIDE Cycling Review*. 'Maybe there was more pressure [at the Giro] but there were also many more people to help carry the burden. The riders, the staff, the directors – there was always someone around to help me out and make sure I had time for myself.'

Potentially, Evans is the full package when it comes to stage racing. He can climb, time-trial and has a handy sprint in a small breakaway group. At 66 kg, he is also light and has a strict work ethic when it comes to training and preparation. He is also meticulous, always a plus in a cycling team when tactics must be carried out with precision – and even more so on a team as disciplined as Telekom. Importantly, as he showed in the Giro, Evans is willing to learn – from both his many successes and from what others may harshly perceive as his failures.

One day Evans may look back at those last painful kilometres of the 2002 Giro, and view the experience as the defining moment in a career that lead him to become Australia's first Tour de France champion. But if not Evans, there is sure to be someone out there who has what it takes.

Honour roll and statistics

Australians in the Tour de France (72 starts by 27 riders)

1. ALLAN, Don

Born: September 24, 1949
Home state: Victoria
Turned pro: 1974
Retired: 1983 (after Six Day track career)
Team: Frisol (Neth)
Tour history (2 starts): 1974 – 103rd, 1975 – 85th
Strengths: Good lead-out rider, domestique

2. ANDERSON, Phil

Born: March 20, 1958
Home state: Victoria
Turned pro: 1980
Retired: 1994
Team: Peugeot (Fra) 1981–83, Panasonic (Neth) 1984–87, TVM (Neth) 1988–93, Motorola (US) 1992–94)
Tour history (13 starts): 1981 – 10th, 1982 – 5th plus 1 stage win, 1983 – 9th, 1984 – 10th, 1985 – 5th, 1986 – 39th, 1987 – 27th, 1989 – 38th, 1990 – 71st, 1991 – 45th plus 1 stage win,

1992 – 45th, 1993 – 84th, 1994 – 69th
Strengths: attacking, handy sprint in breakaway

3. BAINBRIDGE, Ernest

Born: 1891
Home state: Victoria
Team: Ravat Wonder Dunlop (Aus)
Tour history (1 start): 1928 – DNF
Strengths: long distance, endurance

4. BEASLEY, John

Born: July 13, 1930
Home state: Victoria
Turned pro: Never raced as amateur
Retired: 1969
Team: Luxembourg–Australia
Tour history (2 starts): 1952 – DNF, 1955 – DNF
Strengths: climbing

5. COOKE, Baden

Born: October 12, 1978
Home state: Victoria
Turned pro: 2000
Team: Mercury (US) 2000–01, FDJeux.com (Fra)
Tour history (1 start): 2002 – 127th
Strengths: sprint, improving time-trial

6. HODGE, Stephen

Born: July 18, 1961
Home state: ACT (born in Adelaide, South Australia)
Turned pro: 1987
Retired: 1995
Team: Kas (Sp) 1987–88, Paternina (Sp) 1989, ONCE (Sp) 1990–93, Festina (Fra) 1994–95
Tour history (6 starts): 1989 – 83rd, 1990 – 34th, 1991 –

67th, 1992 – 93rd, 1994 – 83rd, 1995 – 64th
Strengths: time-trials, strong domestique

7. JONKER, Patrick

Born: May 25, 1969
Home state: South Australia (born in The Netherlands)
Turned pro: 1993
Retired: 2003
Team: Wordperfect (Neth) 1993, Novemail (Neth) 1994, ONCE (Sp) 1995–96, Rabobank (Neth) 1997–98, US Postal Service (US) 1999, Big Mat (Fra) 2000–02, Van Hemert Groep (Neth), 2003
Tour history (4 starts): 1994 – DNF, 1996 – 12th, 1997 – 62nd, 1998 – 34th
Strengths: time-trials, climbing

8. KIRKHAM, Don

Born: 1887
Died: 1929
Home state: Victoria
Turned pro: 1906
Retired: 1924
Team: Phebus-Dunlop (Fra)
Tour History (1 start): 1914 – 17th
Strengths: endurance

9. LAMB, Richard

Born: 1907
Home state: Victoria
Turned pro: 1928
Retired: 1933
Team: Ravat Wonder Dunlop (Aus)
Tour history (1 start): 1931 – 35th
Strengths: all-round versatility

10. LAWRIE, Bill

Born: August 25, 1934
Died: November 24, 1997
Home state: Queensland
Turned pro: 1961
Retired: 1970
Team: Falcon/Great Britain
Tour history (1 start): 1967 – DNF
Strengths: astute tactician, all-rounder

11. McEWEN, Robbie

Born: June 24, 1972
Home state: Queensland
Turned pro: 1996
Team: Rabobank (Neth) 1996–99, Farm Frites (Neth)
2000–01, Lotto-Adecco (Bel) 2002, Lotto-Domo (Bel)
Tour history (5 starts): 1997 – 117th, 1998 – 89th, 1999 –
122nd plus 1 stage win, 2000 – 113th, 2002 – 130th plus
2 stage wins and green jersey
Strengths: sprint

12. McGEE, Brad

Born: February 24, 1976
Home state: New South Wales
Turned pro: 1998
Team: Fdjeux.com (Fra)
Tour history (2 starts): 2001 – 83rd, 2002 – 109th plus 1 stage
win
Strengths: time-trial, aggressive, improving climber

13. MOCKRIDGE, Russell

Born: July 18, 1928
Died: September 13, 1958
Home state: Victoria

Turned pro: 1953
Team: Luxembourg-Australia
Tour history (1 start): 1955 – 64th
Strengths: all-round versatility

14. MUNRO, Iddo 'Snowy'

Born: 1888
Died: October 27, 1980
Home state: Victoria
Turned pro: 1906
Retired: 1915
Team: Phebus-Dunlop (Fra)
Tour history (1 start): 1914 – 20th
Strengths: long distance, endurance

15. NICHOLSON, Oserick 'Ossie'

Born: 1906
Died: 1965
Home state: Victoria (born in Tas)
Turned pro: 1928
Retired: 1947
Team: Ravat Wonder-Dunlop (Aus)
Tour history (1 start): 1931 – DNF
Strengths: endurance, long distance records

16. O'GRADY, Stuart

Born: August 6, 1973
Home state: South Australia
Turned pro: 1994
Team: Gan 1994–98, Crédit Agricole (Fra)
Tour history (6 starts): 1997 – 109th, 1998 – 54th plus 1 stage win, 1999 – 94th, 2000 – DNF, 2001 – 54th, 2002 – 77th
Strengths: sprint, short time-trial, likes to attack

17. OPPERMAN, Sir Hubert

Born: May 29, 1904
Died: April 18, 1996
Home state: Victoria
Turned pro: 1922
Retired: 1944
Team: Ravat Wonder Dunlop (Aus) 1928,
Australia-Switzerland 1931
Tour history (2 starts): 1928 – 18th, 1931 – 12th
Strengths: incredible endurance

18. OSBORNE, Percy

Home state: Victoria
Retired: 1928
Team: Ravat Wonder-Dunlop (Aus)
Tour history (1 start): 1928 – 38th
Strengths: endurance

19. PALOV, Omar

Born: December 6, 1962 in Brno Czechoslovakia (naturalised
Australian in 1988)
Home state: South Australia
Turned pro: 1987
Retired: 1989?
Team: ANC-Halfords (UK)
Tour history (1 start): 1987 – 103rd
Strengths: hill climber, domestique

20. PEIPER, Allan

Born: March 26, 1960
Home state: Victoria
Turned pro: 1983
Retired: 1992

Team: Peugeot (Fra) 1983–85, Panasonic (Neth) 1986–90, Tulip (Neth) 1991–92
Tour history (5 starts): 1984 – 95th, 1985 – 86th, 1987 – DNF, 1990 – DNF, 1996 – 126th
Strengths: time-trials (short), super domestique

21. STEPHENS, Neil

Born: October 1, 1963
Home state: ACT (born in Melbourne, Victoria)
Turned pro: 1985
Retired: 1998
Team: Santini (It) 1985, Fenchurch (Aus) 1987, Zero Boys (Neth) 1988, Caja Rural (Sp) 1989, Artiach (Por) 1990, Paternina (Por) 1991, ONCE (Sp) 1992–96, Festina (Fra) 1997–98
Tour history (7 starts): 1992 – 74th, 1993 – DNF, 1994 – 52nd, 1995 – 60th, 1996 – 49th, 1997 – 54th including 1 stage win, 1998 – DNF
Strengths: super domestique

22. SUNDERLAND, Scott

Born: November 28, 1966
Home state: NSW
Turned pro: 1990
Team: TVM (Neth) 1990–94, Lotto (Bel) 1995–96, Gan (Fra) 1997, Palmans (Bel) 1998–2000, Fakta (Den) 2001
Tour history (1 start): 1996 – 101st
Strengths: climbing

23. SUTTON, Shane

Born: March 22, 1957
Home state: NSW
Turned pro: 1980
Retired: 1993
Team: ANC-Halfords (UK) 1987, PMS-Dawes (UK) 1988

Tour history (1 start): 1987 – DNF
Strengths: domestique, tactics

24. SWEET, Jay

Born: August 11, 1975
Home state: South Australia
Turned pro: 1997
Team: Big Mat (Fra) 1997–2001, Saturn (US) 2002
Tour history (1 start): 1999 – DNF
Strength: sprints

25. THOMAS, Frankie

Born: November 28, 1906
Died: March 15, 1978
Home state: Victoria
Turned pro: 1928
Retired: 1936
Team: Ravat Wonder-Dunlop (Aus)
Tour history (1 start): 1931 – DNF
Strengths: versatility, endurance

26. VOGELS, Henk

Born: July 31, 1973
Home state: Western Australia
Turned pro: 1995
Team: Novell (Neth) 1995, Rabobank (Neth) 1996, Gan (Fra) 1997–99, Mercury (US) 2000–02, Navigators (US) 2003
Tour history (2 starts): 1997 – 99th, 1999 – DNF
Strength: attacking, time-trials, sprints

27. WILSON, Michael

Born: January 15, 1960
Home state: Tasmania (born Adelaide, South Australia)

Turned pro: 1984
Retired: 1991
Team: Alfa Lum (It) 1984–85, Ecoflam (It) 1986, semi-retired
1987, Weinmann-La Suisse (Swtz) 1988; Helvetia-La Suisse
(Swtz) 1989–90, Ariostea (It) 1991
Tour history (2 starts): 1988 – 50th, 1989 – 69th
Strength: climbing, time-trials

Australians in the yellow jersey (overall leader / winner)

(in order of achievement)

ANDERSON, Phil: 1981 – 1 day; 1982 – 9 days
O'GRADY, Stuart: 1998 – 3 days; 2001 – 6 days

Australians in the green jersey (best sprinter)

(in order of achievement)

O'GRADY, Stuart: 1998 – 0 days, 2nd overall; 1999 – 3 days,
    2nd overall; 2001 – 12 days, 2nd overall
McEWEN, Robbie: 2000 – 0 days, 2nd overall; 2002 – 8 days
    and overall winner

Australians in the white jersey (best young rider)

ANDERSON, Phil: 1982 – overall winner

Australian stage winners

(in order of achievement)

ANDERSON, Phil (2): 1982 Bâle–Nancy; 1991
    Rennes–Quimper
STEPHENS, Neil (1): 1997 Fribourg–Colmar
O'GRADY, Stuart (1): 1998 Valréas–Grenoble

McEWEN, Robbie (3): 1991 Arpajon–Paris (Champs Elysées);
   2002 Metz–Reims, Melun–Paris
McGEE, Brad (1): 2002 Bagnoles-de-l'Orne–Avranches

Australian team time-trial winners

(in order of achievement)

PEIPER, Allan (1): 1991 Futuroscope–Futuroscope
   (Panasonic)
O'GRADY, Stuart (1): 2001 Verdun–Bar-le-Duc (Gan)

Acknowledgements

Anyone who has written a book will tell you it takes a lot of help from many people to get it finished. I am indebted to many people for their guidance, insight, support and friendship. John Wilcockson for his encyclopaedic knowledge and the precious time he dedicated to fact-check my work and his wisdom shared over the years. Graham Watson for his brilliant photos of Australia's contemporary Tour heroes and sharing with me, over many fine bottles of wine, his views on where the book should head. David Halford and the Coburg Cycling Club in Melbourne for being so willing to contribute archival photos and material, and for the many hours he sacrificed to do it. Two of the people David sought were Alan Munro and Olga Rothleithner, the son and daughter of Iddo 'Snowy' Munro. Their support and permission for David to look at the private and personal documents of their father and pass them onto me for publication cannot be thanked enough. Ditto to Carmel Lawrie, 1967 Tour rider Bill Lawrie's wife.

Of course, they are not alone in giving valued material. To John Trevorrow and Barry Langley, thanks for helping me contact those people. As facilitators, they are standout men. One of the people they first steered me to was Don Allan, a man most Australians equate with track racing rather than the two Tours he rode. He was one of the first to submit photos, news clippings and his own time to recall his 1974 and 1975 Tours. Bill Long, a stauncheon to Australian cycling history, was also off and running within minutes

of me first asking for his assistance. His help in accessing anec-
dotes from Sir Hubert Opperman was vital. If anyone knew
'Oppy' in Australia, it was Bill. Another who respects 'Oppy' as
strongly is cyclist Robbie McEwen. He agreed quicker than he
sprinted to win the green jersey in the 2002 Tour to offer his
set of memorabilia and original postcards sent home from
Opperman during the 1928 and 1931 Tours. As did Bob
Thomas, son of 1931 Tour rider Frankie Thomas; and Theo Van
Kalleveen.

Naturally, there are many other cyclists who I am equally
grateful to. Phil Anderson, for inspiring me to cover the Tour
with his yellow jersey feats, and most especially his friendship.
Likewise to Allan Peiper, Neil Stephens, Stephen Hodge,
Michael Wilson and Scott Sunderland. How I enjoyed the nine
years living in Europe to cover the sport in the mid-80s to 90s
before returning to Australia. One thing is sure, without them,
my passion for cycling wouldn't be what it is today. Nor would I
still be covering the Tour every year.

To all my colleagues and friends I have made within the Tour
family since first covering it in 1987, all I can say is a special
merci. That goes to everyone from Jean-Marie Leblanc and
Philippe Sudres at the Société du Tour de France to anyone who
has been a part of the race entourage and has guided me in the
right direction. Two of them are American riders, Greg LeMond
and Lance Armstrong. The two Americans have been inspirational in their ability to win the Tour after fighting back from
their deathbeds – LeMond from a near-fatal shooting accident in
1986 and Armstrong from cancer in 1996. They also showed that
non-Europeans can win the Tour.

Others deserving of special thanks are French journalists Jean-
Luc Gatellier, Philippe Bouvet and the cycling department at
l'Équipe newspaper; Jean-François Quenet and television
commentator 1975 Tour champion Bernard Thévenet, for his
insights into Don Allan. Bravery awards go to anyone who has
ever shared a car with me (and I don't even drive) – or even
worse, a room – while on the road. They include John Wilcockson, Graham Watson, Paul Sherwen, Samuel Abt, David Walsh,

Louis Viggio, Andy Hood, Bryan Jew, Charles Pelkey, Steve Wood, William Fotheringham, James Startt, Luke Evans and Robert Zeller; I hope you will have me back.

It would be remiss of me not to credit Phil Liggett for all he has done. When I was a freelance journalist living in France, he gave me one of my major breaks, recommending me to *The European* newspaper to be their cycling correspondent. A decade later, he didn't flinch when I asked him to write the foreword to this book. Thanks also to Ann McQuaid whose decision to employ me as editor of *Winning* magazine in 1987 gave me the first break to go over to Europe and cover the sport then.

However, as much as I look to Europe to offer gratitude, behind me in Australia there are many who are just as deserving. Firstly, to the current crop of Australian riders who are setting the roads ablaze with their class, personality and spirit. They are not only making *their* dreams come true, but those of so many others – me included. To Gennie Sheer, thanks for being frank, driven and supportive for everything. What can I say but – hey – I really do appreciate it. Really! Michael Stephens of the *Herald Sun*, Phil Latz of *Bicycling Australia*, Rob Arnold of *RIDE Cycling Review*, and Gerard Knapp and Jeff Jones of *Cyclingnews.com* – the advice, sharing of knowledge and contacts has been heartening. The same to SBS Television's Mike Tomalaris and Honie Rowley whose face you never see, only her great work with the camera. Ditto to Melissa Woods, who loaned me her laptop when mine crashed, and Valkerie Mangnall, both from AAP.

Special credit also to those individuals at the *Australian* who backed me to cover the Tour when it would have been easy to say no. They include the paper's former sports editors Stan Wright, Colin Gibson and Louise Evans and past and present senior sport staffers, Chris Stedman, Garry Ferris and those who sub-edit my copy. Ditto for those who finally gave the green light – the paper's editors, first Campbell Reid until he left to edit Sydney's *Daily Telegraph*; the second and current editor, Michael Stutchbury; and of course managing editor, Martin Beesley who signed off on the costs.

Naturally, this book wouldn't even be in existence were it not for the vision and enthusiasm of Jeanne Ryckmans at Random House to back the idea, and my editor, Nadine Davidoff, a former cyclist herself, whose passion for the sport makes the book such a better product. And to Bill Leak and Stuart Honeysett of the *Australian*, thanks for dropping my name at the right time to them.

Finally, special mention to those closest to me: my dearest and ever-so-patient wife Libby, who even dared to follow the 1998 Tour with me; my parents and in-laws; not to mention the many friends I must surely have tested by abusing their interest in the book and letting them waste hours thinking of a title. I hope you, the reader, can understand why I am so grateful.

Bibliography

The Fabulous World of Cycling, Winning, Brussels, volumes 1983–1997.

Jacques Augendre, *Tour de France 2002*, Velo Press, Colorado, 2002.

Pierre Chany, *Tour de France 1992*, Hachette, Paris, 1992.

Roger De Maertelaere, *Daagsen Jours Tagerennen*, Uitgeverij, Ghent, 1991.

Rupert Guinness, *The Foreign Legion*, Springfield Books, West Yorkshire, 1993.

Russell Mockridge, *My World on Wheels*, Stanley Paul, London, 1960.

Jean Nelissen, *La Bible du Tour de France*, Uitgeverij, Maastricht, 1995.

Hubert Opperman, *Pedals, Politics and People*, Haldane Publishing, Sydney, 1977.

Daniel Pautrat, *Le Guide du Tour 1988*, A.S. RMO, Grenoble, 1988.

Daniel Pautrat, *La Guide du Tour de France 1989*, Les Editions de l'Aurore, Grenoble, 1989.

Daniel Pautrat, *La Guide du Tour de France 1990*, Les Editions de l'Aurore, Grenoble, 1990.

David Saunders, *Tour de France 1974*, Kennedy Brothers, Yorkshire, 1975.

David Saunders *Tour de France 1975*, Kennedy Brothers, Yorkshire, 1975.

Pascal Sergeant, *Chronique d'une Legende: Paris–Roubaix 1896–1939*, Flandria Nostra, Zedelgem, 1989.

Harry Van den Bremt and Rene Jacobs, *Velo*, Editions Velo, Oudegem, 1987–1999.

David Walsh, *Inside the Tour de France*, Velo News Books, Colorado, 1994.

Archival material from

David Halford and the Coburg Cycling Club (Aus), Bill Long (Aus), Robbie McEwen (Aus), Bob Thomas (Aus), *RIDE Cycling Review* (Aus), *Bicycling Australia* (Aus), *Velo News* (US), *Cyclingnews.com* (Aus), Canberra Bicycling Museum website (Aus), *l'Équipe* newspaper (Fra), *Velo* magazine (Fra), *Société du Tour de France* (Fra).

Also by the author

The Foreign Legion, Springfield Books, West Yorkshire, 1993.

Tales from the Toolbox, with Scott Parr, Velo Press, Colorado, 1997.

The Dean Woods Manual of Cycling, with Dean Woods, Harper Sports, Sydney, 1995.

A Season for Roche: The Fabulous World of Cycling, with Eddy Merckx, Winning, Brussels, 1987.

The Cycling Year, with Phil Liggett and John Wilcockson, Springfield Books, West Yorkshire, 1990.

The Cycling Year Volume Two, with Phil Liggett, John Wilcockson and Simon Burney, Springfield Books, West Yorkshire, 1991.